ADVANCE PRAISE FOR

Integral City: Evolutionary Intelligences for the Human Hive

Integral City provides an important vision for how we can begin to inhabit our cities with an evolutionary intelligence that promises to allow both people and planet to flourish. With the meta-framework presented here, Marilyn Hamilton joins and extends the integrative tradition of Patrick Geddes, Lewis Mumford, and Jane Jacobs. In particular she helps us understand the myriad connections between behavioral and systemic dimensions of urban landscapes with the psychological and cultural aspects. Drawing on a variety of examples from municipal systems, city politics, public space, cartography, and regional values assessment, she enacts a bee-communication dance instructing us how we too can fly to the nourishing pollen of a new tomorrow.

— Sean Esbjörn-Hargens Ph.D., author of Integral Ecology;
Executive Editor Journal of Integral Theory and Practice; and
Chair of the Integral Theory Department at John. F. Kennedy University.

What will be the most dramatic technological breakthrough of the 21st Century? As Marilyn Hamilton demonstrates in her masterful book, it may very well be a truly integral city. Integral City: Evolutionary Intelligences for the Human Hive is a powerful application of the "meta-theory" of integral philosophy that is bound to change the way we understand our urban environments. And improving the life of our cities may turn out to be one of the most dramatic ways that an evolutionary perspective can advance the human condition. I highly recommend this exciting and insightful book.

— Steve McIntosh, author of Integral Consciousness and the Future of Evolution.

In this era where rapid urbanization is a key driving force behind global change, it is imperative that we find some means for re-creating our cities to be more ecologically sustainable and harmonious with the desires of the human spirit. Marilyn Hamilton has clearly pioneered a vision that does just that. Integral City is a comprehensive and accessible application of the 'integral approach' to city life. It is must read for not just city planners, but also for politicians, scientists, engineers, artisans, change agents and the city dweller.

— Brian Eddy, PhD, President, iGeo Information Consulting Inc.

Advance Praise

Marilyn Hamilton offers us a brilliant and revolutionary new way to examine our cities through the lens of science, ecology and systems theory, to create a new vision of what a city could be — one that supports life on this planet as well as our own evolution as human beings. She helps us navigate chaos and absorb complexity, by turning theory into practical applications. Integral City provides success stories, resources, and a blue print for action based on sound principles.

— Linda Naiman, Founder, Creativity at Work.
Coauthor: *Orchestrating Collaboration at Work*

Hamilton weaves threads of research and practice into a vision for sustainable cities. She illuminates a path toward the future that cuts across cultural, language, disciplinary, political and linguistic lines. Her simple rules give us hope for creating and maintaining productive, livable cities for today and tomorrow.

— Glenda H. Eoyang, Ph.D., Executive Director, Human Systems Dynamics Institute;
Author: *Coping with Chaos: Seven Simple Tools*;
Coauthor: *Facilitating Organization Change: Lessons from Complexity Science*

This is an outstanding book that will create a whole new paradigm for understanding cities and the discipline of urban studies. It moves the discussion from fragmentation and dis connects to wholeness and integration, with the incorporation of several fresh frameworks for research and theoretical explanation, including Spiral Dynamics and Wilber's Four Quadrants Model. Urban studies from here on in will be defined by the rich contribution of this seminal work that will become the definitive textbook in the field. Congratulations.

— Caleb Rosado, Ph.D., Professor of Urban Studies
Director Urban Studies Program, Warner Pacific College

It is a rare occurrence these days to turn the pages of a book and find yourself opening up to a totally new way of thinking about cities – within a local, global, and kosmic context. Marilyn Hamilton amazes us with the depth and breadth of her vision, her mastery of the integral paradigm, and her pragmatic suggestions for creating cities of the future that work for the 60% of the human population now inhabiting them. The book is a seminal work of major importance, from a social entrepreneur whose work will be essential to future generations.

— Nancy Roof, Founding Editor, *Kosmos Journal*
In Consultative Status with United Nations Partner, Coalition for the Global Commons,
Media Ambassador for World Wisdom Council

integral
city

Evolutionary Intelligences for the Human Hive

MARILYN HAMILTON

NEW SOCIETY PUBLISHERS

Cataloging in Publication Data:
A catalog record for this publication is available from the National Library of Canada.

Cover design by Diane McIntosh.
Cover images: Satellite earth – iStock / Mehmet Salih Guler; City aerial – iStock / Djapeman; City condos – iStock / Dean Tomlinson; Row houses – iStock / Steve Geer; Skyline – iStock / Tony Tremblay; Crowd – iStock / Rafael Ramirez Lee; Apartments – iStock / Effinity Stock Photography; Children – iStock / Nicole S. Young; Young woman – iStock / Anna Bryukhanova; Mothers – iStock / photoGartner

Printed in Canada. First printing September 2008.

New Society Publishers acknowledges the support of the Government of Canada through the Book Publishing Industry Development Program (BPIDP) for our publishing activities.

Pb ISBN: 978-0-86571-629-2

Inquiries regarding requests to reprint all or part of *Integral City* should be addressed to New Society Publishers at the address below.

To order directly from the publishers, please call toll-free (North America) 1-800-567-6772, or order online at www.newsociety.com

Any other inquiries can be directed by mail to:
New Society Publishers
P.O. Box 189, Gabriola Island, BC V0R 1X0, Canada
(250) 247-9737

New Society Publishers' mission is to publish books that contribute in fundamental ways to building an ecologically sustainable and just society, and to do so with the least possible impact on the environment, in a manner that models this vision. We are committed to doing this not just through education, but through action. This book is one step toward ending global deforestation and climate change. It is printed on Forest Stewardship Council-certified acid-free paper that is **100% post-consumer recycled** (100% old growth forest-free), processed chlorine free, and printed with vegetable-based, low-VOC inks, with covers produced using FSC-certified stock. Additionally, New Society purchases carbon offsets based on an annual audit, operating with a carbon-neutral footprint. For further information, or to browse our full list of books and purchase securely, visit our website at: www.newsociety.com

 NEW SOCIETY PUBLISHERS
www.newsociety.com

To the *great-great-great-great-great-grandchildren*

of the integral generation.

CONTENTS

xv   **ACKNOWLEDGMENTS**

xIx   **PREFACE: EVOLUTIONARY REFLECTIONS**
xix   A Meta-Framework for the City as a Whole System
xx   The New Science of Human Cities
xxi   Integrating Multiple Disciplines and Sciences

1   **1 – ECOSPHERE INTELLIGENCE: LOCATING PLACES FOR THE HUMAN HIVE**
1   Opportunities and Limitations
5   Lessons from Other Species
7   Location, Location, Location
8   Seeking Resilience
10   Applying the Eco-footprint
13   Relating the Exterior Environment to Interior City Life
17   Growing Capacity versus Outgrowing Resilience
18   The Symbiotic Relationship of the City to Its Ecoregion
21   Conclusion
22   Questions

23 **2 – EMERGING INTELLIGENCE: SEEING WHOLENESS IN THE HUMAN HIVE**

23 Why See the City as a Whole System?

26 The City Has Aliveness

27 Holons Are Wholes

28 The City Survives

29 The City Is a Container with Shape-shifting Boundaries

30 The City Is a Dissipative Structure

31 The City Is a Complex Adaptive System

33 The City Adapts to Its Environment

36 Adaptiveness Roles: Conformity Enforcers, Diversity Generators, Inner Judges, Resource Allocators

37 The City Regenerates

38 Cycles of Renewal

42 Each Scale and Stage of Development Has Recurring Cycles

43 Sustaining the Whole City

46 Emergence: Seeing New Capacities in the City

48 Morphic Fields in the City

50 Conclusion

50 Questions

51 **3 – INTEGRAL INTELLIGENCE: CHARTING PATTERNS OF THE HUMAN HIVE**

51 Integrating the Qualities That Create Optimal Conditions for Human Habitats

52 What Are Integral Qualities of Human Habitats?

56 How Do You Sustain an Integral City?

58 Are We Losing Touch with Our Cities' In-formation?

60 Mapping the Essential Patterns of City Life

60 Map 1: The Four-quadrant Eight-level Map of Reality

65 Map 2: The Nested Holarchy of City Systems

66 Map 3: The Scalar Fractal Relationship of Micro, Meso and Macro Human Systems

67 Map 4: The Complex Adaptive Structures of Change

69 Combining the Maps into a GIS System

70   Going Beyond the Attainment of Quality of Life to a
Vision of City of the Future

71   Adding to the Value of the Earth

72   Conclusion

72   Questions

73   4 – LIVING INTELLIGENCE: LIVING AND DYING IN THE HUMAN HIVE

73   What Is Life? What Is Death?

75   Cities Are Concentrators of Complex Wealth

79   Human Life Cycles: They Will Always Be With Us

90   Fractals Reveal Recurrent Lifecycles, Stages and Spirals in Cities

94   The City Field Has Observable Change States

96   Conclusion

97   Questions

99   5 – INNER INTELLIGENCE: CONSCIOUS CAPACITY IN THE HUMAN HIVE

99   Consciousness: Fundamental to the Universe

100   Subjective Well-being Unfolds

101   Value of Examining a Single Life

102   Mapping Intelligence Capacities

103   Human Emergence: Levels, Lines, Types, States

105   Purpose and Goals

111   Values Vision Mission

112   Leadership

115   Leaders to the Power of 8: Build on Evolutionary Lessons, Catalyze
Interconnectedness, Create Opportunities for Well-being

119   Designing Appropriate Learning and Education Systems

123   Conclusion

124   Questions

**125   6 – OUTER INTELLIGENCE: EMBODYING RIGHT ACTION
IN THE HUMAN HIVE**

125   Mapping Biophysical Necessities for Well-being Basics: Air, Water, Food,
Clothing, Shelter

127 Conditions of Life

128 Biophysical Demographics

130 Managing Energy

130 Dissipative Structures: Processors, Patternizers, Structurizers

133 The Body as the City, the Body of the City, the Body in the City

135 Senses in the City: the Roots of Natural Science and Learning

137 Well-being in the City

139 Embodying Intention, Purpose

140 Designing Appropriate Healthcare Systems

144 Culturally Catalyzing Biophysical Potential, Connections, Well-being

146 Conclusion

147 Questions

149 7 – BUILDING INTELLIGENCE: CREATING STRUCTURES THAT FLEX AND FLOW IN THE HUMAN HIVE

149 What You Get Is What You See: Chemistry, Physics, Biology, Architecture and Engineering

150 Structural Systems for Managing Energy, Information, Matter

151 Carrying Capacity and Other Cruel Facts: The Relationship of Built City to Ecoregion

155 Making Visible the Invisible

156 Differentiating Human Social Structures from Artefacts

159 Mapping Infrastructure for Resource Allocation

161 Taking Responsibility for Renewing Resources

163 Wholes, Heaps and Fitness Landscapes: Intentional Design versus Unintended Consequences

165 Manifesting Relationships: What Matters for Humans and Artefacts

167 Structures Hold the Memory of Patterns and Processes

169 Evolving Structures and Infrastructures for Healthy Education, Healthcare, Workplace Facilities

173 Meshworks, Self-organizing Systems and Hierarchies of Complexity

173 Designing Appropriate Governance Systems

177 Conclusion

178 Questions

179   **8 – STORY INTELLIGENCE: FEEDING EACH OTHER IN THE HUMAN HIVE**

179   The Cadence of the City

181   Relationships: The Bonds of Strength, Resilience and
Transformative Potential

183   City Values

185   Adaptive Relationships: Inner Judges, Resource Allocators,
Conformity Enforcers, Diversity Generators, Intra-group Tournaments

187   Who Is at the Center of the Universe? Eko, Ethno, Ego,
Excel, Equal, Eco, Evo

188   The Blended Family: The Dynamics of Social Holons

190   Mapping Integral Voices: Citizen, City Manager, Civil Society, City Developer

195   Reporting the Voices: The Role of the Media in the City

197   Recreating Cultural Importance

200   Community and Dialogue: Fields of Engagement

203   Communities of Practice: Evolving Cultures for
Healthy Education, Healthcare and Workplace Services

206   Conclusion

207   Questions

209   **9 – INQUIRY INTELLIGENCE: RELEASING POTENTIAL IN
THE HUMAN HIVE**

209   The Quest

214   Mapping Gardens, Deserts and New Horizons

216   The Potential

220   Conclusion

220   Questions

221   **10 – MESHING INTELLIGENCE: ENABLING ORDER AND CREATIVITY
IN THE HUMAN HIVE**

221   What Is Meshworking?

223   Who Is Meshworking?

224   Why Is Meshworking Important?

226   Meshworking Enables Emergence in the Human Hive

228 Conclusion

228 Questions

**229 11 – NAVIGATING INTELLIGENCE: DIRECTIONAL DASHBOARDS
FOR THE HUMAN HIVE**

229 Integral Vital Signs Monitors: Living Dashboards for the Human Hive

247 The Real "So What" of IVSM: Making Informed Choices

250 Next Steps for IVSM

250 Learning to Change: How Vital Signs Monitors Inform Us

252 Vital Signs Monitors Enable the Integral City

255 Conclusion

255 Questions

**257 12 – EVOLVING INTELLIGENCES: IMAGINING THE FUTURE
FOR HUMAN HIVES**

257 Where Did We Start?

258 Where Have We Been?

261 Where Could We Go?

264 How Will We Get There?

270 Conclusion

270 Questions

**271 POSTSCRIPT — APPLIED INTELLIGENCES: RESOURCES FOR THRIVING
IN YOUR HUMAN HIVE**

271 How Can We Help You?

273 Where to Next?

273 Integral City Book Series

275 GLOSSARY

277 REFERENCES

287 INDEX

295 ABOUT THE AUTHOR

ACKNOWLEDGMENTS

The original inspiration for this book must come from my father, Jack Douglas Herbert, one of Canada's seminal museum developers. When I was eight, he told me to write about what I know (and of course, now I know my pursuit of knowing is a never-ending quest). He revealed to me how to bring history alive on his working vacations to archeological digs, visits to historical sites from coast to coast and bantering with museum specialists from around the world at our family dining table.

Next I acknowledge a whole quadrivium of Integral City advisors who signed on early to counsel the website (integralcity.com): Center for Human Emergence founder, Dr. Don Beck; integral ecologist, Dr. Sean Esbjörn-Hargens; Integral Sustainability Director, Barrett Brown; integral LEED building pioneer, David Johnston; integral geographer, Dr. Brian Eddy; integral regional planner, Dr. Ian Wight; integral architect, Mark DeKay; corporate alchemist, Linda Naiman; Ginger Group architect, Jean Singer; Communities of the Future founder, Rick Smyre; integral municipal capacity builder and ED of The Natural Step Canada, John Purkis; integral psychologist, Dr. Bert Parlee; Spiral Dynamics integral wizard and water engineer, Chris Cooke; wizard of Oz, Will Varey.

I thank my urban crucible of learning in Abbotsford, British Columbia (Canada's fastest-growing city for the last decade): John Friesen so graciously introduced me to the importance of community values; Jack Robertson stretched the limits of my old organizational and community paradigms; Peter Andzans invited me into the caregiving sector and introduced me to our local environmental concerns; Gail Franklin shares my curiosity about the writings of Christopher Alexander, the value of community building, and self-organizing systems; Stacey Corriveau is inventing social entrepreneurship and imagining new futures; Debbie Magson embodies social responsibility; Stan Hindmarsh walks the talk of glocalizing care for family, community and world; Carol Uszkalo so ably partners commerce with social justice; Gordon Holloway charts vital signs of city health.

For guiding my research into community, I thank: M. Scott Peck who synthesized from the East and West the technology of Community Building Workshops and assembled the Foundation for Community Encouragement; also Kaz Gozdz for early publication of so many influential writers on community building; and lately the Quantum Women.

On a universal scale, I thank Edgar Mitchell for going to the moon and founding the Institute of Noetic Sciences (IONS) to explore the relationship between science and spirit. His commitment introduced me to a world of explorers who still influence me: Meg Wheatley with the new sciences, self-organization, valuing each other and her Berkana Institute and Community of Conversations that became the case study for my doctoral research and spawned my global cyber-Sanctuary. Meg introduced me to friend Maggie Moore Alexander, (now married to Christopher Alexander and their Living Neighborhood Project in Berkeley, California); Fritjof Capra with the web of living systems; and Etienne Wenger with communities of practice.

In this group of large-scale thinkers, I also bow to Buzz Holling and L. Gunderson, Jared Diamond, Ronald Wright, Rupert Sheldrake, Bruce Lipton, Elisabeth Sahtouris and Marilyn Atkinson for all their research and thinking from the micro to the macro levels of life that has offered vital insights into the integral synthesis I am exploring about the human hive. And thanks to the several navigators who opened my eyes to intelligences I hadn't considered: Captain Rik Krombeen on the high seas; Dr. Jim Logan in intergalactic zones and Mayor Dave Kandal with a much deeper vision of how vibrant a city could be.

I have IONS to thank again for supporting the early work of Ken Wilber whose integral model was foundational to my gaining new lenses for growing capacity in human systems at all scales. Integral Pandit Ken also introduced me to Integral Activist Don Beck, who in turn inaugurated me into the research of Clare Graves and introduced me to the worlds of: Spiral Dynamics; Guru Andrew Cohen and Senior Editor Elizabeth Debold and *What Is Enlightenment?*; Nancy Roof at *Kosmos*; Richard Barrett and Whole Systems Change; and Ervin Laszlo's Systems and Integral Philosophy. Ken Wilber invited me to be a charter member of the Integral Institute, where a crowd of dedicated members and directors continue to enlighten me on all things integral: Gail Hochachka on international development, Michael Zimmerman on philosophy, Genpo Roshi on Big Mind and the wise ones who serve as Integral City advisors mentioned above.

Thanks to Don Beck for introducing me to MeshWORKS™, "Bloom's Pentad" and the work and wonderful bee story of Howard Bloom; as well as the constellation of spiral wizards catalyzing global emergence: like Lorraine Laubscher, Dr. Bruce Gibb, Cherie Beck, Peter Merry and Elza Maalouf; and Steve McIntosh, a rising integral evolutionary philosopher.

In a parallel universe, I thank my Royal Roads University complexity and systematics colleague Barry Stevenson for introducing me to Glenda Eoyang of Human Systems Dynamics; Richard Knowles of Self-Organizing Leadership; and Robin Wood of Integra Foundation. Also at RRU, I am deeply indebted to Ann Dale for her dedication to pushing the edge of sustainability in cities, and all of the grad students who have selected me for thesis supervision and so courageously dug deep for integral insights; special thanks to Rae Ann Hartman who gifted me with the book on honeybees that sparked human hive insights.

Gratitude to my integral community in Canada and the Pacific Northwest: Arthur Gillman, the Delphi oracle who tantalizes me with the great questions of the universe; Michael Dudley, my personal research librarian at University of Winnipeg; the Ginger Group Collaborative, my cross-Canada rhizome of spicy integral imagineers; Karma Ruder and Dana Nunnelly, collaborative artists both; and the integral psychotherapist team of Robert Masters and Diane Bardwell.

I thank the Integral City Capability Network and the integral mesh of people who have made it possible for me to write this book and who are not named here. I make special note of those who dared to offer early critiques: Carissa Wieler, Cam Owen, Kate McLaren, Laura Young and especially Edith Friesen who provided invaluable, inspired, integral editing advice, care and nurturing. Thanks to

Chris Plant, Ingrid Witvoet and Judith Brand at New Society Publishers for being such daring diversity generators, inner judges, resource allocators and caring conformity enforcers in the integral hive.

My final appreciation is due my husband, Peter Dobson, who makes possible my meshworking evolutionary intelligences in the human hive through all the ways he supports my well-being in body, mind, heart and soul.

PREFACE: EVOLUTIONARY REFLECTIONS

*Honeybees are at the top of their evolutionary tree, whereas humans
are the most highly evolved species on our branch.*

— Gould and Gould, 1988 p. x

*All things are global, indeed cosmic, for all things are connected,
and the memory of all things extends to all places and to all times.
This is the concept of the in-formed universe, the view of the
world that will hallmark science and society in the coming decades.*

— Laszlo, 2004, p. 153

A META-FRAMEWORK FOR THE CITY AS A WHOLE SYSTEM

Why is it time to provide a meta-framework for looking at the city as if it were a whole system?

In 100 years cities may, like beehives, be classified as just one of two kinds: wild or designed. Wild cities will be like the cities most of us know today — mostly unplanned, self-organizing, ever-evolving, suboptimal habitats of swarming humanity. But will designed cities be more than the cities that are starting to emerge from the deserts of United Arab Emirates or flicker as CAD/CAMs on the computer screens of developers, architects, engineers and visionaries? Artfully crafted, functionally aligned, technologically advanced and culturally and socially hollow? Or will we have to transcend and include what we assume are the design elements for creating optimal human living environments? Will we need to invite into the design space the very cultural and social people who will occupy the design and so should be the primary co-creators of the city?

How old is the oldest city? Depending on how you define a city, it would appear that the oldest cities date from 3000 to 5000 BCE (Andranonovich & Riposa, 1993; Braudel, 1987; Trager, 1979) and are located in the Middle East (Byblos, Hebron, Damascus). What do we know about some of the lost cities of mankind? The cities from the Mayan culture, Pacific Islands, even the fabled Atlantis (Diamond, 2005; Wright, 2004)? What can we learn about the nature of cities from the nature of man? If the nature of man is self-organizing, evolutionary, developmental, complex, adaptive and co-constructed with his environment, then how does the city reflect this nature holographically (Graves, 2003; Miller, 1978)?

Wild or tame, lost or found, self-organizing or designed, the functionality of the city may have become more of a danger than a service to mankind. We have created megalopolises in excess of 20 million people that are not only impossible to manage or sustain, but that have become massive heat-generating sinks that are changing global climate and sucking up resources at such a rate that they are decimating the ecology in which they are situated (United Nations Human Settlements, 2005; Wackernagel & Rees, 1996).

THE NEW SCIENCE OF HUMAN CITIES

At this stage of human existence, where is the new science of human cities? Where are the successors to the great urban development pioneers? Who has taken up the mantle of Patrick Geddes, Lewis Mumford or Jane Jacobs (Jacobs, 1970, 1992, 1994, 2001, 2004; Meller, 1990; Mumford, 1946, 1970)? Why do we seem to know more about the collective lives of ants, bees and termites than we do of the collective needs of our own species (Johnson, 2004)? Are cities simply physical artifacts of human existence? Or aesthetic expressions of human consciousness? Or giant experiments of calamitous trials and errors and dynamical change that can only be interpreted and analyzed with limited insight? How can cities tell us what we want to know most about human emergence, environmental sustainability and global well-being?

What role do cities have to play in closing the gap between the connected and the unconnected parts of the world that Tom Barnett (2005) so clearly identifies in *The Pentagon's New Map*? How will cities continue to change in the world that is emerging under Thomas Friedman's technologically sensitive gaze (2005)? How will cities develop sufficient resilience to thrive in the face of Thomas Homer-Dixon's converging tectonic stresses of over-population, energy scarcity, environmental damage, climate change and economic instability (2006)?

INTEGRATING MULTIPLE DISCIPLINES AND SCIENCES

How can we integrate the multiple disciplines and sciences to reframe the city as a whole system? *Integral City*, as well as my organization of the same name, tries to wrestle with all these questions by offering a meta-framework for looking at the city as a whole system that optimizes the life of the human species and adds value to the life of our planet. The human species lies at the apex of our evolutionary branch of vertebrates. We are the humans conscious of our consciousness — thus we are not only *Homo sapiens* but *Homo sapiens sapiens*.

The city is the most concentrated form of habitat created by and for *Homo sapiens sapiens*. To explore it within the context of whole and living systems, I use the beehive as proxy from the species that lies at the apex of invertebrate evolution, namely, the honeybee (*Apis mellifera*). On the deepest level of complexity, I apply an integral meta map that reveals, correlates and integrates more insights about the city than any framework we have developed before. While the beehive creates a kind of parable, the integral meta-map deepens the space by which we can understand the intelligence of the human hive.

I use whole-systems thinking to consider the city in the context of the "informed" and ever-forming environment that is the existential ground for defining its economic and social capacity. In thinking about sustainability as a theory and praxis, I find the need to go beyond mere superficial sustainability to consider the implications of emergence. I assume that the human condition is a never-ending quest, involving continuous adaptation and change. I also assume that the city might be like a hologram, and even a fractal of human systems. A hologram is a three-dimensional representation of an entity produced by bouncing laser light off a photographic plate (Laszlo, 2004, p. 72). A fractal is a repeated non-linear pattern that recurs, at infinite scales in nature, arising from the following of simple rules embedded in the nature of the fractal entity; examples include coastlines, cloud formations, trees, villages, bodies, behaviors, hives and cities.

I use a four-quadrant, multilevel integral framework to look at the city's unique capacities and qualities. The key perspectives of this integral framework are represented in all the languages of the world as the first, second and third person voices of I, We/You, It and Its; in other words, the massively entangled mind, heart, body and spirit that experiences life as subjectively, intersubjectively, objectively and interobjectively.

This book assumes that city structures and infrastructures arise from and connect to the natural systems of global ecology. But, I want to explore the dynamics of the city's internal human ecology, in addition to the external global ecology. (So I see myself in the tradition of Geddes and Mumford, both of whom demanded the contribution and engagement of the individual and the collective for the vitality of urban life.) My research shows me that effective city leadership requires an understanding of the dynamics of individual and group human development — that it must embrace the intelligences of mind, heart and spirit and not just the physical body (Hamilton, 1999). Leaders everywhere need such understanding to provide appropriate leadership that is effectively matched to the people being led and/or their environmental conditions.

Contemplating the bees that replenish the pollen banks that support their hives, I think of the city as a human hive within the context of energetic flex and flow — not separate from global energy systems, but an integral part of them. So in that respect, I borrow the mantle of Wendell Berry who so poetically articulates the deep connections between culture and agriculture (Berry, 1977). Cities, like beehives, are urban energetic nodes linked within a global energetic body, which we experience biophysically, psychologically, culturally and socially.

Regrettably, in cities we thought we had tamed, we have evolved to a point where fragmentation and separation have created disconnected silos amongst sectors that ought naturally to function as value-adding systems to the whole city system. To our great risk, loss and danger, we have lost sight of the massively entangled interconnections amongst these systems. So a new form of wildness has emerged that seems unmanageable. This book proposes that we reframe and redesign cities with evolutionary intelligences that integrate the ever-shifting patterns of workplaces, education systems and healthcare systems for the well-being of all. It ponders how we might do this naturally, with solutions that flex, flow and change as people and the city mature. Harking back to Geddes (Meller, 1990), it considers that families, parents, communities and cultural systems all play integral roles in creating the conditions for cities to thrive.

Finally, with deep respect for the brilliant systemic insights of the city by the late Jane Jacobs (1970, 1992, 1994, 2001, 2004), the book considers cities to be full of diversity, full of collectives and full of communities, all of whose members are capable of learning how to adapt and more effectively align their energies and directions to produce a coherent, whole, evolving life experience for all citizens. But we speculate that the quality of life for any given people in any given community goes through natural cycles. The ups and downs of these dance-like cycles cast light on how we can create dynamic conditions for the quality of life in the whole city, rather than an ever-elusive steady state.

The subject of the city is attracting a growing number of authors writing about the city they consider to be vital — the Ecocities, Ecovillages, Creative City, Mongrel City. Others are writing about the aspects and functions of the city — Renewable Energy, Transportation (and its antithesis, Sprawl), Green Building, Planning for the Unplanned. Still others are writing about processes and resources for the city — Sustainable Communities, Sustainable Cities, The Natural Step. Each of these voices and perspectives is important to the discourse about the city; each reflects the insights, wisdom and science of vital niches in the city. But none offers us a big enough framework to hold all the frameworks of human systems at the level of complexity of the city.

Integral City proposes an integral framework as a scaffold to transcend and include the models of the city that emerged from the traditional, modern and postmodern urban eras. As an experiment in applying this integral framework, this book touches only lightly on the massive literature on urban studies from those eras. The review that would recalibrate that literature is a future assignment.

Here I have tried to sketch out how this integral framework can hold the quickly multiplying horizontal postmodern discourses of the city and add to them the vertical, diagonal and relational contexts that make up the Integral City. I propose that the value of the city does not derive just from the survival value to the egocentric individual, nor just to any belonging value of an ethnocentric collective or collectives, nor even just to the ecocentric sustainability value of the region or nation. This meta-framework integrates the multiple disciplines, sciences and arts to reframe the city as if it were a whole worldcentric system that supports the evolution of human consciousness, collaboration and capacity while adding value to Kosmocentric life on planet Earth.

Each chapter explores some aspect of wholeness related to the city and is structured to provide a narrative, sidebar examples of how and/or who is applying the wholeness principles discussed and three simple rules that capture the principles and finishes with three questions for continuing inquiry about the Integral City. Altogether they build an argument and approach for deepening the inner and outer intelligences of the human hive — for practising wholeness in the Integral City.

ECOSPHERE INTELLIGENCE: LOCATING PLACES FOR THE HUMAN HIVE

Nectar and high-protein pollen are found only in insect-pollinated flowers;
species that depend on wind pollination have very little nutrition to offer bees.
...Without bees to pollinate them, most flower species would perish.

Gould and Gould, 1988, p. 20

"Natural capital" includes not only all the natural resources and waste sinks needed
to support human economic activity, but also those biophysical processes and
relationships among components of the ecosphere that provide essential life-support "services."

Rees and Wackernagel, 1994, p. 36

OPPORTUNITIES AND LIMITATIONS

All cities are not created equal. The longitudes and latitudes that mark our locations also demarcate the zones of planetary motion and time. But as efficient as they are, such man-made boundaries defy the cut and thrust of the geologies that shaped the crucibles of city environments and ecologies.

Moreover these boundaries cloud the evolution of geology as a natural process that lies clearly on the map of cosmology and the universe's evolution over the last 14 billion years. Our third rock from the sun is embedded in the energy, matter and light from which all known reality has emerged. And when we view that context of time and space, the environment of cities suddenly becomes exciting, curious and awe-inspiring. Then we can see that the city's true heritage spans the ever-complexifying evolutionary map from the galaxies to the solar system, the lithosphere, the hydrosphere, the atmosphere, the biosphere, the anthropos-phere and finally civilization (see Figure 1.1) (Eddy, 2005). If we consider the start of civilization to be synonymous with the emergence of *Homo sapiens sapiens*, then we are looking at the city within the context of a very short history indeed. For if the first identifiable member of our species dates back approximately 100,000 years, then our first city is only about 5,000 years old.

Cities located in different geographies have emerged by solving the same core problems in different ways. We have lulled ourselves into thinking that the essential services of the city are listed on the directory of any city hall: land use, water management, waste management (solid and liquid), transportation, build-ing. But few city halls concern themselves with essential "off-directory" services like food and energy supply, distribution and management, health care or educa-tion. In the Western (democratic capitalist/mixed economy) world, at least, those functions are left primarily to the private sector. And in the developing world, those

Figure 1.1. A brief history of the world.
Source: Eddy, 2005.

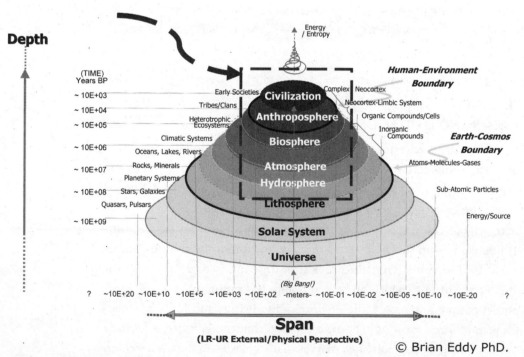

functions are usually governed by another level of government. Thus we suffer from fragmentation and partitioning no matter what form of governance systems develops and maintains policy for cities. This is actually a dilemma of life or death, because we are failing to manage even the external environment of more than 50 percent of the human species (United Nations Human Settlements, 2005).

The point is, no matter where a city is located, these functions are being performed with or without intention. And how these functions are performed is being governed ultimately not by any human decisions but by the geographic environment of the city.

Thanks to the advances in blood-typing technology and the human genome study, we can now trace the journey of humanity (see Figure 1.2) from the savannahs of Africa, around the coastlines of the Indian subcontinent, over to Australia, up into Eurasia and around the shorelines and islands of the Pacific (Wells, 2002).

Figure 1.2. Wells' journey of humanity map.
Source: Wells, 2002.

Note: This map is derived from the science of population genetics, using data from the Y chromosome.

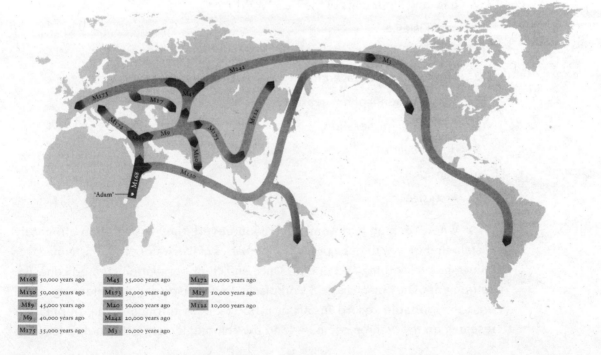

M168	50,000 years ago	M45	35,000 years ago	M172	10,000 years ago
M130	50,000 years ago	M173	30,000 years ago	M17	10,000 years ago
M89	45,000 years ago	M20	30,000 years ago	M122	10,000 years ago
M9	40,000 years ago	M242	20,000 years ago		
M175	35,000 years ago	M3	10,000 years ago		

Geographers differ as to how they categorize the world's geographies. Regardless of the classifications, Wells' map of man's and, therefore, humans' journeys takes him to virtually every one. In a parallel fashion, author Felipe Fernandez-Armesto (Fernandez-Armesto, 2001) rewrites the history of human civilization based on 17 different geographies . He considers the history within the contexts of the following crucibles. (Note that this order reflects the map that Wells' microscope discloses as the journeys' sequence in Figure 1.2.)

1. jungles
2. prairie and savanna
3. Eurasian steppes
4. temperate woodlands
5. tropical lowlands
6. swamps
7. dry alluvial soils
8. hills and mountains of the Old World
9. hills and mountains of the New World
10. small islands
11. Asian seashores
12. Mediterranean seashores
13. southern hemisphere seashores
14. North Atlantic seashore
15. desert sands
16. tundra
17. Arctic ice

Wherever man and woman have journeyed, they have had to ultimately sustain themselves through providing the basics of life: water, food, waste management, shelter, clothing and energy. Once sufficient population created cohesive settlements, they also created workplaces and transportation. Before we could read the portable record in our own body's DNA through Wells' population research on the Y chromosome — and the complementary DNA studies focusing

on the female mitochondria, popularized in *Seven Daughters of Eve* (Sykes, 2002) —
we passed along the stories of these varied environmental life conditions through
song lines, epics and myths or simply discovered the remains of past settlements
in ruins. Those secrets we have disclosed through archeological study and are
always subject to interpretation and reinterpretation.

LESSONS FROM OTHER SPECIES

When we look at other species and their relationship to their natural environment
(often called a territory), we can see that when they have evolved in large populations, like prairie dogs, rabbits or social insects, their histories run in cycles where
overpopulation is balanced against the supply of the basic necessities of life. In
most cases, that balance is maintained by the interlocking cycles of births and
food supply. Where the latter meets or exceeds the needs of the former, births
continue to rise. When it falls below the minimum needs, not only do births fall,
but the population is reduced by deaths through famine and disease. Hobbs'
premodern view of the human experience of this cycle was that life is "nasty,
brutish and short."

However, with the science of systems thinking and complexity, we can find an
example of a living system that transcends the limitations of this food-depletion
cycle by creating an intelligent learning feedback loop. The honeybee seems to have
developed a life-sustaining system that is focused not on the single bee but on the
survival of the hive. The nature of the honeybee is instructive because the co-intelli-
gence of the hive sustains not just a single life or even the hive's life, but contributes
to, i.e., adds value to, the flowers, fields and orchards that the bees pollinate.

I visualize an Integral City that is as much in synch with its environment as
the honeybees are with theirs. An Integral City would live sustainably not just
from resources taken from the environment, but because appropriate resources
were intentionally returned to the environment. Thus a self-supporting seasonal
feedback loop would operate. The beginnings of this possibility are now emerging
through a convergence of positive and negative factors related to the food we eat.

On the positive side, movements like the slow food movement, which orig-
inated in Italy, are spreading around the world. Its tenets are to source your food
locally, cook it in simple, traditional, taste-enhancing ways and share it in socially
engaging dining experiences.

The growing institutionalization of eating locally, reported by Bill McKibben and the 100 *Mile Diet* (Smith & MacKinnon, 2007), are similar movements resulting from experiments by citizens and city agencies to procure locally sourced foods. These positive re-engagements of the city with its region are matched (at time of writing) by the terrifying specters of unsafe food practices in food-exporting countries where safety standards are lacking or unenforced, causing the introduction of everything from herbicides, pesticides and toxins to outright poisons. In addition, the practices of recycling animal parts to feed self-similar species (e.g., cattle offal manufactured into cattle feed) has led to scares like bovine spongiform encephalopathy (BSE) (or its human equivalent Creutzfeldt-Jakob disease, thought to be caused by the same agent). The mysterious and spontaneous appearance of avian flu, foot-and-mouth and other zoonotic diseases raises further concerns about not just where we source our food energy, but how we raise it in the first place.

These bleak experiences cast a garish light on the "end of Nature" argument (McKibben, 2007). Human activity is influencing the functioning of "nature" — but even though we have the hubris to assume that we know what we are doing, our innocence and ignorance about the massive entanglement of natural systems means that, at this stage of human development, we are more often wrong than right. Likewise for those who propose the "end of geography" — that globalization and technological development mean we are no longer subject to geographic constraints — I suggest that this is a premature conclusion. It smacks strongly of domination thinking, without the recognition that geography may be transcended by human systems but will also have to be included. For those who joust at the constraints that geography has offered the human race, I would invite them to expand their view of Earth-centered geography to solar system and galactic geography. Integral geography transcends and includes all these.

Nevertheless, as a result of these positive food-based (energy-resourcing) movements and negative (energy-depleting) dysfunctions, it is time to notice that there are many strategic reasons for the city to renegotiate its relationship with the country or ecoregion. When more people lived in the country than in the city, the relationship of country to city was close and interconnected. Now with this reversed, their relationship is fragmented, disconnected and unappreciated. An intelligent Integral City would nurture its ecoregion with integrity and awareness that their lives were intimately integrated.

As we count the costs and dangers of global warming caused by the burning of fossil fuels generating carbon dioxide, we can look at the food on our plates that has traveled on average 2,000 kilometers (Smith & MacKinnon, 2007) and reassess the real necessity that we renegotiate city relationships with ecoregion resources. It is fast becoming a mark of city responsibility as well as city resilience.

This new appreciation of our interconnections is also a sign of city maturity. It is as if until now we have lived in an era of city centricity, like egocentricity in the individual. And now we are passing into a time of ecoregional centricity, like family, clan and tribal centricity in an individual. If this trajectory of emergence holds true, in the future, cities will live at global centricity. At that time, they will see how and what they contribute to the value of the globe, because they are able to accomplish that without devaluing their region, and/or even adding value to their region. Until cities are able to do that, they are likely not able to add net value to the world.

LOCATION, LOCATION, LOCATION

Just as honeybees adapt themselves to different geographies, human settlements must adapt different solutions to the same infrastructure problems. Each location provides a unique combination of matter, energy and information in its resources. Over time humans have discovered and developed different technological solutions for city infrastructure that are appropriate for each distinctive environment. This has required ingenuity and experimentation. For example, building materials tend to be indigenous to their location; often what has worked or was available in one location either won't work or is not available in another.

Many times in history this has been a costly learning. A modern example illustrates the problem well. On the West Coast of North America in the Sunbelt of California, a characteristic flat roof and deck construction was developed. Two thousand kilometers north, this building design was copied and built into apartments and condominiums in the temperate rainforest of British Columbia. Within a few short months and years, the building envelopes in BC failed because the flat roof design held the rain that rotted the wooden substructures of the walls.

So it appears we have good reasons to accept that different infrastructures are needed to supply the basics of human subsistence in different geographies. Moreover inappropriate infrastructures and/or technologies cannot be imported without due consideration from one geo-region to another. As a result, we realize that a city's capacity to deliver services has serious constraints and limits. Until very recently, those constraints and limits have been attributed to our technologies, rather than to the carrying capacity of the geographic bioregion itself.

The evidence for this is that, virtually without exception, every city on Earth has developed not just to supply the basic subsistence levels of human requirements, but its population has assumed that wealth can be accumulated in its borders without consideration for the costs of producing, maintaining or using such wealth. A perfect example emerges as cities grow from villages to towns to small cities to large urban centers. With every expansion, the settlement creates new requirements for transportation of people, resources and manufactured goods. As distances increase, new transportation dilemmas arise. Humans keep inventing new vehicles as if their operation existed outside the context of energy supplies, clean air, storage space or threats to life. Thus we create the conditions for pollution and gridlock.

If we are looking for an intelligent and Integral City, we can find very few who have attempted to institute any limitations that intentionally match the size of the city to its environmental carrying capacity. (A few resort developments come to mind like Whistler, BC. When the city was inaugurated, a limit to the number of hotel beds was instituted. In a similar way, the Mexican government instituted bed caps and water usage caps for the development of tourism infrastructure in the Baja Peninsula.) Because of this immense failure to match city demands to geo-bio carrying capacity, most cities suck up water, matter and energy indiscriminately. The closest city hall seems to get to practising responsible resource use is instituting lawn watering restrictions in dry summers. But for the most part, cities fail to examine the relevant information that tells us the life of the city is endangering the environment that supports it.

SEEKING RESILIENCE

The recent sciences of sustainability have confirmed that each geo-bioregion has limits to its carrying capacity. The eco-footprint (Rees & Wackernagel, 1994) insight even turned this assumption inside out and demonstrated that, if all cities operated with the level of resources used in the developed world, we would need four or more planets. If we do not respect regional and Earth-based limits to carrying capacity, then human settlements become subject to the same rules of nature that govern other animal species (back to our prairie dogs and rabbits). Some say we forget the lessons of history, but I am not sure that we have ever intentionally learned them in regard to intelligent cities. Often it is only the artifacts of our failed experiments that remind us that we had a lesson to learn. But the reminders show ironically that the teachable moment has existed just after the peak of the city (or civilization's) existence (Diamond, 2005). Once that tipping point is reached, however, it is usually too late for the city and/or the civilization. No doubt every geographic zone has similar tales to tell as those frozen stories in the stones of Uxmal, Ashkenaze and Easter Island.

The experiences of modern-day disasters do not allay these realities. The emergency response systems of the world have provided some resilience to the tragedies of various earthquakes (San Francisco, Osaka, Los Angeles, Mexico City) while being ineffective in the face of others (Pakistan, 2005). They have been partially effective for floods like the Mississippi River (1993) and the Indian Ocean tsunami (2004) but seriously corrupted when the New Orleans' levees failed after Hurricane Katrina in 2005. Our lack of intelligent design in city building, servicing and maintenance means that some day soon multiple disasters striking multiple locations simultaneously will outstrip our capacity to respond and/or rescue.

We lack both a philosophy and a science of sustainable human settlement. That is what Integral City seeks. The State of the World's Cities (United Nations Human Settlements, 2005) should be able to report not just on the major problems of city infrastructure (like poverty, slums and pollution) for which we have data in excess. It should be able to report not even just on the best practices — mainly because they are simply addressing the greatest problems. The State of the World's Cities should be able to report on the relationship of cities to the carrying capacity of their ecoregion and the Earth as a whole.

Integral City and my organization are looking for ways to describe resilience in terms of the parameters to which existing cities can adjust. It is also looking for these parameters to create new cities that enable the emergence and sustenance of human systems at optimal levels so that all human fractals are adding value to the Earth.

We know that we are not the only seekers for better solutions. The deep inquiries of reflective pioneer on the nature of order, architect Christopher Alexander, set a standard still appreciated by few. Cradle-to-cradle eco-aware designer Bill

McDonough has set a design trajectory that embraces living systems. But rarely do other developers dare the experiments where serendipity shows how to create new life-giving designs. Too often the developers of new cities and intentional communities espouse whole-system approaches solely to attract funding or families, while they appear to be missing key intelligences that will truly allow their creations to thrive. (The various developers of Japan's floating city, the desert city of Dubai, and the Baja Peninsula come to mind.)

APPLYING THE ECO-FOOTPRINT

The honeybees' strategy is so sustainable because they have evolved a goal that is supported by coexisting with their environment. Producing 40 pounds of honey per year to support their hive essentially defines the intentions of their operation

Figure1.3. Our ecological footprint.
Source: Rees & Wackernagel, 1994, p. 67.

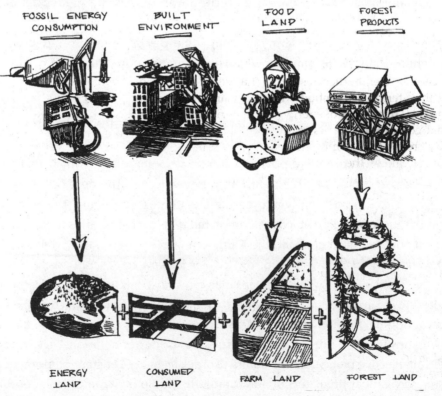

as well as setting limits to it. There is a reason for a beehive's shape and size; it has to do with climate control (Gould & Gould, 1988). When the number of bees generates too much heat for it to keep cool (and thus to support them), the hive swarms and uses its (remarkable) intelligence to send out the excess (properly constituted) bee population to locate and build a new hive.

What is the human equivalent for a city of 40 pounds of honey a year for the hive? Does it relate to what has become called the ecological footprint (see Figure 1-3) (Rees & Wackernagel, 1994) that measures the total per-city load on the environment imposed by its population? It translates into the land area necessary "to sustain current levels of resource consumption and waste discharge by that population" (p. 5). The ecological footprint creates a common denominator of resource consumption (measured in terms of energy use) and land displacement.

The ecological footprint is the first stage of developing true natural-capital-based vital-signs monitors. Eco-footprints provide a wake-up call for cities who measure their resource consumption and equivalent land displacements to realize the extent to which they borrow natural capital from both surrounding and distant geo-bioregions. Perhaps the resource consumption aspect of the equation tells us the equivalent of how much "honey" we think we need to sustain any particular city? At the same time, maybe the land displacement measure gives us the size of the field needed to support this human hive?

After applying the ecological footprint calculations, we actually need the equivalent of three or more Earths to sustain everyone at the level of North American consumption. Clearly such a proposition is neither reasonable nor acceptable. The lessons of nature and culture would seem to recommend strongly that humans take responsible action to reduce the size of city eco-footprints and reframe and/or reinvent what resources are needed in order to operate and survive sustainably. A comprehensive identification of these needs would translate into identifying the unique levels of resource consumption that could be sustained in each of the geographies of the world.

This conclusion is neither new (Rees & Wackernagel, 1994) nor controversial. More recent measures of climate change, after a ten-year trend of record global warming, may well be providing the heat trigger used by the bees to say that it is time to swarm (Monbiot & Prescott, 2007). Because our technology has not yet provided us with immediate access to another one or two Earths, we must "swarm inwards." That means finding ways to lighten our resource consumption and thereby lower the overheating of our local and global environments.

This sounds simple in principle, but it involves a myriad interconnected choices that can work together towards achieving this superordinate goal. But if that is simply to reduce what many people already assume is their right, we are not likely to succeed. Instead we must look for a positive superordinate goal that gives us a target of health and well-being. This demands that we go far beyond simply selecting a national happiness indicator (thank you, Bhutan) to using our intelligence to measure well-being at climatic, geological and biological levels so they can support our levels of consciousness.

Some enthusiasts will say that easy tactics simply require replacing fossil fuels, which are not renewable and consume energies stored in the geology from prior ages, with renewable energies like biomass and methane. This may well be a factor in an overall strategy, but using land to produce renewable fuels diverts energy from food crops and other uses, e.g., shelter. Biofuel also requires the use of precious water resources, about whose cycles and limits we are little better informed than we are about global warming.

However intractable the survival algorithm is, it is not impossible. If a living intelligent system like a beehive can figure out how to balance consumption and productive land capacity, it is an object lesson that human systems can also. Creative energy specialists like George Monbiot (Monbiot & Prescott, 2007) are taking serious aim at amassing the required knowledge to interlink a suite of energy technologies that could address the global warming issue.

Another example of land-use responsibility comes from First Nations methodologies for managing their territories. It gives us some hints about where to look. In the Northwest Pacific Coast, it was traditional for each First Nations tribe to divide up and manage their civilizations by watershed (Durning, 2004). In so doing, not only did they recognize the importance of taking responsibility for the water of life, but this apparently simple act of stewardship focused each tribe on learning intimately how to intelligently live on and replenish the watershed. With this focus, they developed the wisdom to ensure the survival of (seven) future generations and the responsibility to take action based on the climatic-geological-biological crucibles of their civilizations. This was not perfect, but the traditional respect for the interconnection of all systems (along the spectrum of life) far surpassed the Eurocentric mechanistic view of life and the city. Perhaps some of the philosophy of the Integral City is embedded in the First Nations tales of the Great Maker?

The new biology (Lipton, 2005; Sahtouris, 1999; Sheldrake, 2003) shows that life is ever-evolving, and through the human links to all other living systems, our bond with the land is inescapable. Since an Integral City is situated on land (or at least some Earth surface that might also include water, ice or a combination), we have a responsibility to re-examine those bonds and renegotiate our relationship and obligations to them. The ecological footprint is just the beginning of that renegotiation. Once we can measure the total effect of consumption, then we gain perspectives on how to measure the difference between suboptimal and over-consumption. And determining the difference between those levels of consumption will vary with geography. One size will not fit all.

The eco-footprint becomes the starting point for a serious conversation. The climate warming indicators are singing the siren song of the tipping point that may cause climate chaos. Now our own intelligence provides the lenses to go even further upstream and ask, what is the meaning of well-being for the Earth, each geo-bioregion and the spectrum of human system fractals from individuals to cities?

RELATING THE EXTERIOR ENVIRONMENT TO INTERIOR CITY LIFE

When we talk about the external environment of the city as the context for its built environment and for the natural environment that runs through it, we are much better able to see how materially dependent the city's existence is on that environment. For the most part, modern

FLOATING CITY MINIMIZES IMPACT

Virtually managing a small city on the high seas, Holland America Lines has an environmental officer who is responsible for minimizing the impact of the cruise ship on its marine environment. New ships come equipped with smokestack fuel scrubbers and water and waste recycling plants that return potable water to the oceans. However, recent shore-based legislation in California is counterproductive to reducing environmental impact. Although certain ports like Los Angeles are offering rewards for maintaining 12-knot speeds inside local waters, one captain told me that they don't realize or seem to care that, in order for the vessels to comply with that legislation and meet their cruising schedules, the ships race to get inside the reduced rate zone at much higher speeds. This simply displaces the impact of carbon emissions into other locations along the route that don't have the same guidelines. The captain suggested that the legislation needed much wider application in order to achieve the intended results for all cities along the route (and downwind).

city residents just take all that for granted — until the realities make themselves known, usually through forces of nature precipitating disastrous events.

While earthquakes provide vivid images of nature's power for the evening news, the more subtle but even more powerful forces at work in the environment do not provide drive-by photo opportunities. For two weeks in 2006, the city of Vancouver experienced the inconvenience of a boil-water order for two million people, when mudslides, resulting from autumn rainstorms, increased the turbidity of its water into the danger zone. Likewise Toronto in 2004 faced a World Health Organization travel advisory when the SARS epidemic turned up in its hospitals. Both of these are pointed reminders about the fragility of city infrastructures. But they also exemplify two different classes of dangers — the first was apparently a locally caused event, while the second appeared to be a globally caused event. In fact, like the whole-system phenomenon of the weather, both catastrophes are actually embedded in interconnected global systems of weather, disease and transportation. While the appearance of SARS was localized largely to Toronto (with a less severe outbreak in Vancouver), it was nevertheless imported from different environments across the globe.

The reality of the (modern) city is that the issues of consciousness, intention and responsibility are the gateways of understanding, preventing and transforming material challenges because the boundaries of local environments are perpetually porous. When the elements of life can manifest butterfly effects (Lorenz, 1995) half a world away, with disastrous consequences in remote and different environments, then resourceful conscious attention and intention may hold the only keys to survival.

But who is responsible for the stewardship of city resources? With the unfolding of human systems, the answer to that question largely depends which country you are in. International developer Gail Hochachka proposes that people's feelings, beliefs and worldviews affect how they are ready and willing to participate in sustainable behaviors (2005, p. 1). Moreover, she points out that traumatic experiences, like natural disasters and war, can damage people and leave them disabled from appropriate responses. Although these interior realities of a city's population have been largely ignored or discounted because they are subjective, invisible and difficult to study, they are just as real as the exterior physical realties of the city. Interior realities create an interior environment that has just as many or more layers, contours and textures to it as geographic environments. We have studied them through the lenses of psychology, philosophy and the humanities, but until recently we have not recognized that, like our exterior qualities, they evolve and develop. We map the paleontology of our interiors through the shifts in worldviews that enable the growth of our interior landscapes and, therefore, our capacities for response, adaptability and resilience. The key centers of those internal views are the self, the other (family, clan) and the world (society, sectors, spheres of influence, regions, globe).

The subjective and intersubjective realities of these interiors are discussed in detail in chapters 5 and 8. However, here we need to recognize and honor these inner ecologies of being, becoming and relating because, like the exterior world, they are both massively entangled and imbued with patterns that contribute to the reality of the city. We can find examples where ego drives the worldview of rulers, like Ahmadinejad in Iran, Kim Jong Il of North Korea or Chavez in Venezuela, and how their policies affect the lives of everyone in the cities of those countries.

We can point to examples where tribes control cities (e.g., Kandahar or Baghdad) and the relationships of people in those cities are controlled by the power of tribal worldviews. The majority of countries depend on federal governments as dominant landowners, military rulers and governors. Countries with more recent constitutions have evolved multiple levels of government where state or provincial, county/regional and municipal governments take responsibility. Still other cities are influenced largely by dominant private-sector companies that not only are private landowners and developers, but also essentially control the economies of the surrounding area because of their influence. Thus we can see the powerful reality and influence of internal ecologies and their inter-relationship with external environments in the city. We will never be able to change the latter if we do not change the former.

In a few locations where social enterprise and social justice are coming on stream as organizing structures, not-for-profit (NFP) landowners have created intentional communities where the responsibility is shared in dialogic and consultative fashion (e.g., Community Builders Benevolence Society, Vancouver; and Multi-Faith Housing Initiative, Ottawa). In fact wherever any human settlement comes into existence, whether planned or wild, ultimately a form of governance must emerge to make the decisions that living in such close proximity demands.

Modes of governance, ranging from dictatorial to democratic, reflect the interior worldviews and mindsets of both city leaders and citizens. They are ever-emergent and constantly being renegotiated because the stability of cities is forever dynamic. But one thing is becoming clear: some worldviews are more inclusive and more soundly contexted than others. In other words, the internal life of those who coalesce authority, power and influence contributes largely to the capacity of cities to be coherent, adaptable and sustainable. We are fast becoming aware that sustainability means living in the world with mindfulness about our relationship to its realities. Our inner capacities must match our outer intentions.

One of the most perennial proofs of this relationship of the internal human environment to the external environment is the tragedy of the commons. Once an esoteric oddity, the tragedy of the commons has become vividly illustrated by the writing of such authors as Jared Diamond (2005), Ronald Wright (2004) and Thomas Homer-Dixon (2006) who have delved into the startling evidence in the ruins of great civilizations to observe that "progress is hard on the environment." Moreover, they have revealed that the commonly held view is often one that provides the least responsible perspective on how to value and steward a civilization's resources. It appears that history tells us that if we do not choose to learn the fundamentals of sustainability, nature has bold and dramatic ways of bringing the lesson to life (or death in many cases).

Thus we are learning that overcoming the tragedy of the commons requires mindfulness, accountability and vital signs monitoring. Our internal environments need to connect to our external environments in very specific ways, so that we are capable of administering human systems as complex as cities, so that both individual and collective human life can survive. If we fail at this task, for instance, favoring the interests of a few, without considering the interests of the many, once again nature has demonstrated that we lose diversity in the system and, ultimately, resilience. In the face of any disaster, both diversity and resilience are what we need most. What's more, diversity is a major contributor to innovation and the driver of new combinations and inventions (Homer-Dixon, 2006).

Once we see the importance of the mindset and worldview of the city, then we can see the underpinnings of its attitude and relationship to its geo-bio base. And with the largest view possible — these days from external satellites serving global positioning systems and internal maps of human consciousness — we can also see what is working (what's aligned and coherent), what's not working (what's misaligned and incoherent) and what are the city's next natural opportunities and capacities for change.

Then we are able to notice the different perspectives that exist in the city because of different levels of expertise. We can see how the city infrastructure that is managed by expert managers and engineers brings the values of scientific knowledge and experience. And we can also see that despite the value of this expertise and the infrastructure systems, they tend to distance citizens from taking ownership and responsibility for their contribution to the healthy operation of the systems.

Cities are faced with the challenging task of translating this expertise into terms that citizens can understand and take responsibility for. This is why we need to monitor the use of resources at the user level by metering water, fuel, waste production, transportation, land use and CO_2 production. We may even have to adopt rationing for dangerous elements like CO_2 as proposed by George Monbiot (Monbiot & Prescott, 2007) so that we have logical and measureable targets. In the same way that citizens readily adjust their food and housing decisions because they are paying for them, consumers of resources who pay as they use start taking responsibility for waste and inefficiencies that lead to depletion of resources and the tragedy of the commons.

GROWING CAPACITY VERSUS OUTGROWING RESILIENCE

If we are truly trying to be intelligent about living in our cities, we must sooner or later ask where is the consciousness about renewable versus non-renewable resources? Renewable resources like food and biofuels allow us to become sustainable through managed production processes. However, we now know that even renewable resources come with caveats and constraints determined by the inputs to the growth process. Land use, water and fertilizing nutrients are all finite in their availability for renewable resources. In that respect, the inputs are closer to the non-renewable resources we usually associate with carbon-based fuels.

We know from our history that when resources were sufficient we were profligate with our use of them, e.g., food, forests, water, fuel, irrigation channels. However, as populations increase, cities tend to produce less and import more. Cities have a settlement cycle: produce or import needs; produce and self-support needs, reduce imports; over-produce, export excess; import luxuries. This life cycle of cities is discussed in more detail in chapter 4.

When cities are ignorant of their use of resources (i.e., don't stop importing needs and/or don't reduce use of resources), they risk overusing them and depleting them permanently or overproducing waste, e.g., overusing single-person car trips, overconsuming carbon-based fuels and overproducing greenhouse gases. Moreover, the cumulative effect of multiple cities drawing on one geo-bioregion accelerates the depletion of resources and creates the preconditions for the tragedy of the commons, where as one city in a bioregion will fail, all will fail. The resources in question are likely to be water, energy and food. Diamond (2005) describes in graphic detail the demise of the settlements of the Ashkenaze in what is now the American Southwest. He speculates, based on the archeological evidence, that the competition for water, energy and food resulted in starvation (and cannibalism), salinized land (from overirrigation) and a society completely turned in on itself. It is a dire warning of the intimate relationship cities have with their ecoregion. Monitoring protocols and/or systems of vital-signs indicators can tell a city that its policies, created through subjective ways of knowing and inter-subjective agreements, are poisoning its future. If cities do not create or take heed of such warning systems, they will certainly be doomed to suffer and maybe to die. At the time of writing, warnings about global warming are just starting to incur notice and debate in the public sphere (Adger et al., 2007) .

The chronicles of cities show us with certainty that a people who do not know their history are doomed to repeat it. This knowledge combines the subjective and intersubjective life of the populace — the individual and collective con-sciousness — that must be mindful of the biological and structural life of the city.

Only in our conscious awareness (attention and intention) can we engage with the issues that are truly important in the external, visible, physical, objective and interobjective life of the city. It is yet again a reminder of the holographic nature of the city and how *each* of the four integral perspectives (subjective, intersubjective, objec-tive and interobjective) necessarily includes *all* of the four integral perspectives.

THE SYMBIOTIC RELATIONSHIP OF THE CITY TO ITS ECOREGION

It is clear that the city has a special symbiotic relationship with its ecoregion. This is true despite the globalization of trade in every basic commodity from water, food, fuel to all manner of processed and manufactured goods. Even cities like Singapore or those in small trading-based nations like the Netherlands or Costa Rica, who import most of what they consume, are dependent on maintaining relationships with the geo-bioregion to ensure the flow of used matter/energy (a.k.a. waste), manage the access to and/or protection from water (especially ocean systems) and share responsibilities for land-use management with neighboring states.

In chapter 2 we explore the implications that cities are dissipative structures that require and enable the constant flow of energy through structures that are, for long periods of time, basically maintained intact. The enabling of the free flow of energy to build and maintain city structures against the forces of the environment (including all climatic, tectonic, geographic and biologic conditions) is a prodigious task requiring advanced intelligences. Thomas Homer-Dixon has attempted to quantify the immensity of the goal by calculating the energies required "simply" to build the Roman Forum (Homer-Dixon, 2006). He demonstrates clearly the linkages of the city of Rome to the outer ecoregions of the Roman Empire. It is a historical application of the eco-footprint that can remind us how blind we are to the city's current needs to constantly replenish its energy-matter-information flows to sustain the dissipative structures we have created and on which we now depend.

As money is a proxy for much, if not all, of the energy flowing through our cities, we are often reminded that we should "follow the money" to gain understanding of particular commercial situations. Because the city depends on funds raised from taxes, and/or private investment for its sustenance, by following the money, we can usually see that those with power in the city bring vast sums of money into the city from mining (logging, harvesting, exploiting) ecoregions near and far. With ecoregions typically being out of sight and out of mind, and with their declining populations, it is easy to be lulled into complacency that the ecoregions will supply a never-ending bounty for the use of the cities. However, as we have seen in this chapter and will examine further, the infinite resources are a false assumption. Each ecoregion has its own unique carrying capacity, with particular requirements for renewal and sustainability. For the most part we are only just beginning to understand what those investments and reinvestments ought to be. The honeybees could teach us vital principles to put into effect.

GAVIOTAS ADDS VALUE TO ENVIRONMENT

The little Columbian city of Gaviotas is an unusual example of a pioneer city adding value to its environment. Twenty years ago, the high desert plains of Columbia, southeast of the most ecologically diverse jungle park of Serrana de la Macarena, attracted the attention of Paolo Lugari, a visionary and inventor (Weisman, 1998). In the middle of nowhere, a self-organizing community was conceived and emerged as an experiment in sustainability. The founder believed it was possible to create an urban settlement that was self-sufficient with food, water and even power. He invited a core of self-made experts and inventors to join him in this seemingly impossible task. Perhaps their greatest accomplishment was to develop a set of guiding principles that focused on the value of relationships and community. That provided the context for all their manifestation of material progress. Against all odds, they discovered a freshwater lens that had remained hidden to others. They invented a pump to access the water and a solar-powered electrical-generating source. With these fundamentals, they set out to discover what food would grow in the seemingly parched and infertile land. Through trial and error, they developed a productive garden and small-animal husbandry. They went on to conceive of work that would support the community, not only to subsist in Gaviotas, but to flourish. They decided to design and produce versions of the inventions they had created for export to other communities in the world.

People came and went from Gaviotas, but a core of the founding people maintained the vision and the continuity of purpose (i.e., the left-hand quadrants discussed in chapter 3). The growing community managed its own affairs, resolving internal conflicts and reaching out to the outside world for support in distributing their production. But more amazing than their success at handling their internal growth was their success at surviving in the face of the ongoing strife and struggle of Columbia's notorious drug wars. Although Gaviotas was far from any main transportation route, that very fact led the drug warriors to discover Gaviotas as a convenient drop-in point en route to evading the law or invading neighboring countries. Even though Gaviotas was occupied by the drug culture periodically, it maintained an official position of neutrality to both the drug lords and the government. Gaviotas refused to take sides, while at the same time refusing to participate in the drug culture for any gains or convenience. In that way, it earned a grudging respect from the drug guerillas and created conditions that exempted it from destruction.

The story of Gaviotas does not end here. Its greatest success came by surprise. As the budding horticulturists continued their research to expand the garden output, they experimented with trees that would sprout and root. Most of the seedlings they tried survived for a few weeks or months and then died for lack of nutrients, too much sun or too little water. This experiment in forestry seemed futile at best. Nevertheless the Gaviotans optimistically persisted, collecting seeds from various trips to other geographies. Eventually they hit upon a species that would grow long enough to survive beyond the vulnerable seedling stage and develop into a community grove. This came to be taken for granted as it continued to strengthen, until the most surprising discovery of all occurred at Gaviotas. As the grove survived and expanded, somehow it became the incubator for a species of tree that prospered in the jungle swamps of northern Columbia. How the seeds got to Gaviotas no one knows, but one day the sprouted wild seedlings were discovered amongst the plantation, obviously thriving. It appeared that the Gaviotans had discovered how to create tropical rainforest out of high-plain desert. The forest has continued to expand and thrive.

Admittedly Gaviotas is a small-scale, young settlement still. However, it seems to have accomplished what the honeybees have figured out. How can a city add value to the geo-bioregion while using its resources in a sustainable way?

With an increasing awareness that the relationship of city and country depends not only on the flow of resources, but on how we value the relationship, we stand at the beginning of an era when renegotiating that relationship will become critical to our future well-being. If we consider the possibility that our attitudes and values will expand to the point where every city will have a stewardship relationship with its ecoregion and with the overall well-being of the Earth, we may develop an ethic of sustainability with cities playing a leading role.

What if every city took responsibility for the food and energy fields that fed its dissipative structures? What if that was as natural as bees gathering pollen to make the honey that supports their hives?

CONCLUSION

We have come to a stage of city evolution where the scale of our urban development is now visibly exceeding the carrying capacity of bioregions and the Earth to support cities. Our unexamined assumptions about how to support the infrastructure of a city demands that we wake up. It is time to respect the data that is confronting us daily. We need to listen deeply to the recommendations for change that experts are proclaiming; and we need to take action to live in a manner that is coherent with our natural life conditions. If we fail to do so, we will suffer the most grave consequences to our lifestyle and even life expectancy, which will indisputably change our ways. The meltdown of New Orleans in 2005 is just a small example of how vulnerable even the cities of the developed world are.

QUESTIONS

1. What are the geographic, climatic conditions that make my city unique?

2. What would have to change for my city to have a zero footprint?

3. How are cities like the nodes of a global energetic network? What value and special qualities does my city node add to the well-being of the world?

Three simple rules for applying Integral City principles from this chapter:

1. Honor the climate and geography of your city.

2. Steward the environment.

3. Add value to the ecosphere.

EMERGING INTELLIGENCE: SEEING WHOLENESS IN THE HUMAN HIVE

Every species has a niche — a strategy for making its living that is different from those of the other species in its habitat.

— Gould and Gould, 1988, p. 20

How can we fail to appreciate the magnificence of existence?

— Clare W. Graves

WHY SEE THE CITY AS A WHOLE SYSTEM?

This chapter presents highlights from a range of sciences that allow us to consider the city as a whole system. We examine wholeness through the lenses of aliveness, survival, adaptiveness, regeneration, sustainability and emergence. This chapter may seem overwhelming to some readers, and if that is the case, then read around it or sample it as you are inclined.

This chapter attempts to stick to the principles of whole-systems thinking that apply to all four aspects of the Integral City that are discussed in subsequent chapters — subjective, intersubjective, objective and interobjective. Thus it serves each of those chapters, without trying to duplicate what they have to say. Neither is it exhaustive about any of the sciences it references — books abound to do a thorough job of that.

I believe that to truly appreciate the complexity of the city we need to see it as if it were a whole system and have some language to talk about the city as a whole system. In fact we need some language to talk about the city as a system of

METAPHORS OF THE CITY

The city IS a whole. As Manuel De Landa (2006) says, the wholeness is not metaphorical, but it is hard to grasp. So, the images offered by metaphors are a way of holding the whole — and are inspired here by the excellent exploration of Gareth Morgan in his *Images of Organization* (1998).

Metaphors can help us to understand the city as a whole. When we can point to something else and say the city is "like" this, then we get a picture of how we are making meaning of the city. These metaphors are organized according to the quadrants discussed in chapter 3.

At traditional levels of thinking, it has been natural to think of the city in terms of a clockwork or machine. From the Lower Right quadrant, a machine is a mechanical device where all the parts work well when they are well oiled. It may have gears and levers. The machine reduces human labor and is under human control. The city as machine has also been reflected in our language about political machines. Thinking about the city as machine keeps people at a distance from the built structures. The city is outside of us. We live in it or on it. The advantage of this metaphor is that it seems especially helpful to grasping the mechanical, linear, sequential nature of much of the city structures that have been designed, installed and maintained by engineers — the streets, the water mains, the sewers, the telephone lines. The disadvantage of this metaphor is that it doesn't account for the living, non-linear unpredictable characteristics of the city.

A related metaphor for the city is a clock. (Again, related to the Lower Right quadrant.) The city runs like a clock. It has gears meshed together like buses connecting at their hub. It hums and ticks with movement and moves ever-forward with time. The clock metaphor conveys progress and precision. It is more than mechanical — once it is wound up or powered on, it is designed to operate on its own with little intervention. The controls are built in. The advantage of this metaphor is that it conveys the interconnections of the city that make it work well. This metaphor conveys the competence of its creators and the intelligence of its controllers. Like the machine metaphor it is linear but in terms of time rather than space. The disadvantage of this metaphor is that it doesn't leave room for the disconnects, the surprises or the breakdowns that are inevitably part of city life. It implies that citizens all march to the same regimented clockwork, which the vicissitudes of daily life in any individual household clearly contradicts.

From the Upper Right quadrant come metaphors for the city like cell, brain and body, clearly drawing on the living fractals embedded in the city. Such metaphors exist on a smaller scale, making the intricacy of the city more accessible and understandable. We can take what is not generally visible as a whole landscape and reduce the size of the container so that we can understand it. The advantage of these metaphors is that there is considerable truth and alignment to them. When we view cities as having extended human capacities, it makes sense to relate their operations to smaller versions of those same capacities. The disadvantage of these metaphors is that the city is anthropomorphized and made too simple. They convey the impression that the city can be wholly understood, and they downshift the true complexity of hundreds of thousands of people living together.

The metaphor of the city as a garden comes close to conveying the city as a complex container of a living ecology. The garden has a relationship with the gardener(s) and is differentiated from the wild landscape. Gardens generally have zones or areas that interconnect with other parts of the garden. You can walk around a garden. The advantage of this metaphor is it conveys a city that is accessible, beautiful and grown with intention. By extension the gardeners could represent the mayor, council, city hall staff and citizens. However, the disadvantage of this metaphor is that it conveys more control and less complexity than exist in a real city. It also seems to omit the qualities of consciousness and the variety of beliefs that exist in a real city.

The metaphors of the city as a tree, plant or fruit such as "the Big Apple" focus the garden metaphor on a smaller scale than a full garden. They are similar to the cell or brain metaphors in relation to the body. While the tree and the apple make the city accessible as a whole, since we can easily visualize them, they conflate the true business (of enabling human capacity) and never-ending quest that is the city.

Few metaphors come to mind when we look at the city from the left-hand quadrants. Even Googling possibilities like "city as soul" or "city as family" produces negligible results. So we seem not to have associated city with an inner life of the individual or the collective. Perhaps we recognize that the city is a challenging place for reflection or contemplation. In fact the city gives us less opportunity to turn inward, to find quiet, to reflect. Simply to be or belong does not seem to have transferred into metaphors of the city. Sanctuaries, retreats and havens almost seem alien to cities. They are what we seek when we want to leave the intensity of the city.

Finally the last cluster of metaphors — the anthill, the termite colony and the beehive — are all metaphors for the city as a living system with individual and social beings working in cooperation to sustain life. These metaphors convey the complexity of the city as a whole more accurately than the others because they capture the dynamics, interconnections, complexities and even the built environments. The advantage is that they convey a whole system of non-linear, complex adaptive interactions that is visible, quantifiable, observable and even apparently understandable. The disadvantage is that, once again, they seem to omit the realities of the left-hand quadrants. Although we can ascribe intelligence to these social insects, we have yet to find evidence that they are conscious of their consciousness.

Thus it would seem that an adequate metaphor for the city as a whole has not yet been coined. It is a phenomenon for which we can find no equal on Earth and for which we can only imagine a parallel if we built a substitute in outer space that would inevitably have many of the same characteristics.

integral systems. Paradoxically, in order to truly appreciate the integral frameworks discussed in the following chapters, we need to appreciate the worldviews and mindsets that thinking about whole systems can afford us.

By looking at the city as if it were a whole system, we are able to make sense of the space frames in which the city's physical elements exist (both natural and human-made). We can see the time frames in which change happens to all the elements of existence in the city at varying degrees of speed. And we can see the people frames where the diversity of human life in the city evolves and develops across the life cycles of human existence at all levels of scale: individual, family, cultural and historical.

THE CITY HAS ALIVENESS

The city has the qualities of aliveness. It springs from the fact that each person in the city is alive, but also because all the people are alive together in the city. Scientists (Capra, 1996) tell us that the qualities of aliveness are very simple. To be alive means that a system survives, connects to its environment and regenerates.

Architect Christopher Alexander believes that everyone can differentiate spectrums of aliveness. He affirms that if you showed a person or group of people two different designs of common inanimate objects like salt shakers, they could choose the one with the most qualities of aliveness. Alexander proposes that aliveness arises around a center, and that centers are made up of other centers. Centers help one another, and "the existence and life of one center can intensify the life of another" (Alexander, 2002, p. 110). Moreover he suggests that structures, like cities, gain life according to the relationship of density and intensity of centers.

In studying the Phenomenon of Life, Alexander has identified the following 15 properties that help centers come to life. They are intimately connected to the qualities of wholeness and complex adaptive systems we have been discussing.

1. Levels of scale
2. Strong centers
3. Boundaries
4. Alternating repetition
5. Positive space
6. Good shape

7. Local symmetries

8. Deep interlock and ambiguity

9. Contrast

10. Gradients

11. Roughness

12. Echoes

13. The void

14. Simplicity and inner calm

15. Not-separateness (Alexander, 2002, p. 239)

Interestingly, even by embracing a biological definition of life, Alexander's tenets and properties seem to open up other aspects of the integral model — the invisible life of the beautiful (psycho) and the good (cultural) and the shared life (social) of collective support, order and strategy. We essentially come face to face with the ecology of our ancestors, friends, relations, strangers, authority figures, experts, caregivers, politicians, bureaucrats. We realize that not being an island means that we are indeed connected to the environment we have collectively created in the city.

HOLONS ARE WHOLES

Both the sciences of physics and biology have identified ways of describing whole systems. Physicist Arthur Koestler coined the term "holon" to describe a whole system. In the city, each person is a holon. In fact a holon can also be a system of whole systems. The whole systems in the individual person, which biologist James Grier Miller (1978) has documented so well, range from the organelle, to the cell, to the organ, to the functional system, to the person. We could say that holons develop ecologies of systems at different scales.

Moreover ecologies of systems can continue to evolve within the larger whole that contains them, thus further differentiating into subsystems. This is discussed in more detail in chapters 6 and 7. A simple example would be to compare the respiratory system of the whole person to the subsystem in the cell that enables it to exchange oxygen for carbon dioxide waste. The former has not only evolved from the latter, but still transcends and includes it in its overall functioning.

Thus we could create a lattice or matrix of the differentiations and integrations of holons and subsystems at different levels of scale, which is exactly what Miller and his team did (1978).

In examining the ecology of the city as a whole, we are developing a language that contributes to understanding the patterns of life in the city. If we think of the city as the human equivalent of the beehive, we have a useful metaphor for the city as a whole. The survival of the hive is dependent on each bee following the rules and roles that contribute to hive survival, adaptiveness and regeneration. Thus the collection of bee intelligence and behavior that makes up the hive seems to operate like a dynamic responsive hive-mind.

As we look at whole systems, using our microscopes and viewing instruments to zoom in and out, we are able to see the relationships that the various subsystems have developed with one another and appreciate that the ecological relationships are quite inextricably linked. The city is clearly a whole system that cannot be separated into parts without doing damage to the whole, any more than a hive can be cut into without damaging the whole.

THE CITY SURVIVES

So let us return to the three qualities of aliveness and see how survival contributes to the whole city. Let us discover the role of containers, boundaries, dissipative structures and complex adaptive systems.

On an individual basis we can see that the quality of life, or aliveness, determines the quality of survival that a person experiences. Without reference to the integral map (described in chapter 3), usually survival is circumscribed only by biological survival — does a person have the necessary food, clothing and shelter to stay alive? But with the integral map we will expand the meaning of survival beyond the biological external life to include the inner lives of the psychological (emotional–intellectual–spiritual) and the collective external life of the cultural and social aspects of city life. When we enlarge our framework for survival in this way, we can truly see that "no man is an island unto him/herself in the city." Each person is massively interdependent on a living collective system in which he or she is embedded.

Sustenance from this interdependence can take surprising and poignant forms. Barry Lopez (Lopez & Pearson, 1990) suggests that sometimes people need stories more than food to stay alive. Stories lie at the roots of city cultural life. In *Systems of Survival* (1994), Jane Jacobs proposes that two kinds of collective systems are needed to meet the survival needs of the city: the moral system (cultural) and the commercial (social) system. These authors concur that individual survival is dependent on more than meeting basic biological needs. Lopez proposes that the intangible exchange of stories encourages life in people. Jacobs identifies the value of collectively working to create rules for moral behavior and rules for commercial exchange to enable survival.

But in order for us to grasp how an alive wholeness survives in the city, we need some basic understanding about how wholes are systems and how systems work. So let's look at the city as a container. Let's consider its boundaries. And let's see how the city's survival is foundational to its capacity to adapt.

THE CITY IS A CONTAINER WITH SHAPE-SHIFTING BOUNDARIES

It seems like a blinding flash of the obvious to say that the city has an identity. We can identify Montreal, Rio de Janeiro, Sydney and Mumbai as distinct entities. Moreover I propose that these identifiable entities are human systems. And although it is a *human* system, the city, like all systems, is a form of identifiable container with boundaries. However, the city is a very dynamic container with very special boundaries that not only separate it from its background, environment and context but enable it to shape-shift in biological, psychological, cultural and social ways.

The city's shape-shifting boundaries comprise other systems and subsystems that contribute to the city system as a whole. Sometimes these boundaries are obvious from the same plane of observation, like the view of a particular city block on Mapquest®. At other times the boundaries only become obvious when you click on a hyperlink that discloses cascades of subsystems at other planes, like with Google Earth. Exploring the qualities of these subsystems and their boundaries reveals the enormous entanglement of systems within the city. But when we zoom out to consider the city from a high-enough altitude (like we can see from an airplane at 10,000 meters), the boundaries disclose what is considered inside the city system and subsystems and how exchanges across those boundaries may occur.

From a philosophical and psychological perspective, boundaries are identified and interpreted through the lens of the person seeing them. Thus they are to some degree creations and functions of the interpreter. Therefore the boundaries

I have selected to embrace the Integral City are functions of my ways of seeing the world. To the extent that you share these ways of seeing the world, these boundaries will be visible to you too.

Glenda Eoyang classifies four kinds of boundaries in systems: rigid or fixed, fuzzy or indistinct, permeable or porous and impermeable or closed (1997, p. 110). In the city a rigid boundary might be a concrete retaining wall; a fuzzy boundary might be the differences of opinion between school board trustees; a permeable boundary might be the river's edge; and an impermeable boundary might be religious holidays. On careful reflection, we can all think of ways to negotiate, redefine and even reclassify these boundaries, and when we do so, we change the systems they serve and our relationship to them.

When we explore the Integral Model in chapter 3, we will see that these boundaries are not limited to the exterior observable kind from the objective and interobjective world of biology and physics, but they describe patterns of the interior kind in the subjective and intersubjective world of aesthetics and humanities as well. The patterns of our beliefs and worldviews disclose boundaries that grow and expand as we become ever more mindful and make meaning of our personal and interpersonal relationships.

Seeing the city as a whole helps us to realize the massive interconnections amongst its systems and subsystems, the dynamic but frequent stability of their relationships and the kinds of exchanges that can occur amongst them. These interconnections span the subjective and intersubjective along with the objective and interobjective realities of existence in the city. In fact, they reveal how the myriad systems in the city self-organize into stable and unstable patterns and relationships (see Metaphors of the City sidebar). And they also reveal the dynamics of exchange amongst multiple scales of human systems in the container of the city (see City Landscapes sidebar).

THE CITY IS A DISSIPATIVE STRUCTURE

It is always tempting to parse the city into its most visible parts or characteristics: the creative city, the green city, the medieval city, the garden city, the mile-high city. It is only natural with so many cities on Earth that we want to differentiate a city around its visibly different parts. However, the city is not a system of parts but a whole system of the human species that has characteristics as a whole that transcend but include communities, organizations, groups, families and individuals and the built environment that we have created to contain us.

We get fixated on the behaviors and intentions of all these smaller-scale human systems because we interact with them on a daily basis. However, because more than 50 percent of the Earth's population now lives in cities, the functioning of the city creates major repercussions on the quality of life for all people regardless of where they live. That is because, as a whole system, the city functions like a dissipative structure with many characteristics of a complex adaptive system.

What is a dissipative structure? It is an open system where the structural pattern is maintained, even as energy, matter and information flow through it and are dissipated by it. As a dissipative structure, the city is constantly managing the flows through it but, at the same time, maintaining a recognizable pattern from day to day. Obviously cities change over time, as the flow-state of the energy, matter and information reform it, but at any given time, we can point at the city and say, "There it was, there it is and there we expect it to be."

As a dissipative structure, the city sucks in resources from its environment and spews out products, by-products and waste to its environment. That is why, when we take into consideration all the cities of the world, their functioning affects the lives of all people regardless of where they live, inside or outside the city.

THE CITY IS A COMPLEX ADAPTIVE SYSTEM

A complex adaptive system operates far from equilibrium, with non-linear behaviors, always adapting to its environmental context. Within the city, it is clear that each person is a complex adaptive system. When we look at the composite behaviors of clusters of individuals in the city, we see fractal-like patterns in the collective that seem to mirror the complex adaptive behaviors of the individuals.

That means that city subsystems, like neighborhoods, appear to adapt to external and internal life conditions as individuals within them do so, in order to survive. They exist in an ebb-and-flow state, with periods of instability. Thus the city as a whole with its composite of neighborhoods also appears to exhibit the characteristics of a complex adaptive system.

When we look at the city as a complex adaptive system (Stevenson and Hamilton, 2001), we see that many of these qualities are similar to the ones that Alexander relates to aliveness:

- **Scaleable**: Its characteristics derive from the individual human system and any collectives, such as couples, families, teams, organizations, neighborhoods and the whole city. As a container of a collection of individuals, it occurs at scales from 50,000 (approximately) to over 20 million.

- **Quasi-fractal**: The patterns that occur at one level of scale repeat themselves at other levels. Some argue that full fractalness cannot be ascribed because of the differences between social holons and individual holons. (See discussion in subsequent chapters.)

- **Dynamic**: The city is in perpetual motion because its basic elements — people — are living systems adapting to their surroundings.

- **Unpredictable:** The massive interconnections of individuals in the city create conditions where behaviors can be unpredictable because negative and positive feedback loops create interactions that may never have happened before or small differences in the system create entirely new results. For example, the people driving to work may not always make the same decision about what route to take every day of the week.

- **Interconnected:** The city is like a neural network where everything is connected to everything else on a micro, meso and macro scale.

- **Nested:** The relationships of human systems are such that they fully or partially nest within one another (therefore, the nests themselves overlap and interconnect). For example, an individual can be a member of a family, a sports team, a work group, an organization, a community, a city.

- **Uses simple rules:** People within any given city use simple rules of engagement, including forms of greeting, eye contact, respecting personal space and what side of the road to drive on. These vary from place to place but everywhere solve the problem of how large groups of people can live together in orderly ways.

- **Subject to phase shifts:** When people live and work together, they can develop a synchrony of action and/or thought that creates feedback loops that produce a tipping point, which opens the door to an entirely different phase. In short-term positive renditions, this can be recognized as waves of ecstasy at rock concerts or the release of seemingly miraculous community coordination when people respond seamlessly to tragic events like fires, blizzards or accidents. In short-term negative renditions, this can be experienced as mindless crowd behaviors that produce everything from brutish rows at soccer games, to uncontrollable angry strikers at city hall. A long-term example of a phase shift occurred in northern England in the 1950s and '60s with the conversion of coal fires to clean fuels and the resulting improvement in respiratory health.

- **Potentially affected by weak signals:** Complex adaptive systems are so interconnected that a weak signal, like one person's crusade for a change, can create attractors and feedback support that result in change for the whole system. For example, a Vancouver activist's protest in the 1970s led to Vancouver's decision not to build freeways through the city center.

- **Field sensitive:** As a complex adaptive system, the city is a form of container that holds an energy field. That field is sensitive to energy changes from within the container and outside it. For example, it can be expressed as an esprit de corps, like the galvanizing effect in support of New York after September 11, 2001, or even a dissipation of energy, like the staccato chaos that ensued when New Orleans flooded in 2005.

THE CITY ADAPTS TO ITS ENVIRONMENT

Now that we have examined the process of survival in the city, let's move on to the second quality of aliveness: the role of adaptiveness. Let us see how differentiation, integration and resilience enable the city to adapt to its external and internal environments.

Differentiation and Integration

As we examine the patterns of evolution of all natural systems in the world, many scientists are finding that evolution emerges through discrete stages of differentiation and integration. Differentiation occurs when a holon takes on a different role than its predecessors or peers. It is like a division of labor amongst differing contributors.

Integration occurs when different holons come together under one umbrella to coordinate their processes. Integration is precedent to and necessary for the emergence of wholes from other wholes. Alexander might frame this as a new center emerging from earlier centers. One of his most fascinating examples is the 400-year historical evolution of Saint Mark's Square in Venice (Alexander, 2002). In a series of diagrams, he illustrates how the centers in the square have shifted and changed as new structures have been added, but the square has continued to exist as an alive center of the city across the centuries.

While a single holon (whether bee or person) can exist as a separate entity, its capacities are limited to processing its individual inputs and outputs. When holons combine their efforts collectively with intention, they can create a subsystem. Thereby they leverage individual efforts and produce more output with less expenditure of energy. Life likes this equation!! It also builds on it as it evolves by integrating these differentiations.

This starts the basic cycle of complex evolution or the evolution of complexity, through successive waves of differentiation and integration. From atoms, to molecules, to organelles to cells and right on up to ever-greater complexity and consciousness, life differentiates and integrates. When we see the patterns from the scale of least complex to greatest complexity, we are struck by the undeniable evidence of hierarchical differentiation and integration.

Life has evolved through synthesizing holons, systems of cooperation and hierarchies of complexity. Any examination of a phylogenetic map (that any biologist can show you) will demonstrate that the origin and evolution of species has followed these basic precepts, which is why we have such a usable analogy with the beehive and the human city. The evolution of *homo sapiens sapiens* from small family units to cities is no different. Hierarchies of differentiation and integration have emerged in city landscapes, where disorganization has evolved into self-organization and eventually organization. We get hierarchies of emergence and cooperation because it is the natural pattern-making inclination of life to develop them.

Clare Graves (2005) calls this journey of differentiation and integration, for an individual, a "never-ending quest." We stand at this time with a new appreciation that the ecology of human systems we have created is calling forth yet another level of hierarchical synthesis. We need to synthesize our understanding of systems — to move beyond differentiating discrete systems into synthesizing systems of systems. This will enable us to see the impact of clusters of cities and/or ecologies of cities linked by trade, transport and telecommunication. We need to see the impact of city systems on ecoregion systems and evolve new hierarchies of interdependence.

We are living in the age of noetic emergence, as foreseen by paleontologist Teilhard de Chardin (1966; 1972). The inclusive perspectives of hive, holons, subsystems and complex hierarchies give us insights into city adaptiveness and resilience.

Stages of Development Create Resilience

Within the ecology of the city, people are at different stages of bio-psycho-cul-tural-social development. This gives them individually and collectively more or less capacity for resilience. Resilience in the ecology of the city is merely the capacity to survive under conditions of stress. Because each person has different bio-psycho-cultural-social capacities and because life is a dynamic experience, the quality of resilience varies from person to person (and, therefore, from group to group, as discussed in chapter 8 relating to social holons).

The variation in capacities of resilience was highly visible on CNN during the 2005 New Orleans hurricane and flood disaster. In the ecology of that city, those people with greater integral development had more resilience to survive. In other words, they literally had more assets and capacities, in all four quadrants, on which to draw. They had better strength to walk away from threats and had the health to withstand privations; more options to choose from for personal comfort; stronger shared belief systems to buoy their group morale, and access to transportation modes to move out of danger. The poorest and the most disenfranchised had the greatest difficulty sur-viving. And those who were on the margins of survival only did so because eventu-ally organized private and government systems came to their aid — the collective with more assets and resources assisted those individuals with little or no resources.

The Value of the Collective for Resilience

The hive is dependent for its healthy functioning on the healthy functioning of its individual bees (holons). Likewise the city is dependent for its healthy function-ing on the healthy functioning of individual holons in the city.

But at some stage of evolution, neither the hive nor the city is totally dependent on the healthy functioning of every member of the hive or city. One of the values of the collective is that it builds in resilience so that the injury or loss of single holons does not mean the loss of the whole hive. In our individual bodies, this is easy to see — we know that in our different subsystems we are constantly replacing cells. The epithelial cells in our mouths only live a matter of hours. Other cells in our brain and nervous system live for years, but essentially the individual holons are in constant flows of life.

This staggered flow of cell replacement enables life to carry on, even as the cell holons "change guard" on a steady, measured schedule. Only when a minimum critical mass of those cells is destroyed or damaged at the same time do life conditions change. This can happen with injury, like massive burns to the body, or disease, where large numbers of cells suffer a microbial attack, as in cancer, SARS or flesh-eating disease.

It is ironic that, through the assault of stress, we are able to see the value of the collective. When individual holons create a relationship (i.e., a specialized organization or delivery system) to deliver more value to the hive or city, they create new subsystems that improve the quality of life that would not be attainable if each holon subsisted on its own. Frequently the new subsystems improve the quality of life because they create a capacity that is not available to individuals. This means that more resources can be used more effectively and efficiently because of the creation of such value-adding subsystems. (Any such collective subsystem in the city is necessarily a social holon — people working together with a shared intention of creating value for themselves and/or others, as we explore in more detail in chapter 8.) The big examples are infrastructure support systems (e.g., city hall's public works), education and health systems, workplaces and recreational organizations. In purely energetic terms, these subsystems process energy, information and matter with degrees of added efficiency that individuals are less likely to attain on their own (discussed in the following chapters in more detail).

ADAPTIVENESS ROLES: CONFORMITY ENFORCERS, DIVERSITY GENERATORS, INNER JUDGES, RESOURCE ALLOCATORS

Human systems are complex adaptive systems where, like the bees, the roles of conformity enforcers, diversity generators, resource allocators and inner judges seem to create a kind of group mind for survival and regeneration.

Let me explain what the bees have figured out. According to Bloom (2000), about 90 percent of the beehive are conformity enforcers (CE). They match their cues for behavior and use rules that the majority of their peers do. This means they all tend to fly to the same patch of flowers to collect pollen. The inner judges and resource allocators of the hive reward them for successful behaviors in proportion to their contribution to the hive's survival goals, which in bee terms is defined as producing 40 pounds of honey per year. Meanwhile, it is the nature of diversity generator bees (DG) — only 5 percent of the hive — to literally fly to different flower patches than the CE bees. The DG job is to find alternative sources of pollen, and the inner judges and resource allocators of the hive reward them fully for achieving their goals.

Given that any patch of flowers has a limited amount of pollen, eventually the CE bees return with less and less of a full load. The inner judges recognize this lower production by instructing the resource allocators to withhold bee fuel, i.e., they shift resources. This changes the state of the CE bees, so that they become sensitive to the dance cues communicated by DG bees, and they are thus led to discover new sources of pollen.

Thus, in the bee community, both conformity enforcers and diversity generators are vital to survival. And it would appear, according to a composite picture of human systems that emerges from looking at the work of Holling, Adizes and Graves, that similar role allocations within human systems have actually evolved to enable regeneration and sustainability.

THE CITY REGENERATES

With some basic understanding of survival and adaptiveness in hand, we can now explore how the city regenerates as a whole. Through our collective connections, we realize that to regenerate ourselves, and thus the city, is not just a simple act of biological union, which is a collective act regardless of the technology used these days. More than this, regeneration occurs through inner renewal, shared learning and teaching and coaching others in roles, competencies and capacities, inevitably in collective groupings.

If life arises from the three simple acts of surviving, connecting with an environment and regenerating, then ecology necessarily has its roots there too. Ecology is merely the resultant entanglement of lives lived in proximity. It is the enmeshment of the bio-psycho-cultural-social existence with all its myriad demographic differences, life cycles, exchanges and symbiotic relationships.

The experiments that people occasionally try, such as dropping into a city with minimal resources and attempting survival, prove this. Such people quickly discover that the practices of connecting with the city environment culturally and socially are the fastest and truest ways to live in the city. Even those people who choose to sleep rough in the outdoors, in support of the homeless, tap into capacities beyond biological survival that enable them to live in more complex ways on the streets of the city (McQuade, 2005). They bring an intention of inner resolve, spirituality and belief that gives them capacities for connecting with their environment and regenerating hope. In the ecology of the city, like the DG bees, they act as catalysts for change.

CYCLES OF RENEWAL

Renewal in the city depends on many of the capacities people have developed for adaptiveness to their environment. Renewal becomes possible because adaptiveness in the city emerges from massive redundancy in the bio-psycho-cultural-social spheres. For its survival and success, the city does not depend on one ruler or superhero (compared to a castle or feudal manor that did). Instead the city depends on the relationships amongst key roles that have evolved out of a species' group-mind and its ability to shift and flex depending on the life conditions.

Renewal emerges because a city, like all living systems, develops cyclical habits that enable the accumulation, exploitation, distribution and redeployment of resources. Holling (and his colleagues), Bloom, Eoyang, Adizes and Graves all recognize that living systems have natural stages through which they cycle and sequences of super-cycles that result in the evolution of complexity over time. They have identified those stages at different levels of scale: for ecologies, species, systems, organizations and individuals respectively.

Holling, Bloom and Graves essentially identify a trajectory of complex adaptive evolution for living systems. Holling (2001, 2003; Gunderson & Holling, 2002) suggests that wealth (potential), controllability (connectedness) and adaptive capacity (resilience) are the "properties that shape the responses of ecosystems, agencies and people to crisis" (2001, p. 394). Holling and his colleagues propose a four-stage cycle.

Figure 2.1. City fitness landscape.

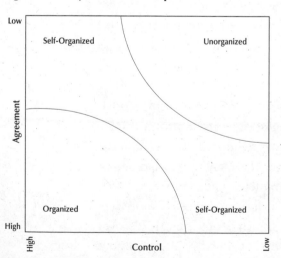

CITY LANDSCAPES: ORGANIZED, SELF-ORGANIZED, UNORGANIZED

As a complex adaptive system, the city is a container. The container exists in a landscape that is the city's ecoregion. Generally speaking, that landscape is relatively stable, unless forces of nature, like earthquakes, tidal waves or forest fires, change the general conditions, or unless forces of humans lead to water shortages, air pollution or climate change.

Inside the city, we can consider that there is also a landscape — not the type we think of as our front lawn, but a fitness landscape. Viewing the city through a fitness landscape, we quickly assess all the complex elements of the city at once.

A fitness landscape measures the city's degree of organization, self-organization and disorganization (Eoyang, 2007). It has two basic vectors: agreement and control, as shown in Figure 2.1.

City fitness landscapes give us readings on how coherently the city is operating as a whole. They can also be used for looking at the subsystems of the city to recognize how coherently they are operating. Fitness landscapes depend on the relationship between control and agreement in a group of people. If the situation is less controlled, it becomes ambiguous and difficult to understand or adapt to. The less we agree, the less we are able to make meaning together.

Where we have high control and high agreement, we can be organized. This is exemplified by driving on the same side of the road and stopping at street lights. When we have low control and low agreement, we can clearly see disorganization in the landscape. This is exemplified by a multi-car pileup on the freeway in a snowstorm, with no one in control and no agreement possible. When either of the control or agreement vectors is in its midranges, we are more likely to behave in self-organizing ways. This is exemplified by traffic with cars moving easily in and out of lanes, keeping at a steady speed.

In the city, by becoming aware of how we can loosen or tighten control and agreement, we can take advantage of organizational rules of the road that give us predictability, standards and dependability. We can also take advantage of self-organization, like real estate market activity (which is not centrally controlled but emerges through individual action like the *Wisdom of Crowds*, that opens up innovation, surprise and flexibility.

While organization usually seems desirable, it can also lead to stagnation and resistance to change. And while disorganization usually seems undesirable, it is a natural state of changing systems. Disorganization comes from lack of control and lack of agreement. When we view the city as a whole system, we can shift the landscape by moving towards either agreement and/or control. This shifts into self-organization and eventually produces sufficient order to create a solution that serves the whole system. Physicist Stuart Kauffmann assures us that, with self-organizing systems, "we get order for free" (1993).

COMPLEX CITY: CONTAINER, DIFFERENCES, EXCHANGES

The fitness landscape of the city system can be better understood when we use a stronger lens to examine the behaviors in the system's container, in terms of differences and exchanges (Eoyang, 2007). As a complex adaptive system, the city's landscape is a container for people who are different from one another and who make exchanges with one another. Differences can arise from almost an infinite number or any combination of variables: levels of development, race, ethnicity, age, gender, birth order, genealogy, experience, cognitive development, training, belief systems or roles. Exchanges could occur with any transfer of energy and/or matter: a kiss, an idea, a contract, a rule, a sale, a song or monetary exchange. If we use the integral map, we can locate differences and exchanges in both of the collective quadrants and at every level of complexity.

Systems theory tells us that we do not have a system unless we have a boundary. So the boundaries of the city define containers in which we can notice differences and exchanges. The city as a container holds individual holons and groups. The uniqueness of each individual holon contributes to the differences in the groups.

The city is obviously a multiplicity of containers that are massively interconnected. It is a complex adaptive system of systems. The enmeshment of these containers means that differences and exchanges from one container can affect the differences and exchanges in many other containers. As we explore in chapter 8, it is obvious that the individual who is part of a family, a sports team, a work group, a community association, a neighborhood and the city as a whole brings their differences and makes their exchanges in all of these containers.

Moreover, the boundaries of those containers (Eoyang, 1997) can be rigid (like a building), porous (like a friendship group), open (like a walk-in recreation center) or closed (like a professional association). Some subsystems in the city will have boundaries with more than one of these characteristics, thus creating an even more complex container (like a government ministry that has aspects of all these qualities).

The dynamics of human systems within city containers can be measured through the volatility of differences and the frequency of exchanges. Those dynamics will tell us the general state of change in any given container and how resilient the system is (as seen in Figure 2.2).

In Figure 2.2, we can define the four states of change by the degree of difference (low or high) and the frequency of exchange (low or high). When we recognize and locate the state of change in the system based on these parameters, we can identify the following options we have for changing the system:

- **Expand (open or make more porous) or contract (close or make more rigid) the size** of the container by changing its boundaries. This can lessen or increase the pressure on the people and their exchanges in the container. An example of the former is increasing the size of a voting constituency to include more people. An example of the latter is moving from school-based education to offering home-based schooling to focus on a select number of students.

- **Increase or decrease the differences** of people in the container. This can be done by bringing more people who are different into the container (like implementing an open immigration policy) or by creating a situation where existing differences are reduced through engagement (like creating a buddy system at a seniors center) or increased through making visible the invisible differences (like exploring childcare value systems with parents).

- **Increase or decrease the number and/or type of exchanges** in the container. This can be done by creating life conditions where people connect more often and/or differently (like pensioners reading to children). Or it can be accomplished by preventing exchange (like building a wall between warring factions).

Thus we can see that the city, as a complex adaptive system, is a mesh of containers with varying amounts of differences and exchanges. Seeing the differences and exchanges can give us insights to the qualities of wholeness of the entire city system.

1. Exploitation (low potential, low connectedness)
2. Conservation (high potential, high connectedness)
3. Release (low potential, high connectedness)
4. Reorganization (high potential, low connectedness)

These properties seem similar to Bloom's explanation of how this plays out in the life of bees, described above. Eoyang echoes these in her analysis of agents and exchanges in the container, discussed in the Complex City sidebar.

In stages one and two, the objectives are to maximize production and accumulation. This would correlate to Bloom's stages of conformity enforcement. The "inner judges" and "resource allocators" of the species enforce activities of members to support production and accumulation of what is valued most.

Eoyang recognizes these system states as the experience of stability and self-organization (see Complex City and City Landscapes sidebars). Adizes identifies

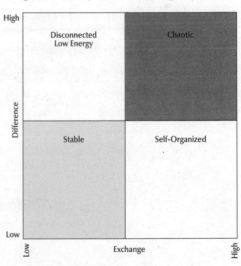

Figure 2.2. City states of change dynamics.

INCREASING EXCHANGES, REDUCING DIFFERENCES ENDS STRIKE

At time of writing, an example of city fitness landscapes occurred in the Vancouver City workers strike. The union and the City could not come to agreement on differences related to work rules for over eight weeks: the union refused to concede more flexibility, and the City refused to concede less flexibility regarding the work rules. Moreover, both parties refused to meet for extensive periods of time. So the exchanges were low, and the differences were high, resulting in disconnection. Eventually the solution was to bring another person in (a mediator) to reduce the differences and increase the exchanges, which resulted in an agreement.

them in organizational life cycles as production and prime. Graves identifies them in individual developmental cycles as the zone of integrating and consolidating new learning and operating and adjusting to maintain steady-state knowing.

Holling then proposes that stages three and four maximize invention and re-sorting (re-deploying) resources. Bloom describes these activities as diversity generation. In fact, using the example of the bees, Bloom proposes that the diversity generation activities are going on all the time, but it is only when the conformity enforcement stage fails that the "inner judges" and "resource allocators" of the species allow diversity generators to catalyze new behaviors for the conformity enforcers.

Holling proposes that success in achieving one objective sets the stage for success in achieving the next objective in an endless cycle. When life conditions change the resource flow through the cycle, his research shows these four stage cycles adapt by shifting upwards to stages of greater complexity or downward to lesser complexity. He defines a "panarchy" as a hierarchy "of nested sets of adaptive cycles. The functioning of those cycles and the communication between them determines the sustainability of a system" (2001, p. 396).

EACH SCALE AND STAGE OF DEVELOPMENT HAS RECURRING CYCLES

As we see in the next chapter, at different stages of development, the capacities of living systems are used differently to sustain life through the processes of surviving, adapting and regenerating. Many keen observers of living systems have noticed that the dynamics at play, within any given scale and at any given developmental level, are essentially the same. (This repeated pattern is an example of fractalness.) In their analyses of dynamic cycles, Holling, Bloom and Eoyang looked more at the stages of adaptiveness that contribute to the resiliency of large-scale whole-living system (ecosystem, species, organization respectively). Within organizations, Adizes looked more at the contribution of key roles; and within individuals, Graves identified the change states and trigger points. Figure 2.3 compares the contributions of each to the four phases that recur at each scale of development.

What we notice is that all five authors have identified the dynamics of recurring sequences that allow the system to survive, adapt to its life conditions and regenerate. Essentially, all five authors agree that human systems are complex adaptive systems where the roles of conformity enforcers, diversity generators, resource allocators and inner judges contribute to the group mind for survival and regeneration.

Figure 2.3. Comparing the adaptiveness components of Holling, Eoyang, Bloom, Adizes and Graves.

AUTHOR	HOLLING	BLOOM	EOYANG	ADIZES	GRAVES
RECURRING STAGES	ECOSYSTEM STAGES	SPECIES ADAPTIVE CYCLES	SYSTEM RESILIENCE STATES	ORGANIZATION LIFE CYCLE	INDIVIDUAL DEVELOPMENT
1	Exploitation (low potential, low connectedness)	Conformity Enforcement Entry	Stability	Production Key Roles: Paei Production administration, entrepreneurship, integration	Delta-New Alpha
2	Conservation (high potential, high connectedness)	Conformity Enforcement Peak	Self-Organization	Prime Key Roles: PAeI Production Administration, entrepreneurship, Integration	Alpha-Beta
3	Release (low potential, high connectedness)	Diversity Generation Entry	Disconnection	Bureaucracy to Old Age Key Roles: pAei production Administration, entrepreneurship, integration	Beta-Gamma
4	Reorganization (high potential, low connectedness)	Diversity Generation Peak	Chaos	Startup to GoGo Key Roles: paEi production, administration, Entrepreneurship, integration	Gamma-Delta

SUSTAINING THE WHOLE CITY

With our criteria for aliveness — survival, adaptiveness and regeneration — we have some criteria available to us to consider what sustainability of the city might entail. (This discussion on sustainability is very abbreviated and limited to the city because the topic as a whole is being explored separately by Barrett Brown In a forthcoming book.)

The active field of sustainability studies is challenged by the same spectrum of definitions, worldviews and frameworks as all other modern issues. How we understand sustainability is very much framed by the level of our conscious development, whether we are thinkers, writers, proponents or activists.

Thinking about the sustainability of the city presents an additional challenge, namely the sheer scale of the complex adaptive system that a city represents. When you consider the never-ending dynamics of behaviors, intentions, relationships and production systems that make up the city, the concept of sustaining a city seems to be more of an oxymoron than a possibility.

Any archeological dig will demonstrate the trajectory of city evolution and confirm the fact that the levels and layers of a city are not merely ethereal or esoteric, but are literally locked into the city streets, buildings and pipes. And although this infrastructure changes more slowly than the people who build or use it, change it does. Moreover it can change in the direction of more or less complexity. Many cities in the developing world, with modern infrastructure that was installed by its colonial rulers, display wide evidence of deteriorating public works. Sadly this is also the evidence that infrastructure requires a level of responsible attention and maintenance equal to the levels of complexity that designed it, and when the colonial governments departed, so did the necessary thinking that was required for modern maintenance.

So when we consider sustainable cities, we have to ask ourselves, what are we sustaining? Regional planner Ian Wight (2002) is attracted to the idea that cities arise from the act of place making — the integration of all the ways that people interact to create a place (discussed in much greater detail in following chapters). Can we relate sustainability to the act of place making? Or do we have to step back far enough from the sustainability debate to recognize that sustaining a city must minimally embrace sustaining order, strategic planning, caring and sharing and systemizing? From this vantage point, perhaps it is easier to consider that all we could sustain in as complex a system as a city is the potential to emerge. This would be key to sustaining the city's resilience as a self-correcting cycle of adaptiveness.

We could even suggest that the preface's description of cities as "wild" or "planned" might be extended into our concepts of resilience. For perhaps, the cycles we are describing really identify cyclical stages of wildness and planning? Wildness may be both unavoidable and necessary — the result of discoveries by diversity generators and the redeployment of resources. Perhaps we can see this quite easily when we look at neighborhoods and how people in them experience the realities of Holling's resilience cycle.

In fact Jane Jacobs' descriptions of the Boston and Chicago neighborhoods in her first book (1992) are graphic examples that the city's resilience goes through cycles, like all living systems. For, as Thomas Homer-Dixon points out, you can even have too much of an apparently good thing if one or more of the stages of the resilience cycle is over-extended because the system will have to over-correct. It seems that any phase of expanded growth will be followed by the contraction phases of maturity and eventual dissolution or reorganization. In other words, when any one of the phases of resilience is out of balance with the whole cycle, then resilience itself is threatened. The stories of tragic and unsustainable cycles in famous cities and societies have been chronicled by Jared Diamond in *Collapse* and Ronald Wright in A *Short History of Progress*.

Thus it would seem that a sustainable city is comparable to Graves' view of the individual person's "never-ending quest." It is perfectly natural that the city, as a collective of mixed human capacity, would mirror the dynamic patterns of the lives of individuals, organizations, systems, species and ecosystems. It appears that what is sustainable is the pattern and process of adaptation, which amounts to the resilience cycle discussed above. This is not a widely accepted wisdom where sustainability is mooted as a steady state of existence. Nor is this a politically acceptable pattern for sustainability, especially because the ebbs and flows to the cycles mean the fortunes of some people are falling while others are rising.

Perhaps the closest that we have come to grappling with the implications of this flow model of sustainable resilience is in the economic realm. However, our attempts are clumsily dependent on a mechanistic model of existence where government policies attempt to freeze the cycles of the stock market and attempt to eternally perpetuate its boom cycle. Little heed is paid to the possibility that the bust cycles might be both a natural and necessary reorganization of resources that will enable the next boom cycle. When any cycle becomes overextended, the ensuing stage is also overextended. The experiences of the 1990s' bursting of the dot-com bubble and the 2007 mortgage-lending bubble seem to prove the point of the reality and the pain of over-corrections. On an equally graphic note, the management of forest practices is learning the terrible lesson of forest fire cycles as natural and necessary to keep forests resilient and emergent (of different species) over long time periods.

With this in mind, it is possible to conceive of a template for cities to develop sustainable practices (defined in such a way that the assets are sustained to serve future generations). But it is much more difficult to develop the minds of decision-makers who can create policies that are not only appropriate to the current conditions, cycles and phases of the city and the diversity of people and exchanges within it, but are flexible enough to change as everything in the city changes.

EMERGENCE: SEEING NEW CAPACITIES IN THE CITY

While I find it problematic to gain traction with the sustainable city, I find it much more promising to contemplate the emerging city. Emergence is a characteristic of living systems that arises from the resonance and coherence of the system. We have seen that resilience arises from the adaptiveness of the system to its environment. Resonance emerges when the system is aligned externally to its environment — it literally resonates with its surroundings. Coherence arises from the alignment of all the elements of the system internally in such a way that energy is optimized. When both resonance and coherence become synchronized, new capacities in the system emerge. This tends to happen at phase shifts, where the internal and external patterns shift from being out of phase, to being in phase with one another. This literally causes a jump into a stronger vibrational quality. We could say the system of the human hive would really be humming a new tune.

We can examine this capacity of emergence from two perspectives. One is holographic and allows us to see how the whole is disclosed from the patterns embedded in all of its parts. The other is morphic fields that emerge from the cumulative repeated activity of like holons and like species.

Holographic City

A hologram is a three-dimensional image that arises from the interference patterns of two wave patterns. The hologram carries information about the whole in every part of its composition.

Thomas Homer-Dixon (2006), in *The Upside of Down*, engages the reader with historical factoids that capture the nature of the holographic city. He derives the nature of three cities from single architectural stones: A foundational stone in the Roman Coliseum; the Temple of Bacchus gate in Baalbek, Lebanon; and the Stone of the Pregnant Woman near Baalbek. Each stone provides evidence for the civilization's values that created them. In that sense they are holographic: a small part of the city that reveals everything there is to know about the city when we uncover how they were created, why they were transported there, who did the work, who directed the work, who designed the structures, how they provided the energy to move the matter and the information to communicate the intentions.

Laszlo proposes that "nature's holograms are cosmic ... they link ... all things with all other things" (2004, p. 71). The evidence for the city as a holographic entity — where any part can reveal the whole — is available because the city is a whole system that arises from the massive interconnections and entanglements of structures, cultures, intentions and behaviors. In this sense, if we laid our hands on any part of the city and traced the connections of that part to all its other parts, we would discover the subsystems and systems that make up the city. If we could instantly draw that map of interconnections and synthesize their patterns, we would create an instant holograph.

The city's integralness arises from the nature of the integration of the city's holons and hierarchies, as well as the integrity that each of those contributes to the whole system. Integrated integrity is one way of describing the alignment and coherence of the city, and its measure of optimization also reveals the city's capacity for emergence.

It is quite possible that the holographic nature of the city reveals the city's capacity for emergence. We see the whole easily when the holograph suddenly shifts into view from any entry point in the city. For instance, this means that if we look at the quality of the healthcare system or effectiveness of the education system we can obtain a proxy assessment of the quality of life or the capacity for development in the city. Each of the quadrants we explore in chapters 5, 6, 7 and 8 offer holographic views of the city.

MORPHIC FIELDS IN THE CITY

Although we cannot always easily gain the insights that holograms of the city could give us, perhaps we can view the whole city through different filters. If we peer through the lenses that Rupert Sheldrake uses, we can glimpse an intangible reality about human existence that has long been known by people who have the capacity to access it. However, this has also been repressed by those who feel threatened by the existence of anything intangible, regardless of the evidence.

Sheldrake, a biologist, has been curious about how species such as homing pigeons, parrots, dogs and horses seem to know how to travel long distances and arrive at specific destinations with pinpoint accuracy. Individual animals even seem to be able to access human intentions and anticipate human behavior with a high degree of accuracy (Sheldrake, 1988, 1999, 2003). Sheldrake proposes that each species over time creates an energetic field, invisible to the naked eye and not registered on any instruments created to date, but which is nonetheless as real as a radio or television signal. He supposes that members of any species have built-in antennae that access that field and gain the knowledge that is stored there. Dogs can even access the field of another species to which they are closely related.

Sheldrake's recent research has expanded to include human phenomena such as the sense of being stared at, telepathy, foresight and predictive dreams (2003). He refers to these energetic fields as morphic or morphogenetic fields. It appears that some people have more capabilities than others to access the information in these fields. In some remote tribes in the Amazon and Indonesia, and in many indigenous peoples like the aborigines of Australia, these capacities are highly developed and widely shared amongst all members of their society.

In the so-called developed world, very few people admit to having skills related to these capacities, and little credence is given to those who do practise them (some exceptions include police departments who quietly use people with paranormal capacities to help solve difficult crimes). Nevertheless, as evidence builds, it is not difficult to speculate that the city may provide a particularly rich ground for demonstrating the existence of these fields. Nowadays we can measure the amount of physical heat generated by the city. We can also control television and radio signals so individual receivers can decode the signals into usable messages that inform and entertain us. If Sheldrake is right about individual people, in the not too distant future we may discover that every city has a morphic field that reflects (and even transmits) the patterns of consciousness that individuals and groups are generating all the time.

Philosopher Ervin Laszlo has similar thoughts. He calls the morphic field the Akashic Record (2004) — borrowing from the Sanskrit word for "sky" or "space." Rather than use biology, he uses the science of physics to suggest that the vacuum of space is not empty, but filled with energy and information that we have simply not recognized nor learned how to access in any sophisticated way. Accessing it tends to be accidental rather than deliberate, notwithstanding the fact that, in every culture throughout millennia, select individuals have been taught the secrets of doing so. Laszlo suggests that the Akashic field holds a permanent record of all human (and Earth) activity — just like the brain apparently holds a record of all individual activity since birth (or conception).

The concept of morphic or Akashic fields creates the possibility that we could harness the intelligence that is concentrated in the city to generate much greater (more complex) intelligence capacities than we have ever dreamed of. If we could truly learn how to think together, we could harness the massive leverage of parallel processing that has enabled us to design modern computers and neural networks (like the linking of personal computers for the SETI extraterrestrial life search project). If we can do this, we will see a significant phase shift in human intelligence that will give cities major new incentives to create optimal life conditions to better support human existence. By the same token, in an optimistic spirit, I anticipate that when this intelligence is harnessed we will finally have the power to add value to life on Earth that is both sustainable (not over-using resources) and emergent (always creating new capacities from existing resources).

In the meantime, whether these morphic fields can be proven or not, people can sense the spirit of a city. This spirit may not translate into a metaphor (see Complex City sidebar), but the core values of a city are frequently translated into qualities that people experience as apocryphal, even before the marketers put labels on them. Toronto is good. Paris is romantic. Rome is capital. Rio is playful. New Orleans was naughty. Dallas is driven. London is finance. New York is liberty.

This spirit is palpable and shared by city residents who sense when it is healthy, stressed or damaged and fight to return it to a state of well-being. We have seen, with the visibility of modern disasters, that outsiders will even rally to restore the spirit of the city. Citizens who have experienced natural or terrorist disasters, such as those of New York, New Orleans, Osaka, and Mexico City, can all vouch for the reality of shared intentions to return a stricken city to health. Such transpersonal support inevitably rallies spirit within the city to rebuild and restore and replace what was damaged.

CONCLUSION

If we don't see cities as if they were whole systems, then we cannot discern their purpose, alignment or coherence. We are blocked from recognizing patterns, processes and structures in the living system that can inform us of the natural emergence of the city's cycles and phases.

If we don't see cities as if they were whole systems, we are doomed not to achieve life enhancing results, supportive relationships or resilient well-being. We look at time frames that are too short, space frames that are too flat and people frames that are too narrow.

On the other hand, if we see the city as a whole system, we can appreciate its embedded wisdom for surviving in its unique life conditions; the mystery of its collective life force; and the tremendous potential it embraces in the energy, information and matter that it embraces. Seeing the city as a whole helps us to truly appreciate the performance of its subsystems and gives us the context in which we can understand and flow with emergence.

Three simple rules for applying Integral City principles from this chapter:

1. Survive so holons serve each other's existence.

2. Adapt to the environment.

3. Create a self-regenerating feedback loop, by interconnecting human regeneration cycles so that they replenish the environment.

QUESTIONS

1. How can all the fractal-like subsystems in the city reach their potential and contribute to the well-being of the whole without centralized control?

2. What supports does a city need at different stages of development? How can we lead any given city into the next natural stage of development for it?

3. How can the cities of the world see how they are connected as nodes in a global network of intelligences, capacities and potentials? How do we develop tools that enable release of blocks to this energy and enable open system flows, within cities and between cities?

INTEGRAL INTELLIGENCE: CHARTING PATTERNS OF THE HUMAN HIVE

That honeybees have a map now does not necessarily mean that
they had one before the dance evolved; the map could
have come later, an economical way to deal with complex information.

— Gould and Gould, 1988, p. 107

What we like from the heart coincides with the objective structure of wholeness or life
in a thing. As we get to know the "it" which we like from the heart, we begin to
see that this is the deepest thing there is. It applies to all judgments — not
just about buildings and works of art, but also about actions, people, everything.

— Alexander, 2002, p. 315

INTEGRATING THE QUALITIES THAT CREATE
OPTIMAL CONDITIONS FOR HUMAN HABITATS

A city is a living system that emerges from the intentions and interactions of individuals and groups to produce both a conscious presence (or spirit) and a habitat (or a built city). Depending on which authority you name, the size of a city can be 50,000 people (like the Romans built, and the number of bees a beehive can contain) or 20,000,000 people (like the Japanese, Chinese and Mexicans have already built).

An Integral City is a way of looking at the city, regardless of its size, to see it as if it were a whole system — a living system that has emerged from an ecology of consciousness and includes (but is not limited to) discursive, political and

51

religious/spiritual contexts together with a specific natural environment (such as mountain, sea or prairie), climate and natural ecology. As such, an Integral City is dynamic, adaptive and responsive to its internal and external life conditions. An Integral City acts much like a complex adaptive human system that concentrates habitat for humans like a beehive does for bees or an anthill does for ants. Like a natural system, it faces all the same issues, factors and challenges that affect the concentration of life anywhere: sustaining flows of information, matter and energy for the survival of human life (Miller, 1978).

WHAT ARE INTEGRAL QUALITIES OF HUMAN HABITATS?

Integral is one word that coalesces all the qualities of the optimal conditions for human habitats. I use the word *integral* to reflect the three confluences of integral inquiry investigated by Ervin Laszlo, Clare Graves and Don Beck, and Ken Wilber. *Integral* means whole, comprehensive, integrated, interconnected, inclusive, all encompassing, vibrant, responsive, adaptive. *Integral* does not mean fragmented, partial, exclusive, frozen, unchanging. *Integral* reflects the conditions of life from which we spring: conscious, complex, adaptive, evolving, developmental. *Integral* is big enough to include all of existence: beauty, truth and goodness; the good, the bad and the ugly; the conscious and unconscious; the positive and the negative; the yin and the yang; the virtues and the vices; body, mind, heart and soul; you and me; us and them.

Integral is a word whose roots are related both to integrity and integration. Integrity has to do with internal consistency and external respect. It implies coherence and alignment and has a moral nuance that connects it to an ethical consistency. *Integrity* seems to relate to the subjective and intersubjective qualities of life. *Integration*, on the other hand relates to the objective and interobjective aspects of life. *Integration* means synthesizing, meshing and combining in a focused way. It means bringing together and blending that which has been separated. (Some people would even associate integration with racial integration, a major social objective of the 20th century.)

In mathematical terms, *integral* relates to a whole or complete number. An integer is even called a *natural number*. In combining aspects of both integrity and integration, integral subsumes the coherence of integrity and the blending of integration. *Integral* is a word that describes the patterns of existence that emerge from the unifying consciousness of the universe — that everything is systemically and naturally connected to everything else; that life on Earth is massively connected from the microscopic level to the macroscopic level. In fact every "thing" or event is not just a pattern of matter, energy or information, but a "system" that is in integral relationship to other systems. The whole universe is a system of systems of systems, ad infinitum.

Some scientists speculate that the patterns of existence that have evolved over the last 14 billion years, since the universe began with the big bang, may even be building on consciousness that pre-existed that event (and that there are other parallel universes embraced by an ever-learning consciousness). Ervin Laszlo describes this super-consciousness as "in-formation" — literally a universal force of connection that "in-forms" all existence (2004). He proposes that information is ubiquitous, vibrational or wavelike and distinguishes it from information that has become grounded or crystallized through connecting matter and energy. (See glossary for Laszlo's definition.)

The patterns of information, energy and matter (in this universe, galaxy, solar system, planet) have produced human systems with a distinct form of consciousness in the last 100,000 years. Within these emergent life conditions (see Figure 3.1), each human carries within them significant evidence of the complex evolutionary patterns of living systems. Our physical bodies are made of the water and "dust of

Figure 3.1. Self-organizing emergence of universe and human life.
Source: Jantsch, 1980, p. 132.

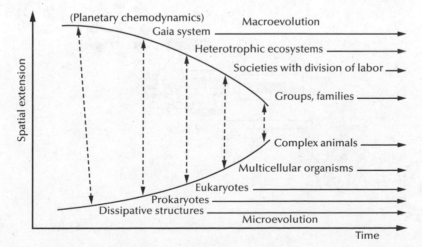

Figure 3.2. Triune brain.
Source: Howard, 1994, p. 34.

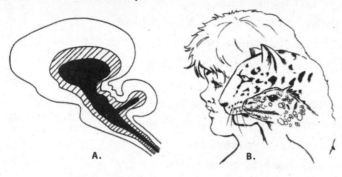

A.   B.

the physical" Earth, and our three-lay-ered brain. Figure 3.2 shows our biolog-ical heritage from reptile to animal to languaging primate (Margulis & Sagan, 1997; Sahtouris, 1999).

Just as our bodies have evolved, so have our social complexities. Regardless of where we have been located on Earth, our diverse human cultures demonstrate evidence that when life conditions provoked us to change, we have changed, generally in the direction of greater complexity. (In this way we are perpetually solving the proverbial conundrum that Einstein described as needing a new mind to solve the problems that our old ways of life could not.) Figure 3.3 shows the iconic examples of the structural complexities of human systems

Figure 3.3. How structures emerge and complexify.
Source: Reproduced with permission from Beck & Cowan, 1996.

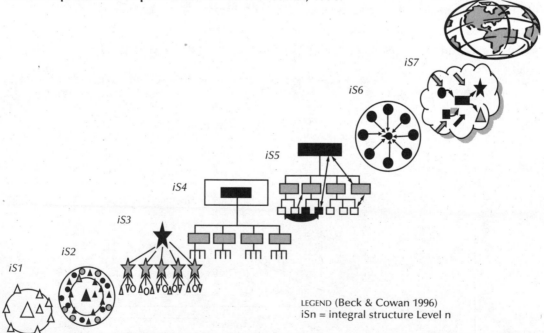

LEGEND (Beck & Cowan 1996)
iSn = integral structure Level n

(from Don Beck's *Foundations Course on Spiral Dynamics*) that have emerged as we have moved from the hearth-based circle of family survival, through the bonding systems of clan and tribe, to the power struggles of chief and king, to the ordering authorities of state and place of worship, to the strategic economies of material exchange, to the accepting embrace of diverse peoples, to the flex and flow of global systems, to a Gaia honoring of all life. (This is discussed in more detail in chapters 6 and 7.) With each of these levels of historical complexity, we have created new artifacts, habitats, structures and forms to contain our human systems. We call the most concentrated and complex of these containers cities.

The life conditions that stimulated our bodies and brains to adapt and survive were accompanied by an evolving consciousness that enabled the evolution of what it means to be human. And it is precisely those life conditions that contribute to the evolution and the state of well-being of our cities today. Like our physical bodies and habitat structures, our individual human life cycles bear witness to the developmental nature of the human system. Figure 3.4 is a fractal map developed by Clare Graves that demonstrates historical development of human consciousness as well as potential individual development. Superimposing the former on the latter shows the approximate historical emergence of these levels of consciousness as *homo sapiens sapiens* has developed.

The nested hierarchies and fractal patterns of life that show up in our bodies and that we extend into the structures of our cities have the potential to show up in every individual life. Whether conceived in the womb or the test tube, we are born helpless and dependent on our parents (or pseudo-parents). They in turn are massively interconnected and both inter- and intra-dependent on the system of friends, work, health, school and community, who are likewise multiply dependent on the social systems of city, state and nation, who are multiply dependent on the cultural norms, who are multiply dependent on the relationships with friendly and hostile cultures and states, who are multiply dependent on the natural ecology of their geography, which is integrated with the global system of climate and energy flow (Barnett, 2005; Diamond, 2005).

We must note that the potential for individual development is exactly that —a potential. As discussed in later chapters, individual physical age is no guarantee of consciousness development. Rather, as we propose in chapters 5 and 8, consciousness development is a function of the life conditions in which the individual lives.

Thus, who we are in the Integral City depends on how we are able to grow the potential of the massively entangled human conditions in each of us. And it is the matching of that human potential to the structures of the built environment of the city, and the social and cultural institutions that creates a dancelike rhythm or coherence we might call "optimal life conditions." We see this as a dynamic flow state, like the shifting patterns of dancers on a dance floor, that may differ from person to person and group to group.

This means that, because of the flow of individual human lives contained in the city, over time, a city appears to go through stages of development that could be identified as infant, child, youth, adult, parent, grandparent, elder. Each stage will translate into a different expression of the city — we tend to call them eras — even though the city will remain the same place. This is the essence of "place making" — it is kind of like creating the spirit or soul of the city as it ages (Wight, 2002).

At the same time that the city's inhabitants are continuously cycling through their life stages, so are the city's institutions and organizations, making the Integral City a highly dynamic system. In fact the optimal life conditions for an Integral City depend more on the resilience of its citizens — or their capacity to adapt in the face of change — than the stability of any of the city's features.

HOW DO YOU SUSTAIN AN INTEGRAL CITY?

Since the Brundtland Report (Brundtland, 1987) was published in 1987, the world has aspired to balance the interconnection amongst the three elements of the Venn diagram, shown in Figure 3.5, of the environment, the

Figure 3.4. Evolving consciousness as mapped by Clare Graves. Source: Beck, 2006; Graves, 2005, p. 181.

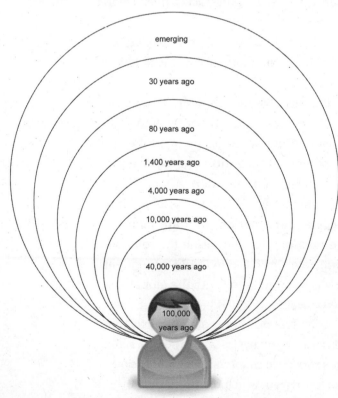

economic and the social. This framing of existence recognized the importance of the three factors, while considering them all equal.

However, all the sciences now tell us that although these factors are massively interconnected, two of the factors are utterly dependent on the third: the human economy and the social factors are encompassed by, rest on and are overridden by the environment as in Figure 3.6. In fact, if we explore the environment we will find it imbued with its own natural consciousness and economy that are the fractal, contextual setting for the city as discussed below.

The evidence for the truth of the relationship amongst the social, economic and environmental aspects lies in the lost civilizations of Earth — the Mayan, Easter Island, Ashkenaze — where the grizzly truths of how the intensity of human systems (a.k.a. cities) overwhelmed the carrying capacity of the supporting environment and resulted in desertification, salinization, drought, famine and even cannibalization (Diamond, 2005; Wright, 2004).

When faced with this evidence, what are the lessons we need to learn for the survival of our own cities? How could these very sophisticated cities fail so close to the peak of their apparently optimal existence? One of the most comprehensive scientific studies of Living Systems was led by James Grier Miller in the 1960s and 1970s (Miller, 1978). This interdisciplinary team concluded that every living system has three major processing systems that articulate the relationships

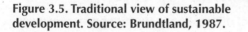
Figure 3.5. Traditional view of sustainable development. Source: Brundtland, 1987.

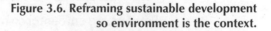
Figure 3.6. Reframing sustainable development so environment is the context.

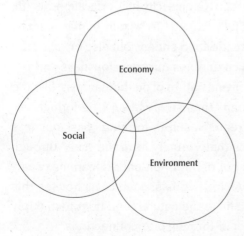

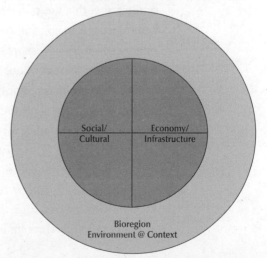

between matter, energy and information. Moreover, they proposed that to process these three constituents, every living system had developed some variation of 19 subsystems (as set out in Figure 6.1).

It appears that the lessons from history teach us that, to some degree, human cities have mastered the flow of matter and energy. However, it appears that our vanished cities of the past lost touch with the information that could alert them to their impending demise. We might also propose that their connections to in-formation became distorted.

And this is the area where Ken Wilber (1995, 1996a, 2000b, 2007)contributes elegantly to the integral discourse. While Laszlo charts the systemic nature of integralism and Beck describes its evolutionary, developmental nature, Wilber gives us the lenses to reunify connections amongst the visible world of matter and energy and the invisible worlds of consciousness and culture. His integral vision demonstrates the co-arising, co-connected realities we have fragmented into individual versus collective and/or internal versus external solitudes. His integral map (discussed below) integrates integrity and integration, holons and wholeness and stages and states. He virtually provides an integral operating system and charting tool that offers a common language to bridge realities and talk about life conditions that require translation, transformation and transcendence.

ARE WE LOSING TOUCH WITH OUR CITIES' IN-FORMATION?

Perhaps, we encounter so many problems of dislocation in the city because we generally forget that the prime importance of city subsystems (city hall, education, health, workplaces) is to support the nature of being fully human? To be fully human not only engages material measures of information, matter and energy, but also engages the in-formation aspect of our existence — which enables our consciousness and our relationships with one another. The ever-evolving nature of our humanness, like the patterns of dancers on the dance floor, means that we are always "in formation." Moreover, our capacity for self-reflection creates a self-in-forming consciousness that generates in-formation feedback loops that virtually form the "self" through reinforcing patterns. Herein lie the sweet spot of our open-ended learning capacity and the secret of our creative talents. As individuals, each of us houses this ever-in-forming treasure, and in the city, we have the natural conditions to multiply its value infinitely through a massive mesh of in-forming interconnections.

However, the cities we currently manage are operating in both external information silos and internal information stovepipes (Dale, 2001). We are far from being aware of necessary information, let alone our in-formation. We make some decisions that interrelate the cities within one bioregion and/or nation in some parts of the world. But what is more surprising (and frustrating and disappointing) is that we seem to make even fewer decisions within any given city with reference to the key subsystems that support, access and inform the human condition. Our separate subsystem bureaucracies for our city management, healthcare systems, schooling (at all levels) and workplaces remain unarticulated or distantly linked at best. A top-down view of our city dance floor indicates considerable chaos.

Is it any wonder that we cannot see the city as a single, wholly integrated and in-forming system that depends on the interconnection amongst these subsystems to serve the well-being of its inhabitants? Ironically, within each of these subsystems (city management, healthcare systems, schooling and workplaces), we are developing progressively more complex information systems to tell us everything we need to know about bricks and mortar, epidemiology, grading systems and performance management. But we are not seeing the integral nature of each of these subsystems nor the integral in-forming connections amongst them. For the most part we are generating and measuring quantitative, objective information to give us reports on the material outcomes of these subsystems. But we are failing to acknowledge the qualitative, subjective information that conveys the realities of our internal, subjective and inter-subjective experience.

WHO UPDATES DEFINITION OF HEALTHY CITY

"A healthy city is one that is continually creating and improving those physical and social environments and expanding those community resources which enable people to mutually support each other in performing all the functions of life and in developing to their maximum potential." This is the definition of the World Health Organization (WHO), one of the pioneers of wholistic thinking about the city. In 2004 WHO's European website distilled its 1986 vision of a healthy city to encompass integral quadrants: UL potential, LL mutual support, UR functions of life and LR physical and social environments. The website prefaces this definition with this mindful context for change: "A healthy city is defined by a process not an outcome .... A healthy city is conscious of health and striving to improve it. Thus any city can be a 'healthy' city, regardless of its current health status. What is required is a commitment to health and a process and structure to achieve it" (World Heath Organization, 2004).

MAPPING THE ESSENTIAL PATTERNS OF CITY LIFE

In order to understand the living-system nature of cities (and, thereby, their fractal, holographic and morphic nature), we must consider four essential maps of city life:

- the four-quadrant perspectival map of reality (Figure 3.7)
- the nested holarchy of city systems (Figure 3.8)
- the scalar-fractal relationship of micro, meso and macro human systems (Figure 3.9)
- the complex, adaptive, dynamic stages of change (Figure 3.10)

Each map gives us a different view of the whole city — thus each is a partial but vital lens of the city container — and helps us to understand the interrelationship of matter, energy and information with an importantly unique perspective. And because each map is a partial view of the same city system, they can be hyperlinked with each other to give us a more comprehensive, complete picture of the whole field of interconnected systems. Let's look at each one in turn.

Map 1: The Four-quadrant Eight-level Map of Reality

The integral map is a four-quadrant map that shows the city has both an outer life that is physical, tangible and objective, as well as an inner life that is conscious, intangible and subjective. It owes its clarity and growing popularity to Ken Wilber who first charted it and has extensively developed it for use in many knowledge domains (Wilber, 1995, 1996a, 1996b, 2000a, 2000b, 2001, 2007). This map shows that reality in the city arises from both an individual and a collective expression (Figure 3.7). The intersection of these two polarities reveals four realities that we can label as:

1. Upper Left (UL): individual — interior/ internal/ subjective/intangible
2. Lower Left (LL): collective — interior/internal/ intersubjective/intangible
3. Upper Right (UR): individual — exterior/ external/ objective/tangible
4. Lower Right (LR): collective — exterior/ external/ interobjective/tangible

The four-quadrant map is a map of city perspectives. Each quadrant represents the view from a different lens: I, We, It and Its. Each of the four perspectives has produced a cluster of domains of knowledge about the city. The Upper Left quadrant holds the knowledge bases of the aesthetics and fine arts. The Lower

Left holds the knowledge bases of the humanities. The Upper Right holds the knowledge bases of the life sciences. The Lower Right holds the knowledge bases of the hard sciences. Thus have our institutions of higher learning organized the knowledge about the transcendent patterns of universal information: Beauty in the Upper Left aesthetics and fine arts (I); Goodness in the Lower Left humanities (We); and Truth in the Upper and Lower Right life and hard sciences (It/Its).

But more than the knowledge content of our reality, the four-quadrant map discloses the four points of view of city dwellers from all world cultures. In the Upper Left, the first person, *Subjective* I, appreciates the beauty of life, the aesthetic quality of living systems. This aesthetic, often hidden from view in the modern city, was more demonstrated and honored in ancient cities, where the scale of human systems was more coherent with the built city. Another description of the *Subjective* I is the psychological (psycho-) reality of the city. The *Subjective* I feels inspired and uplifted by the aesthetic pleasure of walking down a street lined with cherry blooms, imagining the excitement of expressing ideas at the nearby coffee shop.

In the Lower Left, the second person *Intersubjective* We appreciates the Goodness in life. This point of view reveals the moral qualities of life choices that are necessary on every level of human existence and association. These intersubjective perspectives are woven from the everyday stories we tell each other in every informal connection of daily life. They also reflect the tales and myths we create to pass along our archetypal experiences. They represent the formal laws we create for the smooth operation of civic society.

A NETWORK OF HEALTHY COMMUNITIES

In 2005 BC Healthy Communities (BCHC) created a mission to act as a catalyst to enhance individual and collective health, well-being and development by supporting the [WHO] Healthy Communities approach (BCHC, 2005). BCHC based its facilitative activities on principles defined as holistic, strengths based, capacity building, diversity, community engagement, collaboration, integration and learning. It set out from the provincial (state) level to create a network of healthy communities that support healthy actions at a local level, as well as link to the international network, so that learning could occur in all spheres of influence. BCHC also plays a role in making connections across sectors at local, regional and provincial levels and supports local governance that embraces healthy community principles. In building awareness about building capacity at all levels, BCHC introduces an integral mapping system (see Figure 3.11) that explicitly helps communities identify Inner Individual Capacities, Outer Individual Capacities, Inner Collective Capacities and Outer Collective Capacities (BCHC, 2006a). BCHC has applied all three rules for an Integral City from this chapter to support communities to self-organize their own capacities for health.

Figure 3.7. Map 1: The integral map. Source: Adapted from Wilber, 1995, 1996a.

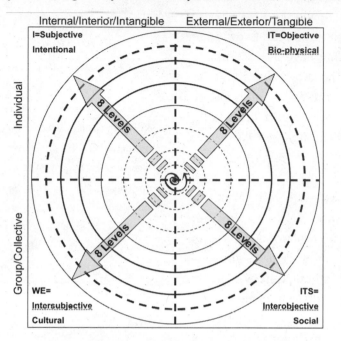

Internal/Interior/Intangible   External/Exterior/Tangible

I=Subjective   IT=Objective
Intentional   Bio-physical

Individual

8 Levels   8 Levels

8 Levels   8 Levels

Group/Collective

WE=   ITS=
Intersubjective   Interobjective
Cultural   Social

Figure 3.8. Map 2: The nested holarchy of city systems.

- 1 = individual
- 2 = family/clan
- 3 = group/tribe
- 4 = organizations: workplaces, education, healthcare
- 5 = community(s)
- 6 = eco-system/country(s)
- 7 = world

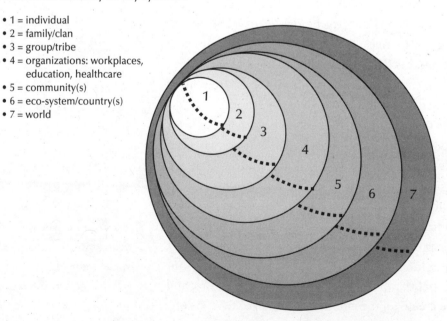

Figure 3.9. Map 3: The scalar fractal relationship of micro, meso, macro human systems.

<<<<<<<<<<<<<<<<<<<<<<<<<Increasing Competencies

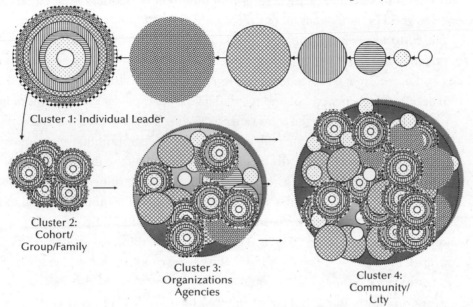

Cluster 1: Individual Leader

Cluster 2:
Cohort/
Group/Family

Cluster 3:
Organizations
Agencies

Cluster 4:
Community/
City

**Figure 3.10. Map 4: The complex adaptive structures of city change.
Source: Beck & Cowan, 1996, Eddy 2003b, 2005.**

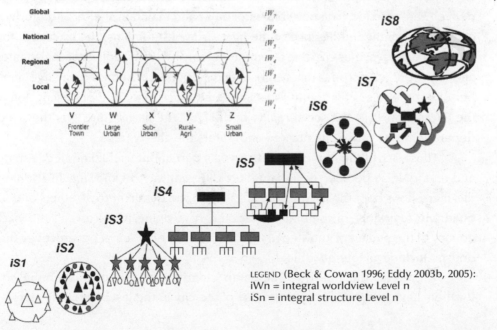

LEGEND (Beck & Cowan 1996; Eddy 2003b, 2005):
iWn = integral worldview Level n
iSn = integral structure Level n

These Goodness perspectives become the crucibles that hold our Subjective Beauty and inform us what is accepted by critical numbers of people in our city experience as good or bad, beautiful or ugly. Another description of the *Intersubjective* We is the cultural reality of the city. The *Intersubjective* We share and discuss their human desires about experiencing the release of stress through greenness in the city and make a moral choice to plant cherry trees on the street, to shade their coffee meeting place, instead of opting for efficiency and paving over the median.

In the Upper Right, the third person *Objective* It appreciates the Truth of life. This perspective demonstrates the actions of life that support material survival in the city. The *Objective* It is the arbiter of material energy of the city that rests on the basics of material life: water, food, waste flow, shelter, clothing. From the *Objective* It, we calculate our individual ecological footprints. And without attention to the well-being of the *Objective* It, the quality of the built life in the city fails utterly. Another description of the *Objective* It is the biological (bio-) reality of the city. The *Objective* It biologically hears the wind in the cherry trees and sees, smells, touches and tastes the blossoms and the fruit.

In the Lower Right, the *Interobjective* Its conveys the Truth that emerges from the material systems that support the *Interobjective* Its individual existences — but by combining multiple material needs, efficient systems can be developed that deliver water and food, dispose of waste, build and maintain shelter and produce clothing. From the intelligence of the *Interobjective* Its domains, the artifact of the built city emerges, thus creating a combined footprint with geological coordinates and an extended footprint that represents the energy consumed for a large number of people to sustain themselves in one city location. Another description of the *Interobjective* Its is the social reality of the city. The *Interobjective* Its is the parks department who physically planted and waters the cherry trees.

Thus each of the four quadrants reveals partial but useful knowledge maps and real, diverse perspectives that reflect different ways of knowing. In addition, this map shows both the inextricable linkages of one quadrant to all others and all quadrants to any one or combination of some. In so doing, it also reveals the inadequacy of the pursuit of knowledge through any combination of perspectives that doesn't include all four quadrants.

Therefore, the four-quadrant map clearly shows us the dilemma city dwellers have faced since the major rise of the city in the last 300 to 400 years. In this same period, the West agreed to split the study of knowledge into left and right quadrants — with the church/spiritual practices (and eventually humanities) on the left and the physical and biological sciences on the right. By coming to this agreement, church and state dichotomized our understanding of human systems of all kinds, including the city. This split underlies the siloing of domains of human knowledge and the failure to grasp the interconnections of all knowledge content and ways of knowing (ontologies and epistemologies). This split lies at the root of our looking at the city as less than a whole human system — as merely a collection of parts — or "de-part-ments."

This map also discloses eight levels of developmental evolution that occur in each quadrant. These correspond to the levels of consciousness identified by Graves (above) and are discussed in the sidebar and in more detail in Map 3 below, and subsequent chapters.

Map 2: The Nested Holarchy of City Systems

The city as a human system is a nest of systems; one cannot just look at the city as a whole or integral system without recognizing that it is made up of a series of whole systems. Gradually in the last hundred years, some scientists have come to realize that their ways of seeing reality have much in common with certain deep spiritual perspectives (Laszlo, 2004; Wilber, 2001). Both scientific and spiritual domains have reframed their traditional worldviews from one described as being the sum of many parts, to one recognized as being entirely wholistic or holistic. Different authors and knowledge centers have gained lenses for recognizing that the universe comprises systems of systems of systems — each one of them a wholeness in itself. Some talk of centers (Alexander, 2004), holons (Koestler), holarchies (Wilber, 1996c) or nested holons (Sahtouris, 1999) or panarchies (Gunderson & Holling, 2002). Regardless of terminology, each observer sees that human systems, as a subset of natural, living systems, are also whole systems (each made up of subsystems) that have gradually become more nested and more complex, as seen in Figure 3.8.

As discernment about whole systems has matured, so too has the recognition that the systems have orders of complexity, so that the holons, wholes and centers are nested into holarchies (Wilber, 1996c) or panarchies (Holling, 2001), where it is possible to see the levels of complexity emerge over time. Miller also tracked these and laid out detailed summaries how the 19 subsystems functioned within each of the levels in the overall nest of whole systems. ·

In many cities, we can see this in the archeological maps that show us in cross-section the built city becoming more and more complex as human systems developed to meet greater and differing challenges. In successful cities, these maps reveal the solutions for the basic functions of cities and how they have transcended and included the solutions that have gone before. (In chapter 7 we propose system structures for cities that support them in their growth along the complexity curve.) In unsuccessful cities, the systems of wholes have been subverted by the failure to see or understand that each whole must be congruent with the other whole systems it interacts with (Alexander, 2004). Alexander (p. 110) notices that successful architecture and living systems have a series of strong centers that interconnect and support one another, so that multiple centers of different sizes serve each other's existence in a complementary way, in the overall wholeness of life.

Map 3: The Scalar Fractal Relationship of Micro, Meso and Macro Human Systems

The third map of the city that casts light on its wholeness is one arising from the insights of non-linear mathematics. Fractal geometry reveals the algorithms of natural systems — the beautiful, repeated patterns that result from the application of simple rules of relationship and association that apply at multiple levels of scale. Figure 3.9 illustrates this and conveys how capacity development in individuals contributes to capacity in families, organizations and communities.

In Figure 3.9, we have an example of an individual who has intentionally enrolled in a competency-developing school system (Cluster 1). Their competencies (identified by different textures and the progressively growing circles) are intentionally developed until they have measurable leadership capacity. At the same time, this individual is in a cohort (group/team) where other individuals are undergoing similar learning experiences (Cluster 2). They associate with one another, drawing on these well-developed competencies. However, when these individuals move out into the worlds of their organizations, they become embedded in social holons where other individuals have different and/or lesser (or greater) capacities (Cluster 3). When the individuals and the groups are embedded in the communities and cities, they become further enmeshed with individuals with mixed capacities (Cluster 4). However, at every level of scale, the basic capacities that were outlined above (by Clare Graves) are the fractal patterns that are repeating themselves in the mixes of human ecologies.

These repeating fractal patterns of human systems reveal that the health of the city is deeply embedded in the patterns or rules that contribute to the health of the individual, families, the team, the organization, the neighborhood, city hall, nation and the world. As discussed in subsequent chapters, we must recognize these fractal realities and their never-ending developmental patterns in the process of seeking congruency amongst them. If we fail to recognize these fractal patterns as natural aspects of human systems, then we fail to appreciate the vibrant dynamics of the city's whole system.

Such is the nature of wholeness that the individual cannot fully realize their potential or goals (for example, to practise recycling) until a critical mass of the individual's membership in social groups takes on the same challenge (for example, enough people recycling so that it is economically rewarded). And one group or cohort will find it difficult to be successful until a critical mass of groups also enlists in developing capacity (for example, recycling as an ordinary way of life).

The saving grace that the new sciences reveal is that only about 10 to 15 percent of a population need change in order that the whole-system shifts towards that change. Thus the non-linear functioning of fractal patterns reveals the power of the diversity generators we encountered in the last chapter. Because recovery patterns that create whole-system change (like homefulness) can be repeated, they create feedback loops that affect the whole system. One of the best examples of this phenomenon came when the world attempted to overcome the shortcomings of the Y2K bug. The over-correction by practically every city resulted in virtually a problem-free rollover for technology systems worldwide in the year 2000.

Map 4: The Complex Adaptive Structures of Change

This final map (Figure 3.10) conveys the stages of change in the city. As a living system, the human system in the city is constantly in the flux of adapting to its life conditions that arise from its external situation in a climatic-geological location. They also arise from the internal situation where the citizens develop consciousness capacities to adapt to the processing of matter, energy and information related to bio-psycho-cultural-social needs. In fact, both external and internal adaptiveness must occur simultaneously.

This view of the city can also be seen in the archeological cross-section but within the vertical context of its geo-bio-region across time. This can demonstrate how coherent the city's use of information is in relation to the sources of its matter and energy.

The dynamics of change are best pictured as vectors that expand the four quadrants of the whole city outward from the seminal center as it adapts to the provocations in its life conditions. These vectors are the outward pointing arrows on Map 1 (Figure 3.7). Beck and Eddy deconstruct these vectors from the geographer's perspective, as in Figure 3.10 where they map out the city's complexifying structures over time.

The dynamics of the city's long-term stages of change are reflected initially in temporary states of change. These states reflect its resilience under duress: how well does it survive in turbulent, chaotic, breakthrough and stable conditions? Historical examples provide apocryphal tales of the most chaotic states of change of city life — and its attendant "ill being": the oceanic submergence of Atlantis, the volcanic burial of Pompeii, the misery of London during the Plague,

Figure 3.11. BC Healthy Community integral map of community capacities. (See sidebar page 61) Reproduced with permission from BCHC, 2006.

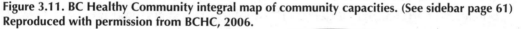

The Inner Individual   *The Outer Individual*

Psychological & Spiritual

- Awareness, thought, feeling
- Attitudes, values, beliefs, intentions
- Inner health & well-being; self-esteem
- Sense of safety, trust
- Sense of connectedness, responsibility & caring for others and the environment
- Creativity, innovation, artistic expression
- Motivation & experience of participation & contribution

Physical & Behavioural

- Physical health and well-being
- Skills & Abilities
- Activities
- Program participation
- Consumer behaviours
- Diet, fitness
- Actions toward others and the environment
- Skills and opportunities for participation & contribution

Cultural

- Worldviews
- Shared meaning
- Collective norms, ethics
- Shared attitudes, values, beliefs
- Shared vision & goals
- Stories, myths
- Shared history, customs
- Shared language, symbols, art
- Co-creativity
- Culture of participation & contribution

Natural Systems / Social Systems

- Natural environment, ecological systems
- Built environment, human systems
- Community institutions (schools, health authority, justice system, religious institutions, etc.)
- Programs and services
- Laws, policies, protocols
- Organizational systems & structures
- Community infrastructure (transportation, housing, social planning council, etc.)
- Governance systems & structures
- Economic system
- Systems & structures for participation & contribution

The Inner Collective   *The Outer Collective*

the demolition of Dresden in WWII. As our world shrinks, modern examples abound, with graphic detail reported on CNN just like the weather conditions such change mimics: the drought of African Saharan cities, the drowning of New Orleans, the bombing of Lebanon.

Jane Jacobs (1970) suggests that city health is highly economy dependent — that cities have control over the means of their well-being by allocating energies to supply their [energy, matter and information] resources from within. But unless cities remain globally aware of their need for adaptive change, they may be blindsided by false economies (like failure to rebuild New Orleans' levies) or mindsets insufficient to surviving their change conditions (e.g., supporting guerrilla worldviews within Lebanon's governance systems).

ALIGNING CITY SUBSYSTEMS

Using the levels of development from the integral map on the subsystems of a city can reveal how the subsystems are aligned or not. Figure 3.12 is a comparison of the capacities within the subsystems (agencies and institutions) that serve the city of Abbotsford, BC, at time of writing.

COMBINING THE MAPS INTO A GIS SYSTEM

When the four maps of the city are combined, they offer a new lens to organize information into Global Information Systems (GIS) maps. A prototype of such a system is discussed in chapter 11 and a preview is offered in Figure 3.13. This

Figure 3.12. Comparison of Abbotsford's centers of gravity in city subsystems, based on levels of development (city is a mini-city with 140,000).

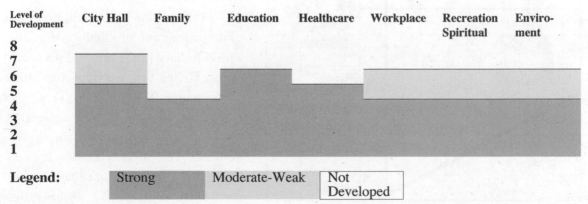

demonstrates how developmental, integral maps can be hyperlinked to reveal integral life conditions for individuals, neighborhoods and whole cities.

GOING BEYOND THE ATTAINMENT OF QUALITY OF LIFE TO A VISION OF CITY OF THE FUTURE

Popular wisdom urges us to examine human behavior so that the quality of human life can be improved. We focus on overpopulation, pollution and greenhouse gas emissions as evidence of the mess and stress that humans have contributed to life on Earth. It is obvious that our behaviors affect not only our own species but virtually every other species with whom we share this planet. However threatening these undeniable conditions are, they are the very signals that indicate our next awakening to a deeper consciousness.

The dangers to the quality of life that now confound our measurement systems can all be attributed to the emergence of the city. Without the rise of the city, we could never have created life conditions for expanded species growth (overpopulation), mindless use of resources (pollution) or climate change (CO_2 overproduction).

We live in a time when we have the knowledge to live intelligently on Earth. This does not mean defining a quality of life as that enjoyed by a relatively privileged portion of the human species or simply arbitrarily raising the quality of life of the rest of the Earth's people. What it does require is creating human habitats where the natural evolution of all peoples can be supported in a way that does not endanger the environment or any people.

The Integral City would make use of the centers of intelligence that exist within its city limits and create conditions of living that are both irresistible and sustainable, because the very act of living this way can be self-organizing, self-reinforcing and self-sustaining. That a city could be not only a center of excellence but a center of intelligence and possibility requires an entirely new

Figure 3.13. Integral GIS map prototype.

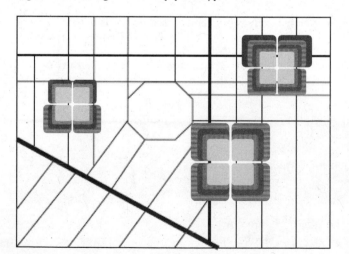

worldview — one that draws on the insights revealed by our four maps. Such an Integral City of the future would respect (by transcending and including) its climatic-geo-bio life conditions, but not be limited by them. The history of our species indicates that the adaptive quality of human intelligences has the capacity to emerge more complex and life-giving habitats. To do so, we will have to "reform" the resources we are currently using and access new resources. Our noetic consciousness not only enables the very idea of an Integral City, but imagines it can be a node of intelligent brilliance that enables the flex and flow of information, energy and matter that adds value to the Earth and even "in-forms" the universe.

ADDING TO THE VALUE OF THE EARTH

An Integral City would go beyond the sustenance of the human systems that it contains and actually add value to its bioregion and/or to the bioregions it is connected to. Ultimately this means that an Integral City would be governed by its capacity to develop, maintain and regenerate life-giving resources. Such a city's health would be measured in the context of the bioregion's health and the planet's health. When we consider that the Earth has many fewer bioregions than it has cities, we can start to see that, by expanding the boundaries of a healthy city into the ecoregion, we essentially demand that the city be governed by its relationship to its life-giving resources.

Even considering the globalized nature of economies, where cities trade with other cities remote from them, tracking the directionality and distribution of the total energy flow of the globe is becoming a "need to know" metric. If human systems are to take responsibility for our contributions to the flow system of global well-being, we need to create monitoring systems that enable us to do so. Because cities are now the habitats of most humans, it appears to make most sense to create a well-being monitoring system at the scale of the city. (Some ideas for this are discussed in chapter 11.)

If we did this with any commitment to intelligent governance, care for natural resources and application of the best of human ways of knowing, the city would move from the immature, undisciplined, unmanaged, unmanageable knot of life that is our current experience into a node of in-forming, free-flowing energy, matter and information. When we arrive at this stage, cities will be recognized for the value that they add to the Earth. If we don't arrive at this stage, cities will putrefy in their own wastes, posing dangers to the rest of the world of spiritual, mental, emotional and physical "dis-ease," that can be exported by air, land and sea.

CONCLUSION

The qualities of an Integral City, revealed by the four maps, challenge us to go beyond a narrow improvement of quality of life. They help us to see that the phenomenon of the city actually adds value to the Earth, because the city focuses and condenses human energy into pulsating nodes of intelligence. The Integral City has the potential to create a quantum leap in human capacities by harnessing the energy created in the intelligence field of human systems in the city. The four maps show us how to see the facets of the field and the wholeness in the city. They help us to understand that it cannot be subdivided into parts. Any parts we label as such are simply elements of an indivisible wholeness that supports the indivisible wholeness of life.

But the models give us insight into the vibrancy of wholeness and help us to detect when that wholeness is out of synch. They help us understand how the city as a whole functions internally, while seeing the commonalities in the patterns of human systems that link them externally to other cities facing the same affronts to their integrality and thus their capacity for integration and integrity.

Three simple rules for applying Integral City principles from this chapter:

1. Map the territory integrally — horizontally through four quadrants, vertically through eight-plus levels of development, diagonally through its change states and relationally through its nested holarchies and fractals of complexity.

2. Create and sustain an integral mapping system at the highest sustainable level of complexity that is appropriate to the capacities of city management.

3. Learn from and update the maps annually or more often.

QUESTIONS

1. What city intelligence field can be revealed by appreciating the intersection of the four Integral City wholeness maps?

2. How do we create the dynamic processes to bridge the silos of city management, education, health care and workplaces?

3. How can we connect the individual citizen to the wholeness of the city?

LIVING INTELLIGENCE: LIVING AND DYING IN THE HUMAN HIVE

The life cycle of a honeybee hive finds its parallel in the life of a single organism.
It moves, feeds, reproduces, even breathes more like an animal than a community of individuals.

— Gould and Gould, 1988, p. 19

Cities are an immense laboratory of trial and error, failure and success.

— Jane Jacobs, 1992

WHAT IS LIFE? WHAT IS DEATH?

In 1961, when Jane Jacobs first published *The Death and Life of Great American Cities* (Jacobs, 1992), she set out to demonstrate to urban planners that cities were much more than inert piles of bricks and mortar, snarls of asphalt or zones of use. With a defiance that was breathtaking, from her first book to her last, she demanded that city planners consider that the life in American (and North American) cities arose from the very human behavior that was born, arrived and lived there.

Jacobs recognized that cities had "natures," were influenced by and generated diversity, died from bureaucratic flow blockages and came alive from civic engagement. She was a proponent of a systems view of the city, while not getting bogged down in the technicalities of systems language. Instead, she relied on her keen sense of observation and challenged her audience to sharpen not only what they saw, heard, felt, smelled and tasted, but to think about the implications of life in the city. Jacobs was notorious for embracing the grittiness of slums, the practicality of public transport and the wisdom of the ordinary city dweller. She honored family and cultural relationships and the power of self-organizing processes to generate natural next steps and innovation.

In her later books, Jacobs built on the systems lenses that showed her the dynamic qualities of modern cities that transcended the mechanistic lenses used by many in city planning departments and city planning professions. An Integral City certainly uses the lenses and language of systems to define life and death. Like any complex system (Capra, 1996), the city as a human system can be considered alive because people in it have these abilities:

- to survive
- to connect with its environment
- to replicate its capacities

Can a city live separate from the people who live in it? If we consider that the substance of the city's energy, matter and information flows through the people of the city, then we realize that the city both "makes up" (as in manufacturing, resourcing, sustaining) the people in it and people make up (as in designing, storytelling, meaning making as well as breathing, eating, consuming and trading) the city. Like other living systems, the city as a whole seems to be a dissipative structure, where the energy flowing through it sustains the structures contained in it — whether they be human, house or hive. This presents us with the paradoxes of interconnectivity and co-generativity when we consider the city. A city's aliveness cannot be considered apart from its citizens, and the citizens' aliveness cannot be considered apart from the city. Both set limitations on the other. So, perhaps, the better question about city life is how can we optimize the life of people in the city? And the life of the city in the people?

A further question might even be how do we reconcile the aliveness of the plants, animals and insects in our city container? Are they indicators of wellness? Does their presence or absence signify a vital sign of well-being in the city? There is certainly enough research now that shows that pets like cats and dogs generally have a positive health effect on people. The invasion of the city by raccoons, foxes and coyotes reminds us that the container of resources we capture in the city are attractive to non-human life forms. (The occasional visit by a larger wild animal like a cougar or a bear brings into stark contrast our expectations for order in the city, with the animal's very wildness and ability to generate chaos by crossing the boundaries between wild and tamed existence.) The presence of trees and other vegetation in the city provide visible reminders of aliveness, and some psychologists suggest they connect us subliminally to an ecological awareness.

Just as we examine the qualities that give life to the city, the same indicators reveal the factors contributing to the death of a city. The living systems perspectives of physicist Fritjof Capra (1996) and evolutionary biologist Elisabet Sahtouris (1999) suggest the kinds of questions we need to ask ourselves to optimize life in the city are similar to these:

1. How vibrant is the health of this city? What do we notice about the vitality of individuals and all the collectives in the city surviving in an integral way? How are they sustaining themselves biophysically/psychologically/culturally/socially? Where is the edge of awareness about how the city connects in a sustainable way with its environment?

2. What is the city's unique value contribution locally and globally? How does the city add value to the ecoregion and/or the global flow of resources and vice versa? How does the city replenish the life conditions that support its life?

3. Where is the city's juice for creating renewal? How are individuals and all the collectives in the city considering the well-being of tomorrow's city unto the seventh generation? How are individuals and all the collectives in the city regenerating their own lives in an integral way? Where are the processes and plans for succession that support people bio-physically/psychologically/culturally/socially?

These "simple" inquiries of city well-being can theoretically tell us the state of city life or give us indications of city illness or death.

CITIES ARE CONCENTRATORS OF COMPLEX WEALTH

A key dilemma of cities is that they are the most powerful concentrators of complex wealth yet created on this planet. Humanity, as a species, is still in its youth. Perhaps then it is not surprising that our cities still exhibit so many signs of early life cycle stages, including the following characteristics of immaturity.

Over-population/Lack of Birth Control

Some cultures have limited their population growth. Western cultures have come to depend on voluntary individual choices. Eastern cultures, most notably China, have chosen to use the compulsory (i.e., involuntary) means of government legislation (e.g., one child per family). By contrast, the fastest growing populations of the world have few indigenous cultural supports for limiting population (United Nations Human Settlements, 2005, p. 23). It appears that the single most effective action a culture can take to improve population control is to educate women. With great courage (and often substantial struggle, as we see in countries like Afghanistan) in breaking away from the traditions of millennia, educated women then find ways to move beyond the value of the family bond and the power of the male-dominated hierarchy. Though often hard won, redefined family and gender relationships recalibrate women's worth as individuals. However, their contributions as more educated members of society naturally curtail their biological/cultural drive to produce children as a means of personal survival (Ehrlich & Ehrlich, 1997).

Urban Immigration Without Ecoregion Responsibility

The imbalance of the world's population distribution is tied to a nation's and culture's attitudes to education and birth control. Sixty percent of the world's population is now urban. The migration of people from rural to urban centers is universal (United Nations Human Settlements, 2005, pp. 77-99). It underlines the symptom of city concentration of complex wealth. But it doesn't explain the failure of the city to value its rural re-sources (sic). Cities have not taken responsibility for maintaining the ecoregions that traditionally would have supported them, because globalization has enabled cities to expand their eco-footprint by importing resources to sustain them. However, the technology of the eco-footprint now enables the human system to understand we need the equivalent of almost four planets if we expect to create all cities equal to the resource-ravenous cities of the first world (Rees & Wackernagel, 1994).

Immature Worldviews

For the most part, cities are still largely "wild." The new cities that are being mapped into existence on designers' blueprints are building infrastructure and structure with little reference to the invisible web of relationships that enable daily survival, family bonds, personal empowerment, civic authority and strategic success. It appears that these human behaviors will be captured and "poured into" structures that have been pre-built rather than self-organized by the human systems that will live in them. These assumptions seem to bear out Jane Jacobs' worst fears about city planning — that it is a process that planners do to and for people but not with them. Misgivings arise even if we give the benefit of the doubt to the planners and developers who are designing new cities (in China, Middle East, Japan, resort towns in deserts, mountains, seasides) to house the bursting populations of the world, from the worldview of flowing (Level 7) intentions. It does not appear that they are considering that the worldview of the people who come to live in such cities will always span the spiral of development (because each of us starts out with minimal capacities that we grow throughout a lifetime. As long as we have a spectrum of ages, we will have a spectrum of human development). It does not appear that they understand the needs for bonding and expression, and even authority must be built one relationship at a time. The engineering approach to new city emergence seems to mirror more of an Orwellian expectation of controlled existence rather than the self-organizing emergence of maturing human individuals and collectives in all their colorful existence.

Inappropriate Locations

The creation of new cities in locations preferred by Modernist success values seems to pay little attention to the capacity of the cities' ecoregions to support such urban centers. Assumptions that water, food, fuel and building materials can simply be imported from elsewhere provide the evidence of severely myopic views of the responsibility cities have to "living lightly on the Earth." It is bad enough that we are faced with the burgeoning dilemmas of our "wild" cities, but to intentionally locate cities without such consideration for the environmental repercussions is not only locally irresponsible but globally irresponsible. It is as if the investors, planners and developers fail to recognize the implications of their city-building decisions that impact space, time and lives far beyond the footprint of the city. While they concentrate on the capital investment for creating new city infrastructures and structures, they appear to remain willfully unconscious of or ignore the operational requirements of such cities — operations that must embrace the bio/psycho/cultural/social realities of any city they build. An integral eco-footprint means that we would measure all such costs and invest in the simulations that would show us the long-term implications of such investments. For it is the long-term investment of the physical/intellectual/cultural/social capital that will prove whether any new city can live or die.

In the meantime, the likes of UN-Habitat, World Bank and World Health Organization struggle with the unending agonies of existing cities in much of the developing world simply just to survive, never mind thrive. While the UN is structured to congregate the voices of nations, it is not set up to focus on the world's cities. As a result all of its efforts through UNESCO and other NGOs, ideas, people and resources spin ineffectively in the informal biannual gatherings of the World Urban Forum. With all our best intentions, the maturity of the world's congress of cities is little better than a Level 2 (bonding) effort. Cities come together seasonally for tribal gatherings (where complainings outnumber celebrations) but are rendered ineffective by their nation's repressive urban governance (even in the most developed nations of the world) and the current state of ineffective global governance.

Thus, location of cities remains a virtual undiscussable. We can examine the entire approach that the United States has taken to the post-Katrina hurricane/storm surge fate of New Orleans as a high-profile example of the irresponsibility of the developed world's approach to city life (Grunwald, 2007). We look in vain in practically every other nation for any examples of enlightened policy or approaches to emergency response and recovery to natural disasters (of all kinds from flood to famine) that befall cities.

The location factor for the life and death of cities is largely undiscussable because it is a political time bomb. It is an issue of power. Those holding elected office fear making decisions that will go against the accepted (read unconscious, default, unconsidered, unexamined) expectations that wherever cities are located they should remain and be supported to maintain their unsustainable existences.

Until now the Earth had sufficient resilience to forgive these human transgressions. But with the overload of human population on Earth resources, it is time for us to take responsibility for our decisions and pay attention with intention to optimize life in the city within context of its natural litho/geo/bio resources.

If *homo sapiens sapiens* develops the will and capacity to do this, it will have moved the species exponentially into an era where responsibility for collective impacts will transcend and include all the civic governance systems yet created.

Doubtless this may take hundreds of years (and as a result will unfold parallel to ongoing disasters, dis-eases (sic) and deaths of existing cities). However, the decision to make choices can start with our becoming conscious that an Integral City must first be awake to its vital signs.

The tracking of its vital signs will give feedback to city individuals and collectives and be the first step in cities becoming adaptive to their life conditions — adaptive in all quadrants and all levels. By growing consciousness capacities, cities and citizens can develop capacities for meshworking (see chapter 10). In this way, the most effective city governance systems will enable adaptiveness through action learning and, in the process, not just map the water and waste management systems that lie below city streets, but also map the information flows and relationship connections that weave the city's true container and underlie the city's real integral identity. It is the powerful combination of identity, relationships and information that results in the phenomenon of place making.

Irresponsible Resource Use

The massive demonstration of low intelligence in regard to responsibly stewarding air, water and food is another indicator of the lack of maturity of the human species. The implications of this are discussed more fully below.

HUMAN LIFE CYCLES: THEY WILL ALWAYS BE WITH US

Bio-physical Life Cycles

Like so much of our science, the human biological life cycle is more visible to us than the invisible domain of human consciousness development. The biological life cycle, therefore, is more observed, studied, researched and reported on. But for the most part, all of this scientific engagement occurs without reference to optimizing biological life in the city.

We do know that the quality of air (or even altitude) in a city affects the most fundamental of human biological processes: breathing. But do we know how to optimize human development so that it thrives in city conditions? Or are we still using a model of optimum human health that might have occurred in a largely agrarian society?

We have long ago learned that the quality of water is crucial to the survival of cities as it is fundamental to human survival. But how have we taken responsibility for the water cycle that flows around the globe and through our cities? Unlike human social rights, the human species has yet to endorse the right of every person to clean air and water and the upstream and downstream implications of such rights.

Can we say anything much different about food? While we can now measure the impact on the planet of a city's eco-footprint in terms of the carbon-based energy it consumes, it is the energy translated into nutrient and caloric food intake that contributes to the health of our biophysical condition. What do we know about the variations in human metabolism that emerged in relation to historic life conditions and how to optimize it not only in the cities indigenous to those life conditions, but in cities far different and far distant to which we have migrated? In general, we pay more attention to the diets of pets for optimizing their health (mostly in cities) in the developed world than we do to the diets of humans (anywhere in the world).

These vital contributors to basic human biophysical health affect every stage of the human life cycle from conception, to birth, childhood, adolescence, maturity, elderhood and death. We do know from our science that each of these stages requires a different mix of nutrients and calories, but the knowledge is not widely disseminated nor easily accessed. Furthermore, health condition is generally a solitary responsibility of parent or citizen, and almost nowhere is it collectively rewarded.

In the developed world, we have lost whatever folk knowledge we had to guide us through human life stage adjustments, and we are stumbling around in the dark of our current ignorance. In most cases the developed world has ceded this ground to institutional bureaucracies like healthcare systems and/or private food distribution systems, both of which are being operated on the value system of profit, not optimization of human health.

Tragically and ironically, as the discourse on sustainability widens, we are becoming aware of the unethical waste of resources that is endemic to the food production and distribution system of the developed world. This is the unhealthy mirror to the massive occurrence of famine and agricultural failure in the developing world. This interlocked global demonstration of low intelligence is another indicator of the lack of maturity of the human species.

Within the context of human life cycles, the failure to optimize our biophysical conditions directly impacts the quality of life experienced in the other three quadrants of our existence. If the body is our biophysical equivalent of the temple (of our consciousness or soul), we have lost the oral blueprints we used to share with each other, and we are building bodies in ways that are blind, deaf, dumb, tasteless and tactileless. Is it any wonder that is how we too frequently experience the cycles of life?

Psychological Life Cycles

The human condition unfolds in natural stages of conscious complexity that have been mapped in many ways by researchers of man's inner life. Whether these are psychologists, philosophers or spiritual guides, in every culture the maps tell the story of individual capacity development that starts with dependence and moves on through co-dependence, independence, interdependence to Intradependence.

Both the sciences of complexity and the sciences of mind development agree that we gain capacity in relationship with others. Thus our learning is quite contextual — whether we are tracking it in terms of emotional intelligence, cognitive intelligence or cultural/social intelligence. It appears that our learning is naturally interpersonal and cannot be advanced without interaction with others. Thus we evolve our intelligence stages from egocentric (self-centered), through ethnocentric (other- or affiliation-centered), ecological-centric (world-centered) to evolutionary-centric (universe-centered).

As in biophysical health, much of our responsibility for this process in the developed world has been abrogated to educational institutions. And, as in the case of healthcare institutions, we have generally failed to ask what we need to learn across the human life cycle in order to optimize human life in the city. What is even more worrisome is the phenomenon that Bill McKibben has identified as hyper-individualism and Ken Wilber has criticized as narcissism. Under either label, the dilemma is that individual development has become stuck in the egocentric stage where individuals fail to appreciate or grow capacity to value others.

The bees in a beehive train and feed their hive members for the purpose of producing 40 pounds of honey a year so the hive can survive — i.e., not just individual bees. But what is the human equivalent of meeting such a definable purpose that can inform our learning and behaviors? (It appears that even the homeless need to be taught the fundamental skills of money management, before they are able to sustain themselves.)

With our knowledge of the impact of our resource needs, eco-land footprint, carbon footprint, resilience and sustainability, we now have sufficient information to take responsibility to live intelligently in cities. To their credit, it is the world's mayors who are stepping up to the plate to support in principle the intentions of protocols related to Kyoto climate change (however flawed its ambitions), sprawl and density, poverty, homelessness and environmental health.

Many mayors are coming to realize that all of these challenges to city health are also challenges to city democracy and can only be addressed through whole-systems thinking.

Cultural Life Cycles

Cities develop cultures through the intersubjective engagement of individuals and groups. Cultural life cycles have traditionally extended over long periods of time because the container of the city has been relatively isolated from the containers of other cities. In these cities where culture was stable, it may have appeared to change little from decade to decade or even from century to century. Traditions, beliefs and relationships developed well-worn pathways within the real city and the citizens' mental maps of the city. Expectations, resources and change would often extend many generations. This web of relationships could become so ingrained that individual cities developed "personalities" or morphogenic fields that still conjure up archetypes or stereotypes of individual cities. To test the strength of these images, think of what comes to mind when you read: Venice, London, New York, Tokyo, St. Petersburg, Rio de Janeiro, Sydney, Mumbai.

However, in the last century, the acceleration of migration from not only the rural to the urban city in the same country, but from one city to another city in a completely different nation, has led to a phenomenon dubbed "mongrel cities" (Sandercock & Lyssiotis, 2004). Cities with mixed cultures are the learning classrooms of today's world. They are also the seat of diversity, pluralism and a myriad of misalignments that make them steadily more ungovernable.

City governance has not kept pace with the rate of change because the governance systems of cities are usually coupled with their states and nations, although the systems tend to develop at different rates. In many ways cities have been the most compact if not stable unit to govern. For the most part, the rules developed from centuries of relatively stable cities have been embedded in higher levels of government like states or provinces and federal systems. As a result, today's cities are being strangled by the so-called higher levels of government, because they are prevented from re-organizing to adapt to their new, often volatile, mix of cultural influences.

Whereas cities used to be populated by relatively homogenous ethnic populations, many cities in Europe and North America today have become mosaics and melting pots of the world's populations. Immigration policies have created cities like London and Toronto and Miami where not only hundreds of languages are spoken, but hundreds of cultural assumptions about the rules of living together are clashing daily in the streets.

It may be that the cities most able to demonstrate adaptive capacity and therefore resilience are the actual city states like Singapore (and laterally Hong Kong), where the orders of government don't dilute the governance strength needed to bind the fabric of mixed cultures, but instead encourage and manage them (Beck, 2007; United Nations Human Settlements, 2005, p. 85).

Social Life Cycles

While each individual can be considered an individual holon, any group of humans becomes a social holon. The qualities of a social holon are the dynamic composite of all the individual holons that make it up. This applies to any human collective, including spousal pairs, families, special interest groups, teams and organizations of all stripes and communities.

The patterns of human behaviors can still be mapped in social holons — they go through life cycles

KATRINA DIALOGUES REVEAL POTENTIAL COHERENCE

It appears that we have the intelligence and resources to address the complexity of thinking about the city as a whole and our capacities to develop coherent solutions even for the most dire of circumstances. Mark Satin explicitly outlined an approach for New Orleans in his article "The Katrina Dialogues" where he brings "some [US] leading thinkers & doers to an imaginary roundtable and [makes] them listen to and learn from one another (using their actually expressed views)." Satin points out that the moral of this story is that we have access to all the best practices that we need to recover from a disaster like this (and even operate a city day to day, by integrating existing resources and practices): "With a little bit of give and take and a lot of vision, WE CAN SOLVE the problems Katrina revealed" (Satin, 2005). Satin's essay can be accessed at http://www.radicalmiddle.com/x_katrina_dialogues.htm.

of their own. However, the social holon is more like a musical duo, quartet, jazz combo or symphony, while the individual holon is like a single instrument. And the human holon is far more dynamic than any actual musical instrument because it is a living system. When we view the ensemble of individual holons, we see in each one a "work in progress." In the human symphony, we are looking at an ensemble of instruments that are at different stages of bio/psycho/cultural/social capacity development; at different states of change; and in diverse roles and relationships to one another.

By playing with the musical metaphor, we can appreciate the challenge that all social holons face in living and working together. If we can imagine a quartet of accomplished master-class musicians starting out to play a challenging composition, we hear beautiful music. But suddenly one of the players is taken ill and calls in a replacement with lesser skills to continue the program. The quartet is no longer made up of the same level of accomplishment as it was to start, even though Replacement 1 is doing their best. Then all of a sudden a second musician is forced to leave, sending in Replacement 2 who is not even the same rank as Replacement 1. The program continues, but the audience can detect that not only is the music more dissonant, the individual performances lack finesse. Within a short while, a third musician is forced to leave, sending in an understudy, who does their best to carry on with the program. But by this time the audience can see as well as hear that the quartet is clearly not performing from the same song sheet (as it were). Finally the fourth original musician must also leave the stage, sending in the last available student to finish the piece. In the last bars, the musical score has not changed, but the capacity of the instrumentalists to perform it has clearly regressed.

In fact, in this story, we have witnessed five versions of the social holon. With each change of musician, the dynamics and capacity of the collective were altered. If we stand back far enough, we can see that the performance was altered not only by the physical replacement of the bodies, but also by the difference in intentions and expectations of each person. When they related to one another in the quartet, they brought different cultural beliefs (e.g., master musicians prove themselves in concerts; second violins are really just second fiddles; students have much to learn from professionals). Furthermore the social intelligence of the quartet was affected because the improvisational nature of the substitutions forestalled any chances to rehearse and improve their systems of playing together.

In short form, we have just described the dilemmas of all social holons. Even with few members of a social holon (as in the quartet just discussed), the dynamics are complex in the extreme. With the addition of each person, the dynamics multiply exponentially. Thus social holons are not just the sums of the individual holonic capacities, but instead demonstrate emergent capacities that arise from the interactions of the individual holons in the container.

However, when we look around us at social holons in the city, we often see more order than we see chaos. How do people figure it out? How do social holons operate despite the intertwining, interacting nature of their experience? For the answer to this, we must look to the natural pattern-making tendencies of life itself.

It appears that we "get order for free" (Kauffman, 1993). Out of the chaos of the origins of the universe, the capacity for self-organizing has been recognized as a fundamental behavior that has resulted in life itself — and thus underlies even human behaviors. In defining a social holon, by definition we are looking at a group of people contained in some kind of boundary. Within this boundary, the individual agents, who are living systems first of all, will interact until they figure out some workable order that allows them to survive, connect with their environment and reproduce.

Thus we set up the conditions for the emergence of human social systems and their capacities to adapt and learn as individuals and groups within the social system in which they interact.

In writing about homefulness, (a social condition where people feel they belong to self, other and place), I have noted that, as humans develop, the complexity of both their consciousness and their societies, the experience of resonance, coherence and emergence changes (Hamilton, 2007a). Humans are forever adapting to changing life conditions.

Moreover, it appears that humans as complex adaptive living systems are evolving a "panarchy" of capacities. As noted in chapter 2, Holling (2001) explains that a panarchy is the "hierarchical structure in which systems of nature ... and humans ... as well as combined human-nature systems ... and social-ecological systems are interlinked in never-ending adaptive cycles of growth, accumulation, restructuring and renewal." Several decades earlier than either Bloom or Holling conceived the systems described in chapter 2, Graves in the 1960s and 1970s (2003) conducted an 18-year study, whose conclusions came to be known as the

Figure 4.1. Levels of complexity.
Source: Adapted from Beck, 2002.

EXPRESS SELF STAGE	ORGANIZING PRINCIPLE OF LIFE CONDITION	SACRIFICE SELF STAGE	ORGANIZING PRINCIPLE OF LIFE CONDITION
AN - Beige	Survival		
		BO- Purple	Belonging
CP - Red	Command & Control		
		DQ - Blue	Authoritarian Structure
ER - Orange	Economic Success		
		FS - Green	Humanitarian Equality
GT - Yellow	Systemic Flex & Flow		
		HU - Turquoise	Planetary Commons

"evolutionary complex levels of human existence." Graves' research showed that human behaviors arising out of one set of conditions created problems of existence that could not be solved at that level (echoing Einstein's proposition of the same nature). As a result new adaptive behaviors are called into existence. Graves identified a group-centric cluster of behaviors he called "sacrifice self" values and an individual-centric cluster of behaviors he called "express self" values. Moreover, his research showed that these behaviors adapted and alternated with one another at an ever-increasing level of complexity, as life conditions changed. Graves used a set of identifiers to represent life conditions (designated by letters from the first half of the alphabet) and bio-psycho-cultural-social human existence (designated by letters from the second half of the alphabet) (see Figure 4.1). Beck and Cowan (1996) and Beck (2002) have devised a system of color codes to identify each level of complexity. Beige, red, orange and yellow (i.e., warm colours) relate to "express self" versions of existence. Purple, blue, green and turquoise (i.e., cool colours) relate to "sacrifice self" versions of existence (see Figure 4.1).

Because the dominant behaviors arise in response to life conditions — as one would expect from any complex adaptive system (Capra, 1996; Holling, 2001; Stevenson & Hamilton, 2001) — each level of existence behaves with increasing levels of complexity in order to maximize the organizing principle (or value) of the current life condition. This behavior results in a tendency to protect the status quo at its current level of complexity. In Bloom's terms, this could be interpreted as conformity enforcement of the organizing principle or value.

Thus a tension in favor of the values and behavior that are most coherent with the current life conditions will be demonstrated as conformity enforcement. The flip side of this behavior is that the dominant culture will also protect itself against diversity generation, until such time as life conditions require the solutions

Figure 4.2. Adizes' corporate lifecycle curve.
Source: Reproduced with permission from Adizes, 1999, 2006.

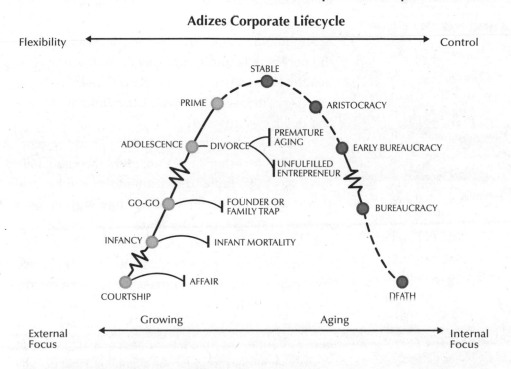

that diversity generation can offer to the problems created by maximizing the values and organizing principles in play at any level of existence. Moreover, we can see the natural evolutionary cycles emerge at all levels of scale: individual, family, organization, society.

With an awareness of the individual human life cycle, Ichak Adizes (Adizes, 1999) has mapped out the trajectory of the social holons in corporate life cycles (see Figure 4.2). He identifies the stages of corporate emergence with the equivalent human stages of: courtship, (affair), infancy, (infant mortality), go-go, (founder's trap), adolescence, (divorce), early prime, late prime … aristocracy, … bureaucracy and death.

Adizes has also recognized that the deployment of strategies and resources at different stages shifts the importance of corporate functions across the life cycle. Four functions serve an organization's needs with different weightings at different stages of growth; production, administration, entrepreneurship and integration. Adizes proposes that the relationship of these functions determines

BURNING MAN: RECURRING CITY

A live, recurring action research process that reveals the reality of creating whole living spaces is the annual experiment of Burning Man (see Figure 4.3). This is a city that is created anew from nothing in the Nevada desert every year. All resources must be imported to the location, and all resources are removed at the end of the mere week's existence. The recent event in 2006 attracted 40,000 people — this is not a trivial experiment in human systems. Virtually nothing is provided except the invitation — even the, by now, civilized arrangement of temporary residences has emerged over time and is passed along to each ensuing year. The citizens create an instant gift economy and in so doing accelerate the self-organizing, creative, innovative emergence of ever-densifying connections. This is the exact opposite of the designed new cities — Burning Man starts from dust, exists in dust and returns to dust. What can we learn from the integral nature of this intentional life and death of a city? (burningman.com)

the attainment of prime (or optimal) performance and its sustainability over time. The value to these insights is not only to understand the vital signs of health in individual organizations, but to recognize the necessity of interconnecting these functions in a healthy economy. The appropriate or inappropriate exercise of these four functions can determine the life and death of a city.

Jane Jacobs (2001, pp. 85-118) used the functions of living systems to explore how the natural life cycle was triggered and controlled through bifurcations, when a system chooses one option over another to survive; positive feedback, when a system rewards some behaviors over others, e.g., doing more of what already works because it works; negative feedback, when a systems punishes some behaviors because it senses continuation would lead to not surviving, e.g., breathing when CO_2 levels rise; and emergency adaptations, like inventing a new response in face of calamitous threat. Jacobs maintained that healthy cities could use all these means to attain and maintain a kind of "prime" level of health through the acts of developing, diversifying and refueling according to the natural laws of living-system survival that apply to termites, forests and cougars as much as humans.

Adizes' approach (1999) seems to recognize both Jacobs' conditions for achieving "prime" but also the primacy of Holling's four functions, because their contributions align the interests of customers, management, capital, organization and labor (p. 143). These are structural alignments that enable appropriate attraction and direction of energies for the sustaining of life in the city for citizens, city managers and city workers.

Figure 4.3. Burning Man city layout. (Source: Reproduced with permission. Burning Man Media and Communications.)

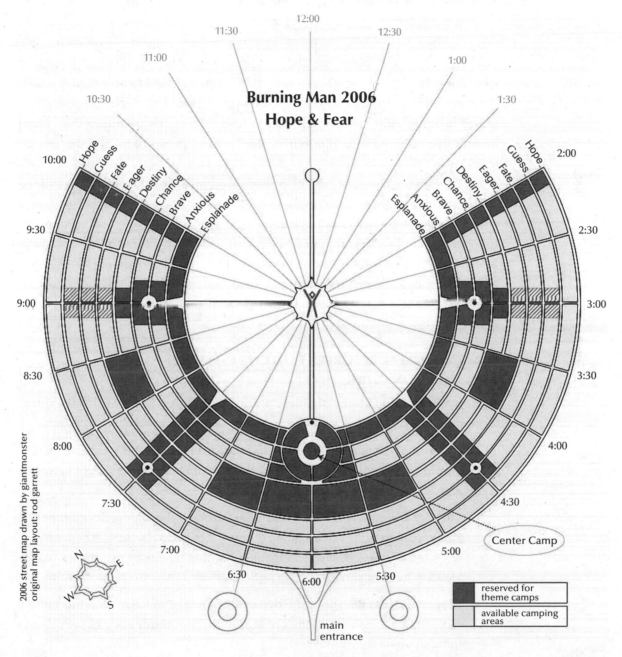

In an analogous manner, the insights of Elliott Jaques reveal the need for what he calls "requisite organization" (Dutrisac, Fowke, Koplowitz & Shepard, nd; Shepard, 2007b). Jaques proposes structural and leadership hierarchies in organizations, based on contexts of the tasks and the longest discretionary time span needed to complete any task (along with quantity, quality and resources available). The longer the discretionary time span required to accomplish a task, the greater the social capacity is required of the leader and department. He proposes layers of differentiation based on the time spans from less than three months, through one year, two to five years, 5 to 10 years, 10 to 20 years, and 20 to 50 years.

Beyond the consideration of individual organizational health across all the sectors from private to not-for-profit (NFP), a city must recognize that how it structures these elements as a system will determine its health and sustainability. The bottom-line question to test right-structures might be to ask, would the bees recognize the roles, responsibilities and cycles that drive the city systems? Is any given city utilizing its conformity enforcers (producers), diversity generators (entrepreneurs), resource allocators (administrators) and inner judges (integrators) in right relationship for sustaining the city?

FRACTALS REVEAL RECURRENT LIFECYCLES, STAGES AND SPIRALS IN CITIES

In their article "The Futures of Cities," Beck and Cowan (1994; 1997, p. 1) explore three dynamics of cities:

- **Horizontal Dynamic**: This dynamic addresses all the possible demographics through categories and classifications of Groups, Types, Norms and Traits.

- **Vertical Dynamic**: This dynamic reflects the evolutionary, developmental Value Systems and value system Memes that produce them. They are represented by the spiral of emergent, unfolding ranges of paradigms, worldviews, mindsets and organizing principles.

- **Diagonal Dynamic**: This is the dynamic of Change which reveals the shifting patterns of transition, transformation and the sequences of complexity through which they unfold.

It is very difficult to keep aware of all these dynamics when considering the city. Only when we picture them as fractal dynamics that exist at every level of scale, can we start to see the effects of dynamic patterns in operation.

In the previous section we explored the qualities of social holons. This is a starting point for understanding the complexity of collections of human social holons in the city, such as families, special interest groups, professions, governments, corporations, non-government organizations, social networks, consortia and self-organizing webs.

From a fractal perspective we can recognize that vertical stages have stage cycles within them. Each one of the social holons has its own criteria for maintaining (or advancing) such stage (life) cycles. Most specialized areas of humanities studies (for example psychology, sociology, archeology and paleontology) have revealed the patterns of stage evolution and their effects on individual performance. For instance Tuckman's stages of team development has become quite apocryphal: form, storm, norm and perform (1965; Tuckman & Jensen, 1977). Furthermore, what this concise description frames for us is that each of these social holons has different life endurance expectations related to their orientation:

- Family: reproduction, care, maintenance of biologically and/or culturally related people — multiples of generations every 20 years

- Teams: project and/or process oriented — days or weeks to years

- Groups: purpose oriented — weeks to years

- Consortia: contract for project completion

- Professions: standards/quality/practices oriented — decades

- Private Organizations: process oriented — years to decades

- NFP/NGO: project or cause oriented — years to decades

- Social networks: purpose or cause oriented — years to decades

- Governments/Justice: governance delivery — decades to centuries

- Self-organizing webs: relationship oriented — years

If life conditions did not change, then the stage cycle might be expected to continue indefinitely as the living system was well matched to the life conditions that supports its life cycle. But when life conditions shift, the living system changes

BUILD SCHOOLS THAT BECOME SENIORS' HOUSING

Demographer David Chalk has proposed that any school board planning for the long-term use of schools should look beyond the needs of the school system. He recommends building links to the healthcare and social service systems. He speculates that when the bulge of "echo" children (the grandchildren of Generation X) no longer populates the elementary schools (and surrounding neighborhoods are filled with empty-nesters and senior citizens) new schools built today will go empty. The solution? Design schools for today's education needs and tomorrow's seniors' housing needs. That means, assuming they are multi-purpose designed, that when the buildings are finished serving the functions of the education system, they can be renovated at reasonable cost to serve the needs of assisted living for seniors.

or adapts to match it, and thus the diagonal dynamic of change comes into play. Through the diagonal dynamic of change, the living system recalibrates its internal energies to permit survival in the life conditions. It shifts upwards or downwards on the scale of complexity until a match is found that allows it to survive.

The vertical record of a city's life or death is often revealed in the archeological layers of the city's history. Cities have a habit of building upon the rubble of past paradigms, where archeological digs from Troy to London, Pompeii to Los Angeles and Xian to New Orleans reveal the demographics of how the city survived at each horizontal layer.

While it is tempting to interpret that each layer contains only one paradigm, in fact each layer probably contains at least three. Each layer would represent the center of gravity of the dominant worldview at any given time in history. But that center of gravity would include evidence of its ancestral roots and leading edge future aspirations. Anthropologists tell us that those remains reveal what was important to people at that time — what they invested valuable resources to eat, wear and build — as well as what was not important — what they wasted, discarded and trashed.

If you want to understand what a city values, look at the bio-psycho-cultural-social connections through which it supports its children's education, youths' coming of age, adults' health and elders' wisdom. Those manifestations will reveal how the political objectives were accomplished through the allocation of resources.

Beck and Cowan (1994, 1997) suggest that political objectives translate across a spectrum of complexity in ways that optimize what the leaders value, i.e., the conformity enforcers, directed and resourced by inner judges and resource allocators (1996, pp. 4-13).

1. Beige — This level of complexity is apolitical. Physical survival takes full energy.

2. Purple — At this level, the group has primacy (either Ethnic or Extended Family or both). The group shares the spoils, jointly owns assets and lives together.

3. Red — At this level, the powerful elite(s) in charge demand the spoils. Everyone else takes second place.

4. Blue — At this level, the righteous earn the spoils they deserve. Everyone else earns by merit of some kind.

5. Orange — At this level, the successful competitors win the spoils. Everyone competes.

6. Green — At this level, everyone shares equally in the process of dividing the spoils.

7. Yellow — At this level, the natural, functional needs present in the life conditions determine and distribute energy of all kinds.

8. Turquoise — At this level, collective individualism preserves all life.

As noted above, Ichak Adizes' lifework has been to research and support the quality of the life cycle of organizations. In identifying the four basic functions that enable organizational life — Production, Administration, Entrepreneurship, Integration — Adizes postulates that if these functions are not used appropriately at each stage of organizational development, then the organization is misaligned and not able to perform at its optimum capacity. He proposes that if people in the organization want to optimize their prime performance, they must coalesce authority, power and influence in order to organize these functions appropriately. In terms of complex adaptive systems, Adizes recognizes that adaptiveness requires appropriate structures to enable survival, environmental connections and future succession. As a social holon, an organization is similar to a dissipative structure through which flow resources to both its individual holons and their social structures — teams, departments, branches, consortia, etc.

When we step back from the organizational context and look at the city as a fractal, can we ask ourselves:

- What are the city's key stages of growth?
- How can we consider the organizational functions that a city needs at different stages to be similar to Adizes' organizational functions? If so what are they and who is responsible?
- What (if any) are a city's natural limits to growth?

Another way to test Adizes' stages of growth is to examine Holling's panarchy model (discussed earlier) to see if it can inform Adizes' approach (or vice versa). One possible framing of this is to notice that Holling has identified the actions that would be the responsibility of each structural role.

Role 1. **Exploitation** (low potential, low connectedness): This is the key responsibility of Production.

Role 2. **Conservation** (high potential, high connectedness): This is the key responsibility of Production, Administration (and Integration).

Role 3. **Release** (low potential, high connectedness): This is the key responsibility of Administration.

Role 4. **Reorganization** (high potential, low connectedness): This is the key responsibility of Entrepreneurship.

Both Adizes and Holling propose, like Graves, that organizations progress from less complex stages of development to more complex stages, and that, given opportune circumstances, at some point there is an up-shift to another level of operational complexity for the entire system. Examples like New Orleans also demonstrate that these tipping points are real, and when minimal critical conditions are violated, a downshift can also occur.

THE CITY FIELD HAS OBSERVABLE CHANGE STATES

In order to make sense of the behavior of any living system, a theory of change inevitably emerges. The fundamentals of change have their roots in the self-organizing nature of the universe, i.e., what has emerged since the big bang? And how is it changing?

At this stage of evolution we know that order does emerge from chaos, and that the universe has stabilized patterns of change so that the litho/geo/biospheres have produced beings conscious of their own consciousness. However, stability is a relative term and can be used as a measure of change. Stability can measure the quality of relationships in a container like a community or a city. We need to ask are relationships between individuals and/or groups stable, unstable or chaotic?

Selecting a model for change in the city is very scale dependent. The effectiveness of any model will be related to what change we want to notice. We need to identify the degree of granularity or resolution that we need, to notice the change amongst different elements. On a fundamental basis, in a living self-organizing system, change must be marked in relationship to its survival, connection to its environment/life conditions and its capacity to regenerate life. Reporting change requires that we track data that is relevant to any or all of these elements.

On Earth one of the most fundamental life conditions that affects human existence — and therefore city existence — is weather. Constantly changing, it is a visible reminder of our sensitivity to its key states: stable, stormy/unsettled, turbulent, clear. These descriptions — with which we are so familiar that we use them as constant reference points in our conversations — turn out to be useful general descriptors about the change state of any system.

As complex adaptive systems, humans in cities are constantly attempting to adjust their individual circumstances to survive in the conditions of the city. We could call this complex adaptiveness "learning." We are constantly learning how to adapt and survive under all possible life conditions: stable, stormy/unsettled, turbulent, clear.

New research (Cummins, 1996a, 1996b; Cummins et al., 2004; Hamilton, 2007b; Wills, Hamilton & Islam, 2007a, 2007b) suggests that our sensitivity to adaptiveness is possibly homeostatic. It appears that we might have a qualitative (or even quantitative?) sense of well-being, to which we constantly try to adjust. Cummins has created a ten-point scale to measure this sense of well-being — and his data suggest that our homeostatic reference point is about 7 out of 10.

Thinking about an Integral City, I speculate that everyone attempts to achieve this rating or condition in their life as a whole. They also, usually unconsciously, seek to translate this state of well-being into their existence as "I, We, It and Its" — in other words, they experience the different perspectives of each of the quadrants of their realities. A measure of well-being, such as Cummins (1996a, 1996b, 2004) proposes, would be a measure of self-alignment with what a person perceives is important in the context of their life conditions. Researchers including Cummins, Wills et al. and myself have attempted to demonstrate that this measure of well-being is not only objective and interobjective, but also subjective and intersubjective.

Semantic differential and structural differential approaches offer a similar qualitative device to gather data from any location. Don Beck has developed surveys asking respondents to rate their observations of local conditions on scales of polar opposites that disclose readings for the locale, by producing a composite picture of conditions that particularize the general conditions as stable, stormy/unsettled, turbulent, clear.

Yet another way of observing change in the city is to use a modified form of appreciative inquiry (Hamilton, 2005), determining what people consider to be important in their community — what are its strengths, difficulties and opportunities. In an Integral City, we can map these responses, based on levels of complexity, and reveal the tensions between each set of data. The tensions reveal the areas most subject to change as people attempt to adapt their experience to optimal conditions.

CONCLUSION

The life and death of the city is linked very closely with all of the maps of the city. It obviously reflects and unpacks the levels of development in Map 1 and the dynamics of city change expressed in Map 4.

As the city complexifies the interplay of micro-individual, meso-organization and macro-community systems interconnect. Life and death and the health of the city are very much reflected in healthy alignment on Map 3. There they reflect each other as fractal patterns and co-exist at different levels of scale. The quality of life in the micro reflects the quality of life at the meso and the macro and vice versa.

However, we must also consider that Map 1 expresses the balance of the inner and outer lives of the city and the tensions between the individual and the collective. Elisabet Sahtouris (1999) beautifully expresses the need that all the holons nested in Map 2 of the city must be in service to both self and other holons. That is the essence of a healthy life in a healthy living city.

QUESTIONS

1. What is the relationship of one person's life cycle to the city's life cycle?

2. If the cycles of life are natural, how do we reframe our experience of surviving the down cycle as difficult but natural?

3. How, when and where do we reintroduce into city life, recognition and celebration of the passages of life? How do we mark the natural life cycles of the self, family, organization, city?

Three simple rules for applying Integral City principles from this chapter:

1. Honor the dance of life cycles in the city.

2. Integrate the natural cycles of change within the city.

3. Learn how to zoom in and out at different scales to dance with the fractal patterns of the city.

5

INNER INTELLIGENCE: CONSCIOUS CAPACITY IN THE HUMAN HIVE

The bee is also wired to time its course of learning in advantageous ways,
so that it learns color and shape before landing and landmarks afterwards....
This innate "preparation" for learning runs counter to traditional
psychological notions, which stress flexibility of the learning process.

— Gould and Gould, 1988, p.185

The city's sustainability is directly related to the city's intelligence.

— Hamilton, 2007

CONSCIOUSNESS: FUNDAMENTAL TO THE UNIVERSE

Intentional consciousness in a city is highly complex and highly dynamic. If we were able to examine the city like a PET scan or MRI scan does a brain, we would see that intentional intelligence is constantly being turned on and off, energized in different centers, and that intelligence is widely distributed. (In fact we discuss the principles of how to monitor a city in exactly that way in chapter 11.) We would also see its sleeping, waking, dreaming cycles as individuals came and went from centers of rest, recreation, work and transportation. We might even start to see a city divided into left hemispheres (where the doing tasks of work and industry are located) and right hemispheres (where the being and belonging relationships of home and recreation are located). Or we might see the city's cognitive, emotional and cultural intelligences (Gardner, 1999; Goleman, 1997; McIntosh, 2007).

It is becoming increasingly clear that consciousness is fundamental to the universe. A growing body of research is demonstrating that consciousness has not arisen from the interaction of matter and energy, but that matter and energy have emerged from and with consciousness itself (Laszlo, 2004, 2006a, 2006b). In our anthropocentric way, we have been ascribing the miracle of consciousness to the human condition. We have viewed ourselves as the center of universal consciousness, just as at one time (in the not too distant past) we assumed that the universe revolved around the Earth. Now, we are gaining faint glimpses of the strong possibility that the universe itself is conscious, and we are just beginning to grasp that our relationship to that vast sea of consciousness is that we are expressions of it, with capacities to witness it, channel it and perhaps even expand it.

In fact, our awareness of the prevalence of universal consciousness is probably at an early stage of awareness, let alone development, in our species. Nevertheless, on this planet we don't know of another species that has become more conscious of its consciousness than *homo sapiens sapiens*. And now that we know that we know, we have created a feedback loop that appears to open up a never-ending journey of conscious awakening.

On this journey, the success of our species and its increasingly large population assures us that we will have lots of company on this journey. But to grasp the apparatus of consciousness and its relationship to the city, we must start with individual people and examine the importance of consciousness in the Integral City, for citizen intentions are foremost held by individual citizens.

SUBJECTIVE WELL-BEING UNFOLDS

In the integral model, citizen intentions reside in the Upper Left Quadrant. This is the "I" space, the seat of intention, attention, interior experience and intelligences or lines of development, e.g., emotional, cognitive, spiritual.

The Upper Left Quadrant of the human condition relates to a person's subjective sense of well-being. Recent studies into subjective well-being by Wills, Islam and Hamilton define the territory by asking questions related to satisfaction with health, safety, relationships, standard of living, achievements in life and future security (Cummins, 1996a, 1996b; Cummins et al., 2004; Hamilton, 2007b; Wills et al., 2007a, 2007b). When related to the insights of Graves, Beck and Wilber regarding the developmental sequences of individual subjectivity, these satisfaction categories seem to align with the very similar trajectory of subjective development through survival, belonging, personal power, order/management, achievement, acceptance and systemic flexibility. Both of these approaches would probably be considered structural approaches to understanding subjective experience in the city.

As Wilber (2000a) has mapped, a remarkable number of psychologists, philosophers, anthropologists, sociologists and organizational developers have disclosed the features of the subjective development space. Although their calibrations vary somewhat, the basic sequences and building blocks of intentional capacity remain virtually the same.

With inimitable thoroughness, Wilber (2006) examines the subjective quadrant, as he does all four quadrants, to propose that we know what we know in this personal interior space, not only through structural ways of knowing, but also through direct experiential ways of knowing. Wilber proposes that each person knows their own and/or others' subjective interior through phenomenological ways of knowing — that is through self-observation and inquiry of the content of one's thoughts and feelings that inform one about reality. The modes of inquiry are typically meditation, contemplation (including contemplative prayer), reflection, journaling, introspection and deep dialogue. These approaches can directly reveal the inner understanding of experience of one's self and be compared to the subjective experiences of others.

The subjective space can also be observed from the outside through structural lenses that map the subject's mental patterns, as illustrated by Cummins, Graves, Beck and Hamilton above. These structures organize the content of subjective experience on ladders of inference that remain largely invisible to the person using them, but which are observable by a third person studying them (Brown, 2006).

Both our inner ways of knowing (phenomenology) and outer ways of knowing (structuralism) create the mental models and maps of our subjective experience of life in the city. They are, in fact, integral aspects of the subjective fabric in the Integral City.

VALUE OF EXAMINING A SINGLE LIFE

The value of examining the intentional, subjective quadrant of a single life is that it gives us the container to appreciate the emergent qualities of consciousness, particularly as they relate to attention and intention. We gain the capacity to make life worth living precisely because we can examine it. Ultimately all attention and intention in the city is experienced at the level of the individual. It is only aggregated into political will through the coordination of multiple individuals — as discussed in chapter 8.

Conscious attention involves the capacity to focus consciousness with awareness. This Upper Left Quadrant, although it is the key focus of philosophers and psychologists, is probably the most forgotten or least valued quadrant of human life in the city. Why should this be? With the visibility of our bodies and the power of our biological drives for survival, it is easy to overlook the invisibility of our consciousness. Like children who act without awareness that their individual actions impact others, we fail to recognize that individual emotions, thoughts, talents and spirituality impact the other quadrants of behaviors, cultures and social systems in the city in a deep and lasting way.

In fact, individual citizen attention and citizen intention lie at the heart of the intelligent city and at the center of the city's capacity to sustain itself. A city that can merely feed, clothe and shelter its citizens lacks the intelligence to sustain itself, because the intelligence for sustainability comes from a commitment to learning about self, others and our shared life conditions. Learning arises from the endless interaction of attention and intention at ever-increasingly complex scales of observation.

MAPPING INTELLIGENCE CAPACITIES

Individual intelligences are indivisibly enmeshed in the psycho-bio-cultural-social capacities of any individual. Wilber (2000b, 2006, 2007) proposes that each quadrant has multiple lines of development. Each line represents a kind of human capacity. We refer to these various lines of intelligence as capital or assets — as in emotional, intellectual, musical, mathematical, cultural, social, spiritual capital. Others have recognized that this capital or these assets are actually intelligences (Dawson-Tunik 2005; Dawson 2007; Gardner, 1999; Graves, 1971, 1974, 1981, 2003). Each of these lines of intelligence has a trajectory of maturity or capacity for further development. Some of these lines of development seem to be especially interconnected, adding value to each other as well as the capacity of the particular line. A trio of particular significance to the Upper Left Intentional Quadrant is emotions, cognition and interpersonal, with a fourth one of spirit drawing increasing consideration (Gardner, 1999; McIntosh, 2007).

In many ways this trio may be special because they relate to our triune brain (reptilian-emotions, mammalian-intellect, human-interpersonal/spirit). Whatever the roots, the general trajectory of development for each intelligence in the trio has been well mapped across a set of calibrations that can be essentially described as follows:

- Self aware
  ° Self manage
  ° Self learn/lead/teach
  - Other aware
    ° Other manage
    ° Other learn/lead/teach
    - Context aware
      ° Context manage
      ° Context learn/lead/teach
      - System aware
        ° System manage
        ° System learn/lead/teach

As one learns to manage and then lead self, other, context and system as a continuous learner, one becomes of necessity increasingly attentive and increasingly intentional. While becoming increasingly attentive and intentional, the individual becomes an increasingly capable contributor to the intelligence of city life. A person who has higher capacities of emotional, mental and interpersonal intelligences has the potential to contribute to many complex social holons, including families, groups, teams, organizations and communities. Each person's attention and intention has a developmental "center of gravity" that provides a potential to contribute to the resilience of the city.

HUMAN EMERGENCE: LEVELS, LINES, TYPES, STATES

When we consider the Upper Left Quadrant as an individual *field* of consciousness, we can more easily see that the field is populated with lines of development, like emotions, cognition, interpersonal, spirit) and levels of development (self, other, context, system). Where the lines and levels cross, we have nodes of capacity that are further influenced by the type of consciousness an individual embodies, e.g., masculine, feminine; yin, yang.

At any given time, an individual consciousness is influenced by the body's energetic states of waking, sleeping, dreaming or meditating. Ken Wilber and Alan Combs (Combs, 2002) propose that states can occur at any time but will be interpreted by the level of development of the person experiencing the state.

In addition, an individual consciousness experiences dynamic change states that can be described on yet another spectrum as open, arrested or closed. In the open state, a person is ready and willing to learn; in the arrested state, he is not receptive to learning; and in the closed state he is resistant to learning. Thus an individual consciousness is highly dynamic. Its awareness is measurable by the development levels of multiple lines of intelligence and accessible depending on its energetic and change states.

As we have discussed in previous chapters (and will revisit), an individual in the city is necessarily influenced by the multiplicity of other humans in the city. The influence each person has on another and on any groups depends very much on their "center of gravity" of developmental levels and lines. When a person has mastered key lines of intelligence to the same center of gravity (e.g., Level 5 or orange), they will have a tendency to "hold steady" at that center of gravity under most life conditions; in other words, they will be resilient in those life conditions. By contrast, when a person is in a growth stage where the center of gravity is changing, it is possible that multiple lines of development will be spread across three or more levels of development, making the person less stable and less resilient.

Consequently any groups (social holons) that include a wide range of people will have a center of gravity, where the majority of people in that group have their center of gravity. Furthermore any immigration to or emigration from the group will affect the social holon's center of gravity and change its subjective (and by implication intersubjective) capacity. Hence the wisdom of crowds can come from the highest levels of capacity in individuals, along with the creative influence individuals have on one another to discover and innovate new consciousness from the interplay of open minds. By the same token, the mediocrity of groups arises from the same phenomenon in reverse — where a critical mass of people at a less developed capacity and/or more arrested or closed attitude can reduce crowds to the lowest common denominator — dumb them down in other words.

PURPOSE AND GOALS

Until very recently, individuals rarely questioned the purpose of their contribution to life in the city and/or never realized that collective life in the city might have a purpose. In the history of the city, human systems have too rarely asked, what ought to be the conscious intention of citizens (or even what is the conscious *duty* of citizens)? Do individuals have a responsibility to raise their intelligence to an optimum level in service to anyone other than themselves? In the developed world (in most capitalist and socialist systems), education of the individual has become an entitlement seemingly disconnected from the purpose of human life. McKibben (2007) describes the most severe manifestation as hyper-individualism.

Whenever I wrestle with this issue of purpose and how it relates to consciousness, I contemplate what I know about bees. Each wild hive has a purpose: to produce 40 pounds of honey per year (a human-managed hive produces even more). That amount of honey is only a fraction of the hives' annual production — the remainder going to production and building functions — but it guarantees survival of the hive as a whole and nurtures all the individual bees in the hive.

Now upon closer inspection, it appears that bees have evolved their roles in the hive to contribute to that purpose, and furthermore they have developed learning processes to support bees in a cycle of learning that spans their life cycle from egg to old age (Gould & Gould, 1988). Eggs and pupae are literally nurtured so that, when the pupae emerge, the young bee has the capacity to start doing simple tasks of cleaning the hive and feeding and caring for eggs and pupae. Gradually it is taught how to receive and store honey, make comb, fly short distances, forage and deliver pollen, communicate its knowledge (through the famous bee dance) and expand its territory and risk capacities. The beauty of this bee world is not only that it feeds the hive, but it sustains the environment that feeds the bees, through their pollination of plants and flowers. It appears to be an elegant self-sustaining system, in which the built-in purpose shapes the bees' behaviors, structures and culture.

For a city to function optimally, its citizens need to practise, manage and lead from a sense of purpose in their collective lives. Such an awareness could coalesce the intention of all learning systems with the relevant application of resources in the city.

What is the equivalent of our 40 pounds of honey? It is likely that any equivalence changes in the city as the values and life conditions of the critical mass of citizens change. From an intentional perspective, the purpose of the city could be to optimize the well-being of citizens at every level of development. Such well-being would be experienced phenomenologically as well as structurally and be represented by the stories shared in intersubjective space. It could also probably be reported by survey (as Cummins' assessments on well-being shows) and would be reflected in the volitional intelligence described by McIntosh (2007).

Using the integral model, we might postulate that well-being is equal parts subjective and intersubjective experience and objective and interobjective action for the individual in the context of shared city life conditions. The purpose of a city is the achievement of what its citizens can manifest together that would not be possible if they attempted it on their own. In the most vibrant cities, this achievement would be the emergent outcome of individual intelligences optimizing sustainable outcomes for themselves as well as the collectives to which they belong, including the city as a whole.

The 40 pounds of honey would represent the manifested outcomes, objective and interobjective results, that are produced from the living of subjective and intersubjective values. This could be translated into something like an overall vital signs monitor of happiness, well-being or quality of life (discussed in chapter 11). In orange language, this would be the city's unique value proposition to the world — its value-added purpose. This would be what the city uniquely adds to the world, what would be missed if it did not exist.

As the city's purpose responds to increased complexity over time, it will change — and what it contributes and how it adds value to the world will also change. In the transition stages from one level of complexity to another, the city will have difficulty supporting the needs of all of its citizens. Some will move away. Others will withdraw. And others will be disenfranchised through some pathology and/or dysfunction, e.g., become homeless.

The larger the city the more likely it will span a wider and wider spectrum of individual purposes; ghettoes of differing purposes and intentions will emerge, and the demands of governance will need to address these discontinuities. Thus the importance for city hall to have clarity about its citizens' values, intentions and purposes is vital to achieving the city's optimal performance as a social holon.

In the history of the city, the relationships that people have had with their key values (a.k.a. purpose) have evolved over time, as have the commensurate structures, cultures and behaviors in the city that have developed to support these values.

As conscious beings, humans use their observations, feelings, thoughts and wants to derive the values that become purpose driven. From these values emerge mindsets, worldviews and paradigms. And centered in the paradigms is a purpose for the human system that dictates what individuals will pay attention to, through observation and awareness of feelings and thoughts, with intention (for achieving their wants/preferences/desires).

Abraham Maslow shone light on the drive for people to address a pyramid of needs that included their survival needs, belonging needs and actualization needs. Maslow's contemporary and colleague, Clare Graves, recognized that this pyramid of needs was continuously recalibrated within individuals as they adapted to the complexity of their life conditions.

Thus, as cities have arisen all over the world, they have evolved to meet key human needs and purposes across a spectrum of complexity. However, it should be recognized that the city did not emerge in the evolution of any of the cultures of the human species until sufficiently complex consciousness had been developed to solve the problems of individuals, families and groups and their multiplicity of artefacts living together. The rise of the city required some form of governance to address and solve the issues of survival, relationships and power in large, spatially confined populations. Ultimately this could only be done through attention to human processes, patterns and structures that contributed to the emergence and management of boundaries, information exchange and the respectful relationship between individuals and groups (agency and communion). This is the essence of Level 4 governance structures.

However, once the values and needs of survival, relationships and power were addressed by intentional governance systems, this set the stage for the emergence of new capacities related to authority and standards, achievement and results, caring and sharing, flex and flow, and global mindfulness (Levels of Complexity from 5 to 8).

INTEGRAL EDUCATION

While members in the integral community are designing integral learning systems for children, we can get a glimpse of what an intentionally designed integral learning system might look like. Real-life examples are starting to emerge in the International Baccalaureate (IB) schools, many of which have developed their approaches to education from a globally informed and internationally experienced faculty, curriculum and students. (The IB in Westlake, Texas, or in Monterrey, Mexico, are prime examples.) Some cities in British Columbia have been following the research focus of Clyde Hertzman's early childhood development project that addresses the factors that contribute to human development before age six (Hertzman, Kohen, Dunn & Evans, 2002). The School Board in Calgary, Alberta, has been developing an integral public education system that embraces the developmental levels of learning from kindergarten to Grade 12.

At Royal Roads University, an adult-oriented, post-graduate, competency-based leadership degree has been delivered with a developmental model since 1996. Kegan's, Gardner's, Torbert's and Scharmer's research and models of adult development at Harvard and MIT have slowly been reaching outward, influencing the design of curriculum and delivery modes in public, private and corporate universities.

An Integral Learning System for business leaders has been designed by integralist Jean Trudel in Ottawa, Canada (see Figure 5.1). They have mapped out the project plan to create a learning process for business leaders to develop self, supervision and management of others and organizational strategies for global success. They are utilizing all that they know about integral project management to create an integral learning process that embraces levels of development for individual and social learning, using integral principles of practice, management and leadership.

As each city evolved within the Petrie dish of its geographic/biologic life conditions, it tended to develop unique manifestations of the spectrum of values held by its citizens. Commensurate with the rise of the city, the emergence of trade, through water and land routes, and long-distance economies introduced the dissemination of ideas and influence of attention and intention from other cultures amongst cities situated on the trade routes.

Thus conscious exchange occurred between people with ideas who solved the key challenges of cities differently. The realities and natural delays of intentions communicated and delivered at the surface level of the Earth allowed for gradual assimilation of change that affected individuals and groups (and city governance).

However, once transportation and trade routes took to the air, the distance and time collapsed so that assimilation of conscious choices became more demanding and difficult. When this acceleration of interaction was followed by large-scale immigration of people with different capacities for attention and intention, the nature of cities changed quickly. Today, in countries that encouraged large-scale immigration (or were target destinations because of war and/or natural disaster), cities contain such a mix of cultures (collectives of people with distinct belief, relational and communication systems) that the attention of the individual citizen is largely unfocused (but over-stimulated) and the intention is obscured (or private in order to protect source culture).

So it is not surprising that we are at a stage of history where the misalignment of attention and intention in the city is rampant and growing. Dissonance is an unintentional and unintended reality of current city life and national immigration policies. In few countries did federal policy-makers consult with their city counterparts on the ramifications of implementing decisions to open up borders to other nationalities. Thus, countries like Canada are now populated with cities where major resources of the local education and social systems must be devoted to teaching 40 percent of the population who have a first language other than French or English. By contrast, professionals who attained their credentials from foreign countries are frequently employed far below what their qualifications indicate is their potential for contribution in their new cities. This is frustrating, humiliating and de-energizing for everyone. Decision-makers who failed to align the impacts of their open immigration policies with city, state and nation now have the evidence that such coherence is desperately needed.

In the history of the modern city in the developed world, public schooling emerged to serve the rise of the Industrial Revolution and the location of manufacturing capacity within the city. As factories standardized work, they encouraged widespread standardized schooling to prepare students for the factory. As a result, for a short period of time (a century?), the intention of citizens was relatively well aligned with the intentions/purpose of the industrial city.

At the beginning of the 21st century, now that the complexity of the city must address such a mass and mix of individuals with attentions and intentions influenced by such a mosaic of cultures, the purpose of the city is not clearly defined. Commensurately the purpose of many individuals also appears murky.

Ironically, we live at a time where the lack of conscious purpose at the scale of the individual and the scale of the city create ricochets of side effects. Sandwiched between the individuals and the city exists a multiplicity of organizations — profit, not-for-profit, government agencies — that ostensibly have a variety of stated purposes. However, few if any are aligned with one another for the well-being of the individual citizen, and without a purpose higher than their

Figure 5.1: Leadership learning framework.
Source: Reproduced with permission of Jean Trudel.

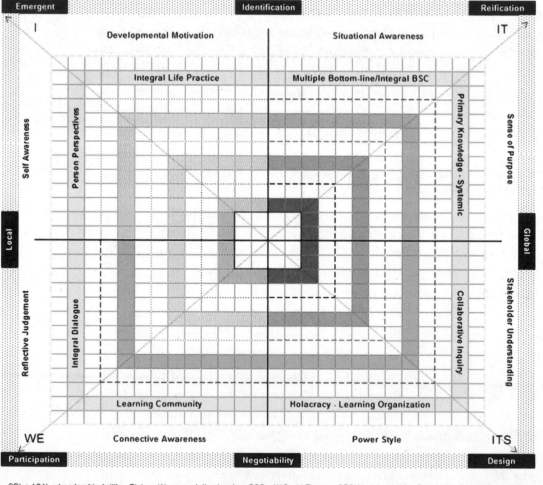

SDi ◆ AQAL ◆ Leadership Agility ◆ Eteinne Wenger ◆ Action Inquiry ◆ BSC ◆ MAP ◆ U-Theory ◆ SECI Model ◆ Nothing Extra ◆ ICM Framework & Matrix

© 2007 Copyright Integrated Channel Management Inc

own, virtually none are aligned with the well-being of the city.

But now more than ever, the very sustainability of our cities is intimately dependent on the intelligence and intentions of its citizens. In order to attain the former, we must address the latter.

It is a paradox that as the percentage of humans on Earth living in cities surpasses 50 percent and is moving quickly toward 60 percent (United Nations Human Settlements, 2005), the purpose of cities is not explicit. People choose to move to cities, but as a result, many individuals and cities suffer. It appears that without espoused city purpose the misalignment of people and organizational purpose and priorities will fail to serve any individual city, as it will fail to serve the planet. The matching of the individual and group behaviors of bees in the beehive is guided by the hive's over-arching purpose. How will we make the purpose of any given city explicit, so that alignment is natural and supported?

On an individual level, the need for felt purpose may be the reason that one of the most popular books in the United States right now is entitled *The Purpose Driven Life*. On a group level, the scale of homelessness in cities may also be an indication, not about what structures and services are most missing, but rather what is the conscious purpose of the self and the city that is most missing in peoples' lives.

VALUES VISION MISSION

A citizen in any given city will hold a spectrum of values to which she pays attention and for which she will form intentions or purposes. A critical mass of these individual values sets contributes to the values a city holds for itself. For example, people can value safe streets and erect buildings with windows, doors and decks that enable "eyes on the street" as Jane Jacobs proposed. For example, people can value gossiping and trading stories, so they set aside park space and attract coffee shops or tea houses where they can do so. For example, people can value the aesthetic expression of energy and joy and set aside time and space for artists to thrive.

A city's values make possible the vision(s) that people dream for themselves and how the city can change. "Without a vision, the people perish" (Proverbs 29:18). When enough individuals and groups share their dreams, the human hive starts to experience a form of internal resonance because, from these dreams, the city's vision and mission or purpose can emerge.

An integral perspective on the city helps us to recognize and honor the necessity of conscious awareness. It ought to train our attention on the city's needs as a whole — and realize the need for a meta-framework that can hold sufficient complexity to explain the behaviors, cultures and structures existing and needed in the city. An integral approach to consciousness enables us to see the evolution of hierarchies of capacity. It helps us focus attentions on what is valued and intentions on behaviors and outcomes that match those values.

LEADERSHIP

When I first started my quest to understand the relationship of community to leadership, I was very frustrated by the parochial attitude of the mayor and council in my city. The city was growing rapidly and needed new solutions for everything from rush-hour traffic to school locations, cultural resources, recreational facilities and environmental policies. But no one wanted to change the old ways of maintaining the status quo. It seemed as though the city could never change as long as that mayor and those councilors controlled the decision-making. And even though their decision-making focused largely on the built environment of the city, their lived values effectively controlled and influenced the lived values of the city's residents. In other words, the personal values of the mayor and council determined the filters through which decisions were made and the ceilings that limited citizen aspirations.

My driving question was, does the capacity of community leadership determine community capacity? Or does the capacity of community determine the capacity of its leadership? How do the vision, values and mission of one influence the other?

I have come to realize that this question is the classic chicken-and-egg dilemma. The capacity of community and leadership are co-determined. Each arises simultaneously, with the community being the container for holding the emergence of leadership and leadership being the catalyst for emerging community.

Leadership in the city is needed now more than ever before. Leadership, within an integral context, can be defined as a never-ending quest for personal capacity development. In terms of the Integral City, this necessarily implies that

MAYORS AS LEADERS

In recent years many mayors have stepped up to the demands of Level 8 leadership because of dissonances in their own backyards. The terrorist assault on New York on September 11, 2001 brought Mayor Rudy Giuliani on to the world stage. In the glare of crisis, he followed many of the simple rules of leadership that spoke to the hearts, minds and souls of his city constituents, while using all the resources at his disposal to minister to their bodies and the city's broken infrastructure. Whatever shortcomings may have emerged in his subsequent run at the US presidency, in that extended moment of crisis, he seemed to demonstrate capacities of a peak state of awareness: seeking information and counsel from expert others and ordinary citizens alike; being available 24/7 to communicate on all levels; embracing the city as a whole; receiving and integrating resources from around the world.

In Curitiba, Brazil, Jaime Lerner, former architect, urban planner and three-term mayor, thinks and acts systemically (Level 7) in terms of children and citizens designing the city, so they will understand and respect it. As a Level 8 designer, he considers that change is not a question of scale but a function of co-responsibility. He is responsible for designing a mass transit surface bus system that can transport two million passengers per day and is used by 75 percent of the city's citizens (despite the fact that they have one of the highest private car ownerships in Brazil). Other cities now learning from his solutions that transcend and include eco-ethno-egocentric solutions include Seoul, Honolulu and Bogotá (Mau & Leonard, 2004).

In Bogotá, Columbia, Mayor Enrique Peñalosa became more interested in the happiness of city residents than the traditional economic indicators of well-being. He asked the Level 7 questions, How do we want to live? Do we want to create a city for humans or a city for automobiles? With the answers to these questions, he inspired the design and implementation of the Transmilenio Bus Rapid Transit system. Improved quality of life became measured by reduced: travel time for users (32%), citywide violent crime (50%), traffic accidents (80%), fatal traffic incidents (30%), noise pollution (30%) and parent time away from children (37%) (Mau & Leonard, 2004, p. 57).

Chicago Mayor Richard Daly intends to transform the city of Chicago, known variously for its railroad hub, commodity exchange, tall skyscrapers and perennial wind, into the greenest city in the world. Surprisingly the landscape he is intentionally transforming is the rooftops of the city. Ironically from the stereotypical outer space of the concrete jungle (so criticized by Jane Jacobs), he is creating not just urban forests and skyscraper meadows but green open spaces that expand the inner space of hopes and expectations for all citizens.

city leaders must take a conscious approach to individual development (as shown in Figure 5.1) that prepares them to deal with the levels of complexity that now exist in the city.

As many have recognized, with the tipping point of the majority of humanity living in cities now passed and with the rise of the megacity, human realities have become concentrated within the boundaries of the city. And those boundaries are broken, breached and bleeding.

Complexity science tells us that all living systems have a boundary. One of the great dilemmas of the city today is that its boundaries are as ambiguous and/or contentious as the multiple consciousnesses who are identifying them. It is no wonder that it is difficult to manage, let alone lead a system that is the city.

Epigenetic biology has been instructing us to reframe our understanding of the most basic living system — the cell. Until recently, conventional biology has assumed that the cell was "managed" or led by the nucleus. However, new discoveries (Lipton, 2005) have disclosed that a cell can live for a long time without its nucleus; but it cannot continue to exist without its membrane ("membrain"). In other words, like all systems, cells require boundaries in order to manage internal and external information/nutrient exchanges and internal/external relationships.

Thus the consciousness that city leadership now requires may reveal that, while positional leadership may be vested in one or several people (e.g., mayor and council), true leadership is actually practised by those who interpret, negotiate and create the boundaries within which the city functions. Who are these leaders? They are the people who with attention and intention take responsibility for themselves, organize care for others, lobby positional leaders and power structures and consider the global implications of decision sets. They tend to be informal and unorganized leaders working consciously in civil society. Paul Hawken (2007) recognizes their growing number as a glocalizing force, with an impact globally as well as locally, that is gaining power and influence through non-traditional means.

Their biggest challenge is a failure to have sufficient conscious "altitude" to see the potential of the system-shift from single leaders who manage boundaries to shared leadership who define and hold boundaries. While they work prodigiously as individuals and in small pockets, the current lack of leadership alignment prevents the leveraging of their consciousness and behaviors.

The city has key leadership needs in every fractal: individual, family, education, healthcare, workplace organization, community/recreation, city governance.

LEADERS TO THE POWER OF 8: BUILD ON EVOLUTIONARY LESSONS, CATALYZE INTERCONNECTEDNESS, CREATE OPPORTUNITIES FOR WELL-BEING

Today's cities need leaders who have developed their consciousness to the "Power of 8," a reference to the developmental levels in Maps 1 and 4 of chapter 3. Leadership to the Power of 8 calls forth leaders who have the consciousness of the eighth level of development, where the worldview is Gaiaic, the paradigm is global interconnectedness and the individual sees herself in terms of service to the evolutionary well-being of the world.

Leadership to the Power of 8 understands the infinite qualities of adaptiveness that enable human systems to thrive (and reproduce themselves) in endlessly changing life conditions. Whereas Leadership to the Power of 4 depended on authority, Leadership to the Power of 5 depended on competition, Leadership to the Power of 6 depended on equality and Leadership to the Power of 7 depended on complexity, Leadership to the Power of 8 transcends and includes all of those and depends on integral evolution. Through interconnection and cross-collaboration on a truly global scale, we can see that Leadership to the Power of 8 enables the global flow of people, energy, security and resources.

Today's cities need leaders who have developed their consciousness to the Power of 8, so that they can see the world of cities seen by Jared Diamond (2005), Ronald Wright (2004) and Thomas Homer-Dixon (2006). They need a consciousness that understands the interconnected, evolutionary, developmental nature of city life.

Leaders to the Power of 8 have consciousness with a sufficient altitude that they gain the widest lenses and new capacities. Leaders like Al Gore (2007) have a worldview that is mindful of the largest Earth-based climate systems so they have an awareness of Diamond's transglobal climate contexts. Leaders like David Suzuki (1989)understand that each of Earth's 17 habitats has a limited carrying capacity for life of all kinds, and that if we overtax it for our basic resources of water, food, shelter and clothing, we doom our own survival. Leaders like Don Beck (2002, 2004, 2007) are mindful that our set of bio-psycho-cultural-social values can become intentionally developed to the level of complexity equal to the Power of 8. These values represent the capacities of how we are able to respond to environmental problems individually and collectively, as cities, organizations, countries, trading blocks and world governance systems. Leaders like Tom Barnett (2005) recognize, care for and counsel the health of friendly trading partners, because the conditions of our friendly trading partners are intimately connected with our health as cities, countries, organizations, trading blocks and governance systems. Leaders like Gro Brundtland (as Chair of World Health Organization, 2004) recognize, care about and protect cities from hostile neighbors because they can directly affect the health of human systems (e.g., SARS, Avian Flu), those of our trading partners (e.g., DDT), the environment (e.g., deforestation) and even the climate (e.g., desertification/water).

Our planet is only just developing leaders to the Power of 8. We are starting to see leaders who have grown sufficient intentional capacity that gives them the credentials to speak about matters that impact the whole world. This capacity arises from their struggles to align their personal commitments, challenging life experiences, dedicated research and continuous learning and education (thank you, Ann Dale). Just for starters, they are likely to have taken the trouble to learn the science of climate change and what factors contribute to global warming (thank you, George Monbiot). They will have had the courage to develop and/or propose environmentally sensitive ecologically based governance policies — maybe even where one size does not fit all, but policies are appropriate to the life conditions of the habitat (thank you, Thomas Homer-Dixon and Steve McIntosh). They will develop lifelong learning programs that integrally teach bio-psycho-cultural-social values that respond to the life conditions of cultures and environments (thank you, Ken Wilber). They will influence trading partners to integrate ecologically sensitive policies for climate variance, environmental impact and continuous learning (thank you, Thomas Friedman). They will challenge and/or set boundaries for hostile neighbors to limit and correct climate, environmental and human systems damage (thank you, Tony Blair). In other words these leaders make their invisible consciousness and conscience visible every day.

Today's cities need leaders who have developed their consciousness to the

Power of 8 so they can catalyze interconnectedness. Such leaders can embrace the uneven distribution of power in the city and between cities and countries. Barnett (2005) reminds us that leadership to the Power of 8 must recognize that global economic power trumps military power. He suggests that governance rule sets need to be appropriate to the level of complexity of the society they serve. This means that it is not appropriate to implement leadership in Afghanistan and Iraq that is the same as leadership in North America. The societies that those leaders serve are at very different stages of development, and they need leaders who respect that.

In assisting appropriate leadership in developing countries and cities, leaders to the Power of 8 need to support leaders to the Powers of 4, 5, 6 and 7 to integrally embrace security for the person as a bio-psycho-cultural-social living system. McIntosh (2007) explains why this will look different in Amsterdam than it does in Bali or Sri Lanka. Leaders to the Power of 8 can also assist cities in developing nations by recognizing that rules and laws must be designed so that they embrace the globalization of economy, technology and communications. This means new opportunities for commerce and accelerated redistribution of resources of all kinds, but especially the resources that wash the hearts, minds and souls of the Upper Left quadrants.

Barnett's final injunction to leaders is to balance work flows between the movement of people, access to energy, long-term direct investments of one country in another country and security (2004). He sums up the needs for the Level 8 well-being of the globe: "Nothing in the global system should be allowed to prevent the flow of any of the resources from regions of surplus to regions of deficit. In effect, labor, energy, money and security all need to flow as freely as possible from those places in the world where they are plentiful to those regions where they are scarce" (p. 198).

Leaders to the Power of 8 need mindsets that have the capacity to design systems that flex and flow on a global scale. Ironically they need the basic training that military provisioners learn to master for those who are most disconnected and disadvantaged: how to deliver the basics of life, how to ensure access to energy, how to ensure security of person and property. In other words, they need to feed the babies and the families. They also need to know how to educate people who are most disconnected and disadvantaged about key leverage values of life —

especially how to educate women, to shift the balance of personal power between men and women and enable the release of more capacity for both genders.

Leaders to the Power of 8 need strength where necessary to ensure security for people who are connected and advantaged from the threats of people who are disconnected and disadvantaged (while creating plans for the latter as noted above). This will prevent the unnecessary downshifting of people with the capacities to build new assets. This means identifying and removing blocks for people who are most disconnected and disadvantaged so they can improve their lives.

Finally leaders to the Power of 8 must also support exchange with friendly trading neighbors. If economics trumps military power now, then we must foresee that information will eventually trump economics. Enabling fair and democratic exchange may be the most powerful strategy leaders to the Power of 8 can promote to change the world. Leaders to the Power of 8 who enable the transparent process of exchange (of products, people, values, processes, ideas and information) allow people in the city naturally to come to think and act in terms of whole (world) systems change. This may be the most effective way to encourage advantaged cities to invest in cities that are disconnected and disadvantaged.

Thus leaders to the Power of 8 improve the flow of products, profits, people, priorities, energy, security and resources for all. Today's cities need leaders who have developed their consciousness to the Power of 8 so they can create conditions of well-being for all citizens. According to Thomas Friedman (2005), such leaders will need the wisdom of Solomon in the "great sorting out" between the haves and the have-nots. In the life conditions of 21st century economic realities, city leadership must move from command and control to connect and collaborate. To do so, leaders will have to work on their own bio-psycho-cultural-social capacities to the Power of 8 and educate others on the same capacities. Instead of using command and control, city leaders need to enable connections and collaboration at all levels of scale: personal, teams, organizations, communities, cities, regions, nations, trading partners and world bodies.

Power of 8 city leaders will need to redefine leadership, boundaries and identities within the city. This means understanding the changing landscape of work, politics, economics, security, technology and communications and informing and engaging their cities, people and organizations in developing proactive responses to globally interactive life conditions at the Power of 8. This will mean seriously renegotiating old relationships and continuously rebalancing new relationships.

City leaders to the Power of 8 will create the conditions for the development of new governance systems (the judicial, legislative and executive governance structures of Steve McIntosh and the rule sets of Thomas Barnett). This will be a multidimensional challenge because it will mean finding ways to realign power with other levels of government that do not have the same pressures to change. This building of bridges across traditional city and national boundaries will probably mean renegotiating allegiances, loyalties, treaties and alignments. This could even mean developing social contracts for horizontal collaboration with unusual partners, like the City and First Nations tribes.

The transition of jobs from the developed world to the developing world might also provide the impetus for cities to recalibrate existing governance systems (judiciary, legislature, executive) and step into the realm of rule sets that haven't traditionally been their purview — like redefining intellectual property rights, developing global labor standards and tracking shifting job pools.

It is highly conceivable that city leaders to the Power of 8 will challenge the priorities of values worth preserving. For example, when research shows that happiness plateaus when personal income reaches about $10,000 to $13, 000, then the Bhutan measure of gross national happiness instead of gross national product might prove to be a rallying value for city leaders.

The new bottom line for leaders who have consciousness to the Power of 8 will be to enable emergence and evolution in people, organizations, cities and the world simultaneously. They will lead through informed ecological action, massive, continuous and integral connection, continual adaptation and respect for all living systems. Leadership to the Power of 8 is not for the faint-hearted or the unprepared.

DESIGNING APPROPRIATE LEARNING AND EDUCATION SYSTEMS

How do we prepare leaders who have the consciousness and capacity to lead to the Power of 8? When we consider what we now know about human learning; how much we invest in the technology of human entertainment in terms of innovation, time, materials and effort, and the costs of our public education systems, we must come to the sorry conclusion that we are squandering our resources for designing and delivering powerful education. However, we must also recognize that we have immense resources to apply to this task.

INTEGRATING LIFE PRACTICES

One of the most comprehensive practices that has been developed integrating the individual, heart, mind, soul and shadow is the Integral Life Practice (ILP), created by Ken Wilber's Integral Institute. In addition to the practices (for developing outer intelligence) described in the next chapter, ILP demonstrates the practices of developing inner intelligence. It provides instruction for an AQAL (all-quadrants, lines, levels, types) framework, meditation, awakening/enlightenment, compassionate exchange, non-denominational spiritual engagement, shadow work and developmental curriculum for leaders and seekers. This resource is especially designed for the Western mind, while incorporating psychologies, philosophies and practices from both Eastern and Western cultures (Morelli, Leonard, Patten, Salzman & Wilber, 2006).

Leaders with intentional capacity to the Power of 8 have achieved that level of performance by developing capacities at powers from 1 to 7. I think of leaders whose military experience has demanded that they achieve these levels of performance — people like Colin Powell in the US and Rear Admiral Roger Girouard in Canada. Or leaders who have viewed Earth from space, like astronaut Edgar Mitchell, Founder of the Institute of Noetic Sciences. Or leaders who have ministered to the spiritual needs of the world, like Nancy Roof, cofounder of the United Nations Spiritual Caucus and publisher of *Kosmos* magazine. All of these leaders have the (emotional, cognitive, interpersonal) capacity to interact with the challenges of cities at a global scale. But what city in the world has developed a course of study and practice that enables a person to methodically progress from cradle to peak performance at the defined levels of complexity that deliver leadership to the powers of 1 through 8?

The challenge we now face as a species is not only to define what is the human equivalent of the bees' 40 pounds of honey (a Lower Right systems purpose), but what are the bio-psycho-cultural purposes that align with that intention? And what is the course of development that will support our achieving those intentions?

On the broadest scale, we are talking about creating a lifelong learning system that optimizes human potential with appropriate attention and intention. Developing our citizen intelligences will determine the extent to which our cities will be sustainable. Moreover, if we are to do this in an evolutionarily respectful way, we must design it so that it allows individual, family and cultural variation. Such variation needs simple rules (rule sets) that allow learners to experience learning unique to their potentials (i.e., not one size fits all) while at the same time creating citizens able to contribute to the achievement of city purpose.

The work of fully exploring such a system is beyond the scope of this book (and begs another volume devoted to this topic). However, my recent research with Ann Dale and her team (Dale, 2001; Dale, Hamilton et al., 2007; Dale & Onyx, 2005; Dale, Waldron & Newman, 2007) gives us some insight into the examination of learning practices for leadership to the Powers of 4, 5, 6 and 7. Our research focused on the practical purposes of defining learning trajectories to implement the practices of sustainable community infrastructure.

In that research, we concluded (Hamilton & Dale, 2007) that in order to mobilize the flow of intellectual and social capital for learning about the city these key steps must be taken:

1. **Find out what is important to key stakeholders in the city.** Leaders need to know where the value systems of city stakeholders fit on the eight levels of development. Values reveal the "center of gravity" of the thinking systems in the city and help identify what decision processes leaders can use. When we know the relative strength of traditional, modern, postmodern and Integral value systems (leadership to the powers of 4, 5, 6, 7), then we know how to engage the players.

2. **Identify the change state of the city.** Leaders need to be able to lead regardless of whether the city and/or its neighborhoods are stable, disturbed, blocked, chaotic or inspired. (We discuss this in more detail in chapter 8.) However, what leaders must know here is that they need emotional intelligence so that they can connect to people and situations. Mayor Rudy Giuliani was an excellent example of a mayor who was appropriately matched to the evolving change states of New York after September 11, 2001.

3. **Identify and align the key structures of the city.** City leaders to the Power of 8 must be effective in coordinating structural combinations of dynamic centers and dynamic edges (like council meetings and citizen delegations), as well as strong or weak centers (such as the judiciary or public works) and strong or weak edges (such as executive corps or social services). This

means appreciating that structures need to be aligned with values and priorities in the city for effective service delivery.

4. **Map the knowledge systems the city uses.** City leaders need to know how each city department utilizes its specialized experts and accesses knowledge from relevant domains, e.g., planning, fire, police, public works. The intellectual capital applied by city departments and leaders enables them to be effective (or not) in a variety of situations from the predictable to the complex and chaotic. Without mature, continuously updated knowledge systems, the leaders and the city will lack the information to match resources to city needs. Such leaders will also likely lack the capacity to interconnect one system's interaction with those of other systems to see the ripple effects of change.

5. **Correlate values, change states, structures and knowledge.** Leaders who can assess these factors together will identify the capacities and deficiencies of the city's operating systems. Figure 5.2 shows how all these elements

Figure 5.2. Creating the design space of knowledge, structures, values and life conditions.
Legend: K=Knowledge, S=Structures, V=Values, LC=Life Conditions

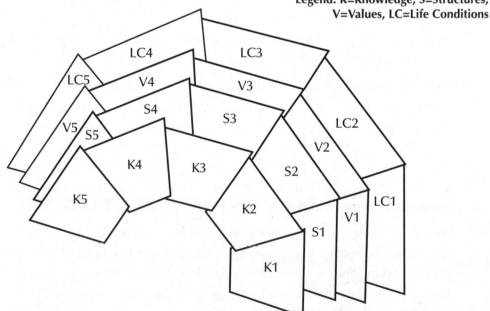

are correlated in a design space for creating an appropriate learning/change strategy (for leadership to the powers of 4, 5, 6, 7).

6. **Design an appropriate learning/change strategy that shifts the system towards integral sustainability.** Leaders who want to enable integral cities need to consider the key realities which contribute to bio-psycho-cultural-social change in human systems. Effective learning design will be determined by the fitness of the learning process to the players' values, their operational context (change state and structures) and access to relevant knowledge resources.

In the end, preparing leaders to the Power of 8 involves capacity development with a curriculum and experience that aligns knowledge, values, structures and life conditions. It is ultimately about learning experiences in the classroom, online (and/or with other media) and on the job that gives leaders the opportunities to build dynamic, resilient and adaptive bridges between silos, stovepipes and solitudes that can operate to the Powers of 7 and 8.

The four-quadrant, all-levels model defines for an integral learning system the developmental sequences, curriculum structures and maturity models that city educational systems now need. With the plurality of cultures as city reality, we should anticipate and encourage that all of these learning models will coexist in the city: private, public, cooperative, for profit, not-for-profit. No longer is a one-size-fits-all approach to education sufficient to the complexity of the city. However, what is needed most of all is a city vision that coalesces the intention of all learning systems with the relevant resources to emerge, maintain and evolve the purpose of the city.

CONCLUSION

Citizen intentions create the true spirit of a city. The expression and realization of intentions lie at the heart of the city's energy — its joie de vivre, its esprit de corps. Citizen intentions dictate whether individuals experience happiness, well-being and quality of life in the city. It is imperative for cities to nourish the capacities of citizen consciousness, so that the ever-increasing levels of complexity that exist in today's cities have minds, hearts and spirits equal to living optimally under these complex life conditions.

The expression, exploration and evolution of individual citizen feelings, thoughts, wants and values make possible the sharing of those same qualities with others and the creation of shared intentions. Ultimately the capacity of the social holon, which is the city, is totally dependent on the capacity building of individual citizens. So paying attention to the content, process and context of intentional development is vital for a city to develop adaptiveness, resiliency and ultimately sustainability.

QUESTIONS

1. How powerful is individual intention? shared intention?

2. How do we allow for individual optimization in the context of collective optimization? How do we design education systems that enable both?

3. How do we plan for the "never ending quest"? How do we capitalize on ever-increasing intelligence? How do we not leave people behind?

Three simple rules for applying Integral City principles from this chapter:

1. Show up and be self-aware, present, mindful.

2. Notice the city intelligences and map them integrally.

3. Grow leadership in heart, mind, soul.

6

OUTER INTELLIGENCE: EMBODYING RIGHT ACTION IN THE HUMAN HIVE

Bees have been working effortlessly through the algebra of foraging since before
our ancestors came down from the trees. Such is the potential of innate
wiring, honed and polished by countless generations of natural selection.

— Gould and Gould, 1988, p. 91

We need to consciously redesign the entire material basis of our civilization.
The model we replace it with must be dramatically more ecologically sustainable,
offer large increases in prosperity for everyone on the planet, and not
only function in areas of chaos and corruption, but also help transform them.

— Alex Steffen, cofounder of Worldchanging, as quoted by Robertson, 2007

MAPPING BIOPHYSICAL NECESSITIES FOR WELL-BEING BASICS: AIR, WATER, FOOD, CLOTHING, SHELTER

This chapter is about life in the city seen through the Upper Right quadrant — the biological "It" space of the city — the space where the body acts and behaves.

Behaviors demonstrate our intelligence in action. We have a great track record of being able to study behaviors in general through empirical science, but we have a much more dismal track record of changing them on purpose. But we do have a few accomplishments that should encourage us that expanding intelligence is possible by changing behavior. Key examples of changed behaviors in the 20th century testify to this — specifically, smoking reduction, "particip-action" (practicing regular physical activity) and car seat-belt use. However, these examples also demonstrate that behavior in the city does not change in isolation of intention, culture and social systems. Without the support of educating messages, cultural peer pressure, legislated distribution or installation and judicial enforcement of practice, even these logical behaviors would not have happened. We can see the evidence for this in cities located in countries where a whole-system approach was not taken to change behaviors. For example, even in "enlightened" Europe and emerging Asia, smoking still occurs in public places. And where seat-belt enforcement does not exist, the body count from highway accidents is demonstrably higher.

It seems trite to say that individual citizens require basic necessities to maintain life — but the lived truth of this statement lies at the heart of everyday biophysical well-being in the city. In some respects the eco-footprint (Rees & Wackernagel, 1994) provides a measure of the effectiveness of the city's purpose. Each person needs a definable amount of clean air, water, food, clothing and shelter to survive. Therefore, the city must supply to its citizens the amount of the necessities required to sustain its population. Each person or household essentially has a "home" economy that arises because of the need to supply the basics of life to the individual cells in the household body. The only source of those necessities is the environment in which the city sits — a range that now extends from the center of the city to the furthest point around the world.

The economies of households are well illustrated by the economies of the beehive. Economies in the natural world are rarely steady-state flow systems but rather rise and fall like the bees' pollination cycles that deliver peak energy incomes for a few crucial weeks a year (from mid-April to late June in the northern hemisphere) that allow the hive to survive. In the rest of the year, the hive barely breaks even, or may even run at a loss, consuming more food than it gathers (Gould & Gould, 1988, p. 21). Many individuals and city managers would recognize the need to manage such resource ebbs and flows.

When I say "the city must supply" the basics of life, I mean the systems of the city. These will be discussed in chapter 7, but it is worth noting here that, like the beehive, all the essential systems of the city exist to support the direct or indirect survival of its citizen bodies, relationships and exchanges.

De Landa considers that the biological history of cities demonstrates that for "an urban ecosystem to work, food chains must be shortened" (1997, p. 153). When cities grow beyond a certain size, the shortening of these food chains becomes difficult and/or impossible. In the past this has led to mass migrations. De Landa goes on to describe with considerable interest how the colonization of lands has replicated biological ecosystems as well as social ecosystems, thus literally affecting gene pools of both humans and their environments.

The actual basics of life have their own order of complexity that are represented in our most basic biological needs. The order of the basics — air, water, food, clothing, shelter — represents an evolving sequence of evolutionary needs (and thus, an order of complexity), with a recognition that the first items on the list have primacy over all the needs following. Therefore, in a crisis, these are exactly the sequence of needs that must be addressed to ensure survival. The realities of these empirical truths are becoming the stuff of daily newscasts. The citizens of New Orleans were reduced to fighting for these necessities when the city systems failed them. The citizens of China's over-polluted cities are dying at a rate of 750,000 per year simply for the lack of clean air (McGregor, 2007).

CONDITIONS OF LIFE

All living systems have three basic qualities: they survive, they connect with their environment and they reproduce themselves (Capra, 1996). As living systems, humans share these qualities and, as mammals, require interaction with other human beings. Thus the roots of our living together in groups arise from the very fact that we are living systems.

The biophysical facts of life then set up the conditions for individual survival and species survival. The city is just a natural and inevitable outcome of human behaviors that have resulted in human evolution. But it has also become a life condition itself that directly impacts citizen well-being.

Even as the city represents the most complex creation of humans' combined efforts, its ultimate health and functioning rest on the health and functioning of individual citizens. To understand the city, we must understand citizen behaviors; to understand citizen behaviors, we need to understand citizens as individuals in the context of the many.

BIOPHYSICAL DEMOGRAPHICS

The biophysical features of individuals in the city are the raw material of the city's demographics. The composition of the city from these aggregated qualities gives the city its granular face.

The demographic condition of the city determines what and how it will interact with its environment. The mix of gender, age, generations, race, height, birth weight, mortality, country of birth and location define the physical characteristics of our dissipative structures. They determine what raw materials we need to optimize our well-being from conception to death. Demographers claim demographics determine the destiny of cities and societies because they embody human well-being and enable the manifestation of human intentions.

Demographics are key determinants of our intentional, cultural and social capacities, because they represent the bodies through which our intentions, cultures and systems are delivered. We ignore them at our peril; but we can learn from them to our advantage. If we do not learn from their messages, our bodies moan, whisper, nag and protest with ever-increasing volume until they are heard.

The city is an ecology of demographics. As a dynamic container of complex adaptive systems, the city's objective qualities change as citizens are born, live and die. Certainly the strength of the generation of the baby boomers born after 1945 has brought a fascination with demographics to the forefront, because the population bulge embodied in the boomers has made demands on city systems like no prior generation (Dychtwald & Flower, 1989).

Horizontal Traits: Hardwiring for Preferences

Biologists and brain scientists are in a hotly contested war of research publications about the meaning of life at the genetic level. On the one hand, materialists like Stephen Pinker (2003) assert that all human behavior can be accounted for through the electrochemical, biophysical architectures of the brain and protein analysis of the gene. On the other hand, developmental/evolutionary biologists like Rupert Sheldrake (1988) and Elisabet Sahtouris (1999) and microbiologists like Bruce Lipton (2005) propose that more is going on in the cell than simple genetic manipulation. The cell itself (and its DNA) creates an energetic field and is itself embedded in energetic fields to which it responds or adapts. The cell is able to learn and thus demonstrate consciousness. This can be seen on the most fundamental level in an amoeba or any of the single cells of our body.

Thus it appears that both realities are true: the cell has a material existence *and* a conscious existence. And since the human individual is made up of cells, it follows that that human systems at every level of scale encompass the objective (material) and subjective (conscious) qualities of life.

All that being said, some aspects of the biophysical patterns have become habits of form (i.e., information) that we consider more or less hard-wired behaviors. For instance, the psychologist Eysenck (Gregory, 1987, pp. 245-247) proposed that extraversion and introversion arise from cortical stimulation — extraverts can tolerate more stimulation to their reticular activating systems (RAS) than introverts, who have more nerves in the RAS. Eysenck's extensive cross-cultural research disclosed that extraversion and introversion seem to be present at birth. Howard describes the "big five" personality dimensions in terms of bipolar behaviors that indicate biophysical underpinnings: Extraversion/Introversion, Resilience/Reaction, Openness/Preservation, Agreeableness/Challenging and Conscientiousness/Flexibility (1994, p. 137).

In a similar manner, certain other traits appear hard-wired, like the preference for right- or left-brain dominance. Right-brain preference is a kind of analog thinking capacity, seeing big pictures and patterns; left-brain preference is a kind of digital thinking capacity, seeing the details and analytic aspects of reality. Many systems of trait theory (from Jung and Myers Briggs, Herman Brain Dominance, 16 Personality Factors, Costa and McCrae (Howard, 1994), build on the recognition that humans appear to have shared behavioral patterns that can be clustered into groups — even from the times of the Greeks, and maintained by current traditional Chinese medicine practitioners (Porkert & Ullmann, 1988).

From the perspective of our understanding of human systems in the context of the city, these traits are more like second- and third-level demographic features. They relate to the horizontal capacity of human systems that is carried throughout life. These capacities influence how we develop — and will give us, for example, preferences for everything from individual expressiveness versus collective expressiveness, first- and second-order change and tasks versus relationships. The character or personality of groups (social holons) is influenced by these preferences, as are the effectiveness of team performance, organizational strategy and community spirit.

MANAGING ENERGY

The value of any demographic data to individuals and groups in the city and to its governance system is that it provides the physical data for calculating how to manage energy in the city. Managing energy in the city comes back to clocking the flows of energy through our dissipative structures — determining what we consume on an individual basis and translating it into an energy-based common denominator.

The eco-footprint was designed to provide such a calculation (Rees & Wackernagel, 1994). (See footprintnetwork.org/gfn_sub.php?content= myfoot print to calculate your footprint.) It calculates the number of Earths that would be needed if everyone lived at the level of the person completing the calculation. (For most people in the developed world it is currently three Earths and increasing.)

A calculation like the eco-footprint provides a level of self-awareness that becomes the first step of self-management. Even though critics observe that the eco-footprint has data gaps, those very gaps indicate information we need to fill in the whole picture. As more data becomes available, current models may prove inaccurate, and even the eco-footprint algorithm may have to change. However, the concept of the eco-footprint is vitally important to the entire discourse of climate change. The value of using it (or another equally full-system model) cannot be underestimated, because it highlights both the individual behaviors that contribute to possible climate change and attempts to compare the collective behaviors of different groups of people.

It should be noted that, while this calculation focuses on the energy it takes to sustain the biophysical well-being of an individual, managing energy is an integral process that is intimately connected with intentions, culture and social systems.

DISSIPATIVE STRUCTURES: PROCESSORS, PATTERNIZERS, STRUCTURIZERS

If, as we have previously proposed, the city is made up of fractals — entities whose patterns repeat themselves at different levels of scale — then the biology of life appears to be the most logical source of exterior city patterns. The biology of humans starts with a single cell, which through processes of division and differentiation develops into the miraculous structure of the human body. Throughout its development, the human pattern is sustained and maintained by the metabolization of nutrients from the environment.

Moreover, the processes of sustaining and maintaining structures are accomplished with the cooperation of groups of cells that function as a whole (holons) — in organs, body systems and human bodies — in the family, clan and community — in educational institutions, workplaces and civic society. At its most fundamental functioning, home economy in all these holons, starting in the cell and finishing in the city as the whole, is about processing, patternizing and structurizing in dissipative forms.

Thus the city is not a static place of bricks and mortar. Rather it is a dynamic dissipative structure, capturing environmental resources in a flowing process of ever-emerging embodied behavior patterns. These patterns are so consistently repeated across cultures that they have become virtually universals. Brown (as quoted in Pinker, 2003, p. 435) has listed a set of surface and language-based universal behaviors that identify behavioral patterns. Pinker proposed that even this comprehensive list needs to be expanded to include deeper mental structures.

This realization brings new appreciation to our short list of the basics of life. It would appear that the first three items are the inputs of human economy: air, water and food. These are the true inputs to our dissipative structures. Clothing and shelter are the primary outputs of our biological systems, for we cannot survive without them in any city. But while the air, water and food are internally processed by the human being, clothing and shelter are externally created.

So the nature of the human being is defined by two classes of necessities: the first group supports our prehuman reality; the second group supports our distinctly human reality. No other life form produces both clothing and structures to protect and contain its biophysical form. What is more, because of the invention and creation of these two extensions of the human system, the whole stream of all other human creations and artefacts has gushed forth!! What an amazing (re)discovery.

If Eden represents our unembellished biological state, then banishment represents not a fall from grace, but instead is a metaphor for the marriage of intention and behavior. Once we leave Eden, we must source our biological necessities and create and supply all other elements of our survival, i.e., clothing and shelter.

Figure 6.1. Biological systems.
Source: Adapted from Miller, 1978, p. 365.

KEY BIOLOGICAL SYSTEMS	DETAILED BIOLOGICAL SUBSYSTEMS
1. Subsystems that process both matter-energy and information	• Reproducer (eggs, sperm, sex glands, genitalia and accessory structures) • Boundary (membranes, skin, hair, cornea)
2. Subsystems that process matter-energy	• Ingestor (mouth, nostrils, skin, jaws) • Distributor (blood, lymph, vascular systems) • Converter (mouth, teeth, tongue, facial muscles, salivary glands, stomach, liver, gallbladder, pancreas, small intestine) • Producer (unknown) • Matter-energy storage (fatty tissues, liver, gall bladder, bone marrow, muscles, bones, spleen, urinary bladder, lower bowel) • Extruder (kidneys, ureters, urethra, rectum, anus, lungs) • Motor (muscles, fascia, bones and joints of arms, legs) • Supporter (skeleton, tendons, ligaments, joint capsules, muscles, fascia)
3. Subsystems that process information	• Input transducer (eyes, ears, chemoreceptors in nose and tongue, nerve endings and receptors in skin, specialized receptors in skin) • Internal transducer (postsynaptic regions of neurons, receptor cells in central nervous system that receive and transduce signals about chemical and physical states of the bloodstream) • Channel and net (blood and lymph vascular systems that convey hormones, central nervous system network of neurons, peripheral and neural network) • Decoder (cells in sense organs, ganglia, nuclei, cortical sense areas, linguistic brain centers, temporoparietal area of dominant hemisphere of brain) • Associator (not known) • Memory (being determined) • Decider (neurons, pituitary and endocrine glands, ventral horn nuclei of spinal cords, motor nuclei of all parts of brain, cortical motor areas, nuclei of cerebral cortex, limbic areas, nuclei and cortical areas of cerebellum) • Encoder (exocrine glands, pheromones, beta coded information, gamma coded symbolic information processing area of dominant hemisphere of brain) • Output transducer (exocrine glands and parts of extruder which excrete pheromones; components of motor including lips, tongue, soft palate, larynx, lungs, hands, feet, muscles of chest and abdomen)

The parable of Eden is a fractal (or archetypal) story itself. It represents humans' evolution as a species as well as historical emergence and development as an individual.

If we had not left Eden we would not have cities. In Eden we were only what we breathed, drank and ate. After Eden we were what we created as well.

Systems and Subsystems in the Biological Quadrant

In the book *Living Systems*, systems scientist and author James Grier Miller (1978) documented in considerable detail the critical systems and subsystems of the human body. His interest was to demonstrate the similarity of subsystem functions across all kinds of living systems. In doing so, he also charted the extent and importance of process (and symbiosis) at every scale of living system from cell to nation.

Like a growing number of scientists (Capra, 1996; Prigogine, 1997; Prigogine & Stengers, 1984), Miller discusses the body in terms of a dissipative structure — one that is constantly recreating itself by processing or metabolizing energy through self-sustaining structure. His emphasis on the dissipative structures of biophysical life provides a useful way of charting the 19 subsystems in the human organism (which parallel the same 19 subsystems in all other living systems) and the awesome complexity of our biophysical experience. Miller's (1978) 19 subsystems are grouped into three categories related to matter, energy and information. The key biological systems and their detailed subsystems are summarized in Figure 6.1.

THE BODY AS THE CITY, THE BODY OF THE CITY, THE BODY IN THE CITY

Let us now examine how the health of the body can reflect the health of the city. In this regard a model used to illustrate integrated medicine (T.W.H. Brown, 1989) presents three major states of health: disease, dysfunction and health.

In the disease zone, pathology manifests itself in changes at the cellular level in structure and function. The body is in a danger zone that if not corrected can lead to dysfunction or death. The body requires acute care and/or crisis intervention.

If the city were a diseased body, it might be Chernobyl with its meltdown of (nuclear) energy-generating systems, New York with its devastating structural collapse on September 11, 2001 or New Orleans with its boundaries breached by broken levees.

Within the zone of dysfunction, the body's health ranges from disintegration to disharmony. The worst deficiencies rarely occur as single dysfunctions, but work in collaboration with one another, debilitating the body in multiple ways. Dysfunction can manifest deficiencies of:

- nutrition
- structure
- toxicity
- psyche
- emotions
- spirit

Dysfunctions in the body can deprive it of proper nutrition (as resulting from today's over-refined foods or outright starvation). They can interfere with cranial, spinal, soft tissue and appendage structures (as in arthritis, nervous disorders, AIDS or osteoporosis) and toxify bodily tissue (as in mercury poisoning, air pollution from leaded gasoline, water pollution from solid waste leaching or substance addictions). Finally dysfunctions can debilitate the body with pain, trauma and

INTEGRATED PHYSICAL PRACTICES

Developing their research on *The Future of the Body*, Michael Murphy and George Leonard co-developed the Integral Transformative Practice, one of the earliest integrated practices developed for optimizing outer intelligence (Leonard & Murphy, 1995). The authors combined optimizing body practices from Eastern and Western traditions, including martial arts, flexibility, strength and aerobic training. They also offered objective measures of progress and proposed full optimization could not occur just with the individual, but had to embrace a community of practice and even service to the community.

In recent years more integrated physical practices have emerged such as Neuromuscular Integration Action or NIA (Rosas & Rosas, 2005), developed by a husband-and-wife team in Portland, Oregon. They combined three practices each from the traditions of dance, healing and martial arts.

One of the most comprehensive practices that has been developed for integrating the body with heart, mind, soul and shadow is the Integral Life Practice (ILP) created by the Integral Institute. In addition to the practices described in the previous chapter that develop inner intellignce, ILP describes the practices of developing outer intelligence by exercising the three bodies (causal, subtle and gross), weight and interval training and eating key foods (carbohydrates, proteins, fats) appropriately to support and expand energy levels. Practitioners report increased health and energy not just in their physical beings but also in their inner lives, work and relationships (Morelli et al., 2006).

ineffective survival techniques, as in physical abuse, war, schizophrenia, or worry.

Murphy describes the degenerative state as one of negative transformation, suggesting that society can choose to operate in such negative manners that whole groups are diminished (e.g., slavery, apartheid), others are isolated (e.g., women, homosexuals), others are denied (e.g., immigrants from some countries) or others are never properly recognized (e.g., aboriginal peoples). He alleges that outcomes from these practices result in "self-mutilation, dissociation, or lack of help from our secret [evolutionary biological] resources ... [and] we will cut ourselves off from many of our creative attributes" (1992, p. 562).

If the city were a dysfunctional body, we would see a place without sufficient tax base to support its infrastructure; consuming its own land and energy resources beyond its willingness or capacity to replace them; with impassable roadways, inoperable transit systems, sporadic and poor telephone and media services; polluted air, water, soil and unhygienic waste management; characterized by conflict, tyranny and intimidation by its governance system. Extreme examples can be selected at different times from around the world: Shanghai (air pollution), Mexico City (soil pollution), New York (waste management), Baghdad (conflict) and Delhi (water pollution). Many examples of less extreme dysfunction can be pointed out in most cities.

SENSES IN THE CITY: THE ROOTS OF NATURAL SCIENCE AND LEARNING

In order for us to change from "dis-ease" and/or dysfunction, we depend on our senses to provide the data to make observations and choices. Our senses are our biological evidence-gathering mechanisms. They gather the data that stimulate both automatic behavior (like eye blinking, flinching, sneezing, gagging) and intentional behavior. Intentional behavior involves choice and therefore consciousness. With sufficient repetition, it can become habituated, but when we bring conscious attention to the data gathered by our senses, we weigh the options of what to do next. Continue as we are? Change (direction, speed, frequency, intensity, etc.)? Stop what we are doing? When we make the choice, then more data floods in to help us evaluate the value of that choice.

While Rupert Sheldrake has been studying what he calls the sixth and seventh senses, we would do well simply to appreciate the value of the "usual" five senses in the city: sight, hearing, smell, taste, touch.

We know from maps of the brain that the sense of sight is the most highly demanding sense from the perspective of the percentage of brain cells allocated to its performance. This is followed by touch, with heavy emphasis on the hands. But we also know that the primal sense of smell is the fastest route to brain engagement. The sense of hearing continues when we sleep, and the sense of taste awakens not just when we eat but when we think of eating.

The senses are inextricably linked with one another, often even able to replace one another when one is damaged or destroyed (a condition called synesthesia). The senses emerged as embodied survival strategies from the time before our consciousness could become objectively aware of them.

The senses are our personal biological data-gathering tools with many automatic interpretation capacities so tightly connected to them that we experience the output indicators (bright, loud, hot, sour, soft) almost simultaneously with the input. In the city, our senses are bombarded with stimulation, frequently to the point of over-stimulation and even pain. When senses are over-stimulated, their data-gathering and interpretation effectiveness plateaus, and we start ignoring the signals they are sending us. This is not only stressful, it is dangerous because we lose touch with information that can be essential to our survival.

This plateauing of our senses is captured in the apocryphal story of the frog in the pot of water on the stove. The frog fails to notice that, as the heat under the pot gradually warms the water to a boil, he is actually being cooked to death. Increasingly our biological experience of the city is that we are being cooked to death by the malfunctioning of a set of nested dissipative structures, with block-ages in the flow of nutrients. The city has grown to a scale where the metabolizing processes are blocked at many junctures causing toxic backup. The toxins become pollution that is not being cleaned from the system. So we suffer from air, water and food pollution and/or toxicity. Our senses suffer from incessant bom-bardment of our visual cortex, sustained and often painful decibels of noise, toxic fumes, unnatural foods and abrasive materials.

While the over-stimulation of our senses in the city can initially be exciting, lit-erally and figuratively, over time this wears down our receiving apparatus and tires out our interpretation centers. And our eyesight, hearing, touch, taste and smell all dim. The capacity for absorbing stimulation varies with disposition and age. It tends to decline in adulthood, unless we learn how to de-stress and become mindful of our environment.

Roots of Natural Science

Ultimately our senses provide the tools for observation, without which we would not have the data for feelings, thoughts or wants. The senses provide an unending stream of data for our personal (albeit informal) scientific experiments, also known as living.

When we formalize the data gathered by our senses, we shift into science. But the basis for science is simply the formalization of the learning process that evolu-tion has developed through our basic sense-gathering, dissipative, structure-oper-ating system. Without the senses and without the data, we would literally be without intelligence.

A city without intelligence is an oxymoron. However a city without intelligence sufficient to its complexity is a city that has lost touch with its senses. A senseless or sense-deprived city does not make sense and is ultimately not sustainable.

Senses Enable Learning Through Dissonance

A final comment about our observation capacities relates to dissonance. Our sensing faculties are the first source of information about change in any given aspect of the city. They tell us whether we are experiencing pleasure or pain.

When we are comfortable (with a majority of sensory input confirming our experience of pleasure), we have little incentive to change. The human condition is disposed to maintain the status quo when life conditions support us in doing so — it uses less energy.

However, when our senses tell us that life conditions are changing, we attempt to adapt by restoring our comfortable state of stability. When change triggers are not too intense or frequent, that strategy makes sense from an energy-conservation point of view; for to change requires that we change behaviors, and thus the amount of energy and how we use it.

As long as we pay attention to the sensation-based evidence, we will have the tools to notice if returning to our comfort zone is an option or whether life conditions are shifting so much that a new behavior is required. When the data from our senses tells us that we cannot return to our usual way of doing things, we experience bodily discomfort and cognitive dissonance. What we observe, think, feel and want are no longer aligned. The longer this misalignment occurs, the more discomfort and dissonance we experience, until we finally reorganize our energy, through rethinking, deep feeling, reframing our wants and relationships and finally changing our behaviors. This is the simple map of the learning journey. It clearly shows us the important gatekeeper role that our senses play in the process of learning.

Through learning we expand the capacity of intelligence in the individual and thereby the intelligence capital of the city. Learning is not simply a matter of intellectual engagement, but embraces the reorganization and reapplication of energy for changing behaviors and taking action.

WELL-BEING IN THE CITY

The sense-based indicators of wellness in biological life are related to the dynamic balance of all the systems and subsystems in our dissipative structures. Because biology co-creates its environment, wellness is a process always in flux, as individual organisms at all levels keep adjusting their relationships to find what works. Symbiosis and structural coupling are characteristics of living systems and are fundamental to community and city well-being. They are the biological equivalent of the cultural expression of acceptance. Effectively, no complex biology and no micro- or macrocosm exists without symbiosis and structural coupling (Maturana & Varela, 1992).

Indicators of biological alignment and coherence thus emerge from a healthy dynamism. Biological health, characterized by wellness (or wholeness), emerges from the capacity to find nourishment from one's environment (the basis of what scientists call structurally coupling with the environment), metabolize such nourishment (i.e., derive sources of energy from it that allow one to sustain one's physical identity and structure) and reproduce or regenerate.

Health also emerges from resilience — a capacity to flexibly relate to one's environment, including relating to others in it — so that sourcing nourishment, sustaining life and reproducing may continue to occur despite conditions of change in the environment.

When the body approaches the health zone, it moves from dysfunction into a state of integration and optimal functioning. It has a strong immune system, structure and processes. It is receiving physical, psychological, emotional and spiritual care that assists it to resist disease and breakdown and to repair systems degradation, structural breakage and tissue damage. The body responds with assurance, confidence and positive demeanor. In the health zone, the body seeks to establish not just balance but buoyancy or resilience on all levels, including spiritual, psychological, emotional, physical and interpersonal. It integrates all structures and processes in harmony with its environment.

Michael Murphy (1992, p. 562) suggests that the optimal state of health is the starting point for the body to achieve metanormal functioning — which would be the equivalent functioning of bodies in an Integral City. His research indicates that you can create new capacities — even metanormal capacities — by improving intra-system communications that enhance performance.

In a healthy city, where system and subsystem structures and processes are clearly defined, metanormal functioning would provide multiple controls (like city/state/provincial and federal laws; judicial, legislative and executive balances of power), utilize great diversity (like providing for multiple cultures in one city) and ironically operate without awareness of control (as when citizens are satisfied and able to take the social infrastructure for granted).

If a healthy body were a city it would have perfectly balanced respiratory, circulatory, skeletal, digestive and autonomic nervous systems. It would be an athlete in peak condition. The closest we can come to naming healthy urban centers today are the Organisation for Economic Co-operation and

Development (OECD) candidates for the most livable city in the world: Vancouver, Zurich, Sydney.

Developing a wholesome body and developing a wholesome city requires that we promote general practices of health (and healthcare systems, as outlined below). Moreover, whether we are developing an optimal city or an optimal body, Murphy reminds us that healthy biophysical functioning is intimately connected to healthy intentions: "We need many virtues and traits that help produce good societies in general, among them charity, courage, forgiveness and balance" (1992, p. 562).

EMBODYING INTENTION, PURPOSE

Just as consciousness has complexified as the human species has evolved, so has the body. Biologists and medical students have a saying that "ontogeny recapitulates phylogeny." This simply means the natural life cycle of a single being reflects the stages of the evolutionary cycle of the species. This can be seen in the growth of the fetal body through stages that reflect the evolution of plant, fish, reptile, mammal and human. Vestiges of these stages appear to remain in the triune human brain, which is now recognized to have layers of complexity related to its reptilian past (the amygdala, seat of the emotions and the fight/flight response), its mammalian ancestry (the cortex) and the foundation for higher learning (the neocortex related to consciousness aware of itself).

While we tend to think that the body and brain we have now have not changed since the emergence of *homo sapiens sapiens* as a distinct species, both have in fact adapted to life conditions. As a result of the remarkable discoveries still unfolding from the mapping of the human genome, we now can trace the sequence of the emergence of morphologies (Abravanel & Abravanel, 1983), blood types (O, A, B, AB) (D'Adamo & Whitney, 2000) and genetic family groupings through both male and female lines (Sykes, 2002; Wells, 2002). We know even that gender types are largely influenced by life conditions in the maternal womb (Baron-Cohen, 2003; Moir & Jessel, 1991). Other studies of neurobiology have revealed the secrets of brain architecture (Braverman, 2006; Pinker, 2003) and cell functioning (Lipton, 2005) .

In fact the more we study the gene, the brain and the body, the more we realize that the human being's basic condition is to adapt and change. No longer can we assume that genes, the most basic building blocks of life, are not continuously adapting to life conditions, as epigenetics is now informing us (Hamer, 2004; Lipton, 2005; Ridley, 2003).

Furthermore the mysterious linkage between intention and biophysical performance is being tested. Rupert Sheldrake has been investigating a cluster of phenomena that defies the assumptions of classical biology and psychology. He is researching conundrums whose solutions seem to draw on explanations from the quantum physics of Einstein and Heisenberg and the quantum biology of Lipton (Sheldrake, 2003). These questions open the doors to the "spooky" effects of intention at a distance, like telepathy, premonition and awareness of being stared at. And while classical science has attempted to sideline such phenomena as superstitions, it appears that humans are not the only species with these capacities. If the conduct of dogs (who know their owners are coming home before they arrive), cats, birds and horses are any indication, these behaviors may have evolved as survival strategies. Humans may also have previously developed these capacities, which today lie largely untapped in individuals and collectives in cities but may be available for reawakening. Certainly some indigenous peoples seem to have high access to these capacities and continue to practise them in remote, un-citied places like the jungles of the Amazon, the outback of Australia and the river banks of Borneo.

This research seems to indicate that, even though we don't yet have all the technology to discern the evolutionary structures of our body and brain, we soon will be able to see that the developmental levels of increasing complexity will be visible and identifiable. Thus the effects of living in the city where the opportunity for intention and purpose are so individually embodied and collectively contained may soon disclose entirely new possibilities for evolving human experience. If, as Sheldrake proposes, the human system has the capacity to naturally receive signals from a distance (and be aware of embodied states as well as cognitive understanding), then we may be standing on a whole new threshold of human capacity emergence that will make the Level 8 leadership competencies (explored in some detail in chapter 5) look primitive.

DESIGNING APPROPRIATE HEALTHCARE SYSTEMS

In this biological quadrant of the Integral City reside the roots for the appropriate design for healthcare systems that create and sustain biophysical health for citizens.

Similar to the situation discussed in chapter 5 regarding integral education systems, integral healthcare systems deserve a whole book on their own. But we can describe a thumbnail sketch of such a system here because the need to see healthcare systems integrated into the fabric of a healthy Integral City is urgent.

Healthcare systems in most countries (even the most developed) are currently in considerable disarray. The reasons are easy to list and very difficult to fix quickly. So to build some positive momentum for how to design integral healthcare systems, here are some suggestions.

We need to get clear on the vision and the purpose of the healthcare system in the city. The city's vision and purpose will tell us the purpose of the healthcare system. The two need to be aligned so the resources needed to maintain the healthcare system are made available through the governance systems in place. Is the purpose of the city's healthcare system to enable an optimal dissipative structure, processing sufficient energy to sustain its citizens with a minimal eco-footprint? Is the purpose simply to respond to acute care? What role does the city and healthcare system play in promoting health? Preventing disease? Enabling longevity? The process of answering these inquiries will reveal a vision and purpose for the healthcare system.

We need to ask how citizens define health. This may seem a trivial question, but until we conduct a cultural and developmental scan of the city with a focus on how citizens define health, we will not realize that definitions of health are values based. When we consider that values and culture determine the actual

GLIMPSES OF INTEGRAL HEALTHCARE SYSTEMS

Vestiges of full-city integral health systems are emerging on the horizon. Most cities in the developed world have clinics that offer some form of integrated health medicine. For example, the integrated health practices offered at Integrated Health in Vancouver, BC, provide traditional Chinese acupuncture, chiropractic, nutrition and a pharmacopeia from Eastern herbology, Western homeopathy and nutraceuticals.

Some locations like Carbondale, Colorado, have community-based integral health societies, like Davi Nikent, that aspire to implement integral health frameworks, like that developed by Elliott Dacher's Integral Medicine. Wilber's Integral Institute has a special interest group focused on Integral Medicine.

Taking advantage of world-class events like the Olympics has opportunities for impacting local health. In BC, where Vancouver and Whistler will host the 2010 Winter Olympics, the Province identified key strategies to improve the (physical) health of citizens before the 2010 Olympics — increase exercise, eat more fruits and vegetables, reduce smoking (Pointe, 2008).

geographies that we use to describe the biophysical body, it becomes apparent that we literally see, sense and serve our bodies differently, depending on how we define its health. Do we measure health by the chi flowing through our meridians? By the consumption of foods that energize our chakras? By the practice of exercise that strengthens our muscles? By the ratio of our diastolic and systolic blood pressures? By eating selections from all the food groups defined by the FDA? Discovering the myriad interpretations of health reveals the cultural and developmental sensitivities to health and the related modalities that would be supported by citizens. This can provide the evidence about what combination of health care modalities should be resourced and how much diversity (and hence resilience) can be built into the healthcare system.

We need to integrate, educate and support citizens' preferred approaches to health. We can see that health definitions are not limited to physical health. But the ways that we could embrace emotional, mental and spiritual (i.e., intentional) health along with biophysical health vary by culture. This in turn impacts the social system and facilities we develop to deliver healthcare services. Such services need to take into consideration even our developmental natures. We need to be able to deliver the biological basics of life, but also heal ailments that are rooted in developmental breakdowns. Treatments matched with developmental needs accelerate healing. For instance, for broken physiques, a surgeon might replace a hip; broken relationships, a shaman might restore health in a sweat lodge; disempowerment, a herbalist might administer a decoction that restores centeredness; disorder, an acupuncturist might rebalance energy; overexertion, a physiotherapist might relieve back pain; depression, a psychiatrist might prescribe neurotransmitters; systemic burnout, a nutritionist might create a new diet; world weariness, a spiritual counselor might lead a retreat. In a city with an ecology of biological needs, a spectrum of modalities are needed to create an appropriate healthcare system.

Design healthcare from at least a Level 7 (yellow) worldview, so that it is systemically responsive, adaptive and flexible. When we consider the variety of services just itemized for a healthcare system, it is obvious that ideally the design requirements must come from a worldview that is systemic, respectful of the spectrum of development, cultures and biological variety. If Level 7 or higher designers are available, then they will have to articulate across all the levels of health delivery systems. If Level 7 designers are not available, the system will be designed from the center of gravity of the designers (and stakeholders). Where Level 7 designers consult to cities where less complex health delivery models are appropriate, they can help to align the system so that it can meet current needs and evolve into greater complexity when the time is right.

We ought to understand the demographics of the city. An understanding of demographics in the city will help determine the flex and flow of health needs in the city. If we scan the city for different definitions of health (as suggested above), then we also need to know how many people hold those expectations, their ages, genders, races, etc., so that health care can be informed by all this data. These factors will indicate how resources should be programmed to serve demographic needs.

We should inventory the integral (four-quadrant, all-level) health of the city. This data will indicate the strengths and weaknesses of health in the city. By including all quadrants, it is possible to see how capacities or deficiencies in one aspect of the city's existence are impacting other aspects. For example, the program Success By Six®, developed by United Way, maps the factors that contribute to childhood health in the city. This focuses health resources on a demographic that research shows has critical impact for future health of the community. However, six-year-olds are inevitably members of families whose adult life conditions impact the children. Thus the bio-psycho-cultural-social health of the primary-care adults must be considered for success before, by and after six.

We need to inventory and map existing health facilities and human resources within the city and the region. This will disclose how resources should be adjusted to align demographic needs with actual conditions of health. As noted above, to achieve biophysical health, assets in all of the quadrants of the city's reality need to be mapped so that the psycho-cultural-social aspects of health care are correlated. When any one of the quadrants is not operating at the same relative capacities as the others, distortion and disease occur in the human system. A healthy healthcare system would consider the resources that serve the health of all quadrants.

Design a healthcare system that addresses the bio-psycho-cultural-social system of health of the city that addresses the key cultural sub-populations. This horizontal approach to health care is parallel to the modes of delivery. With an understanding of the cultural mixes of the population, special attention can be paid to differences that are not trivial. For instance with the four major cultural groups in Singapore, health care ought to match the food, medicines and even gender practices of the relevant cultures. This would overcome natural resistances (such as for Muslims against pork products, alcohol and inappropriate nursing staff) and create environments where people can heal without fear of breaking important cultural taboos.

We should set up benchmarks and vital signs to monitor the health in the city in terms of well-being. If the purpose of the city healthcare system was to create the conditions for well-being in the city, it would have to establish criteria for defining well-being. It would then make sense to monitor the performance of the healthcare system in terms of creating and supporting well-being in the city.

We need to research ongoing states and stages of health and develop healthcare systems that are able to adjust to the continuous adaptive condition of the states and stages of human health. This will enable appropriate messaging, education and healthcare modalities. The ailments of every level of development have related modes of treatment, and they evolve over time. We need health care that addresses needs appropriately at beige, purple, red, blue, orange, green, yellow and turquoise. Like education, health care is a never-ending quest.

CULTURALLY CATALYZING BIOPHYSICAL POTENTIAL, CONNECTIONS, WELL-BEING

A final note about our healthcare systems relates to the multiplicity of maps of the body and how they can expand our intelligence. We tend to take the mental models of our bodies for granted, and unless we are guided to do so by elders, mentors and experts, we take our behaviors as givens. But our senses, our learning and our science now tell us that behaviors in the city can become more intelligent. Our aspirations tell us that we must become more intelligent.

The fascinating discoveries of brain science reveal more to us every day about the biological, physical, chemical and energetic capacities of our brains and bodies. The merging of the sciences from the East and the West has demonstrated that different cultural approaches to health sciences have produced different geographies of the body. Now that we are finally able to compare notes about these culturally influenced health maps, we can better appreciate the traditional Sufi parable of eight blind men with their hands on different parts of an elephant, giving them very different data and interpretations about what they are sensing.

In modern cities, understanding the differences of these culturally varied maps is vital so that the multiplicity of cultures can manage the boundaries, resources and expectations for biophysical survival that divide them but at the same time potentially inform them. The realities of these maps appear to create fields of intention that unite like-minded citizens even though they vary from group to group.

The empirically measurable reality of these fields of intention is only becoming visible as communities of practice participate in research that discloses their effects. Practices like Reiki and therapeutic touch explicitly involve the intentional and energetic influence of the practitioner on the patient. Even the effects of prayer and peer support groups on the treatment of disease have demonstrated the impact of intentions and relationships.

The research of Rupert Sheldrake (1988, 2003) on morphogenetic fields suggests that intentions are most influential between people who are emotionally connected or connected through relationship. His serious study of many anomalies of human biology, like the sense of being stared at, telepathy, precognition and visions, suggests that these capacities are natural biological survival processes. Like other biological capacities, people don't possess them all to the same degree. Some have more than others. However, the studies do reveal that biophysical existence appears to create a measurable energy field in and around each person that is able to transmit and/or receive effects not just locally but at a distance.

The fact that empirical worldviews and science have ignored or even repressed this evidence has not prevented the continual recurrence of these effects, but it has marginalized practice and practitioners, even to the point of state suppression at some stages of history.

An understanding, let alone a genuine curiosity about the effects of energy fields in the city, has come more from the implicit fear of massive energy infrastructure (like power lines and telecommunications antenna) on human energy systems than from curiosity about the capacities of the energy fields in our own bodies. Becoming aware that human energy systems can be harnessed for the good, as described by Hagelin (2007), is still a novel idea. But it certainly opens up the question, oft repeated here, what is the purpose of the city? Perhaps the answer becomes imbued with unimaginable possibility when we consider that at least one potential for people living together in urban density could be for intentionally embodying a unified energized field for the purpose of destressing others and enabling optimal biophysical health for the collective of humans in the city.

CONCLUSION

What is important about citizen behaviors? Citizen behavior is the action mode of the city. It is the realm where the cognitive domain of intention is embodied and made manifest. In the city, the quadrant of the biological and physical is experienced in the presence of others essentially like us. We sense their behaviors; they sense our behaviors. Individuals are temporally and spatially linked and even coupled with others so that whatever groups we form, we create a multiplier effect.

With all the stress, tension and terrorism in the world, it is ironic to consider that cities could not exist if some minimum level of acceptance or tolerance did not exist. Acceptance is a behavior that can be charted on a scale measuring the degree of tolerance for others more or less like us. The more the citizens of a community accept people who are visibly different from them, the more biological diversity can contribute to the resilience of a city.

Well-being in the city requires that we pay attention to how we manage our individual and group energies. By doing so, we serve the patterns, processes and structures of well-being that support our city intentions, cultures and social systems. If we fail to do this, Diamond cites the repeated blindness of societies to grasp the implications of their short-term behaviours for their long-term survivability. He describes in horrific detail the histories of societal "collapse" from the South Pacific to the North Atlantic to Latin America. He cautions that these historical instances may be more than metaphorical warnings for the continuation of life on earth (Hamilton, 2007a).

QUESTIONS

1. How can we design healthcare systems that serve multiple levels of well-being in a holistic values-based and culturally sensitive manner that support the purpose of the city?

2. How powerful are our energy fields? How can we learn to use them for well-being?

3. How do invisible biological electrochemical transmitters affect positive and negative behaviors in the city?

Three simple rules for applying Integral City principles from this chapter:

1. Manage personal energy.

2. Seek biophysical well-being for self and others.

3. Nurture healthy leaders.

7

BUILDING INTELLIGENCE: CREATING STRUCTURES THAT FLEX AND FLOW IN THE HUMAN HIVE

The life of the bee is like a magic well:
the more you draw from it, the more there is to draw.
— Karl von Frisch, as quoted by Gould and Gould, 1988, p. 225

We are the first [society] to enjoy the opportunity of learning quickly
from developments in societies anywhere in the world today,
and from what has unfolded in societies at any time in the past.
— Diamond, 2005, p. 23

WHAT YOU GET IS WHAT YOU SEE: CHEMISTRY, PHYSICS, BIOLOGY, ARCHITECTURE AND ENGINEERING

This chapter connects to the realities of the city, represented in the Lower Right quadrant of the integral model. It explores aspects of the city that we are most familiar with through the receptors of our senses. This is the city that we see, feel, hear, smell, touch, taste. It is external to us and at the same time contains us.

City structures and infrastructures arise from natural systems. When we reframe the city from being merely the built environment *outside of* us to the built environment as simply an extension *of* us, our relationship with the "objective" city becomes ever so much more personal.

The most livable cities have been created so that the building blocks of matter, information and energy serve the human system in compatible and coherent ways. These building blocks rest on the realities discovered through the hard sciences of chemistry and physics: What is the chemical state of water? What is the life cycle of H_2O? What causes water pressure? What are the constraints of water flowing through pipes of certain dimensions? How do you collect and process sewage? How do you build an arch? How high can you construct a building of wood or brick or steel and glass? How long can you store food? How do you move people and goods on a daily basis?

The answers to these questions have been translated by engineers and architects into the built environment of the city. We have essentially created exoskeletons, muscles and organ systems to capture and contain our biological functions. The realities of our biological functions dictate and determine that the structures of the city are mere enablers of the flow of matter, energy and information to individual human systems. Individuals in turn personally process the matter, energy and information through their individual systems in a never-ending flow. As long as people are part of the city, they will call forth an infrastructure that supports them to the extent that they are maintaining and developing their human capacities.

To the extent that invisible human capacities of consciousness and culture develop, the visible human capacities described in biology, archeology, anthropology and sociology help us understand the behaviors of individuals and groups related to such developments. Essentially, in the city, you get what you see. And we see what we get (consciously).

Because of their nature, the structures and infrastructures of the city, grounded in matter, tend to be much longer lasting than the manifest intelligences in the other quadrants. They appear frozen in time, but effectively matter and energy just move through the structures at a much slower rate than through individual biological persons. The scale of the city is different than individual humans, and its measures need to be calibrated for effectiveness at the city scale.

STRUCTURAL SYSTEMS FOR MANAGING
ENERGY, INFORMATION, MATTER

The structural systems for managing energy, information and matter are essentially the same as those mapped out for the individual biology in chapter 6. James Grier

Miller (1978) summarized them for a society. They are adapted for a city as set out in Figure 7.1. These systems demonstrate the actual existence of a city state (which Miller has subsumed in a society) and make a very strong case for the clear value of managing a city as a natural human system, derived from a natural human system. Thus it argues for special considerations in the management of its governance systems.

As human capacities for processing energy, matter and information have evolved in complexity, we can see that the city has always responded to reflect these evolving capacities. This is reflected in Map 4 of chapter 3 where it is obvious that the city complexifies its structures as it matures and/or grows. If we want documented proofs of the changes to these functions (in scope and location), we can look to the city's archives (if they exist) and/or the historical buildings and archeological record of the city (as noted in How Infrastructures Change with Invention sidebar).

CARRYING CAPACITY AND OTHER CRUEL FACTS: THE RELATIONSHIP OF BUILT CITY TO ECOREGION

Even as cities become increasingly adept at creating built solutions to

Figure 7.1. Comparison of major subsystems for an individual and a city. Source: Adapted from Miller, 1978.

SYSTEM	SUBSYSTEM FUNCTION	INDIVIDUAL MANIFESTATION	CITY MANIFESTATION
1. Deals with Matter-Energy and Information	1. Reproduction	Genitalia	City Declaration, Constitution
	2. Boundary	Skin	Bylaw Enforcers City Limits
2. Deals with Matter-Energy	1. Ingestor	Mouth	Importer (public, private, NFP)
	2. Distributor	Vascular System	Transportation firms
	3. Converter	Upper GI Tract	Energy refiner (gas, oil, electricity, ethanol)
	4. Producer	Eye/Hand	Factory Coordinator
	5. Matter-energy Storage	Fatty Tissues	Warehouse
	6. Extruder	Urethra	Waste Manager, Sewage Treatment Dept.
	7. Motor	Leg Muscles	Trucking firm, taxi firm
	8. Supporter	Skeleton	Land and building developers and maintainers
3. Deals with Information	1. Input Transducer	Sense Organs	Communications infrastructure: telephone, computer, wireless, etc.
	2. Internal Transducer	Homeostasis Monitor	Polling and monitoring organizations, e.g., audit firms, public opinion pollsters
	3. Channel and net	Neural Network	Communication networks
	4. Decoder	Cells in sensory nuclei	Interpreters, translators, e.g., editors, language translators
	5. Associator	Distributed cellular connectors; GABA	Teaching institutions; cultural relationships
	6. Memory	Brain/mind	Libraries
	7. Decider	Cerebral cortex (part)	Government, Voters
	8. Encoder	Tempoparietal Lobe	Media Specialists; bloggers; digitizers
	9. Output Transducer	Larynx	Media Reporters; PR firms; Bloggers

serve human demands, they seem to be disconnecting from the ultimate infra-structure on which their systems depend — namely the planet's carrying capacity. The carrying capacity for each city is intimately tied to its ecoregion, even though cities have attempted to import their needs from increasingly distant locations (e.g., the average food on your plate is reputed to travel 1,500 to 2,000 miles) and to export their excess to destinations as remote as possible from the creation of the problem (e.g., garbage and sewage).

If the city's structural roots were clearly visible in its ecoregion, the city would see its best interests protected by assuming a stewardship role for its ecoregion. However, because the history of many of the most powerful societies have roots in the over-populated cities of 19th century Europe, the habits of cities die hard. Like beehives that are induced to swarm, populations exploded out of the European cities in the 1800s and became colonizers in what De Landa (1997, p. 152; 2006) calls "neo-Europes" — the temperate zones of North America, Argentina, Australia and New Zealand. These were locations where the life conditions replicated the old home and enabled the recreation of a pseudo-European society, complete with culture, crops and livestock. Effectively the new world societies were able to cultivate veritable European-style ecosystems. De Landa notes that any urban ecosystem requires a shortened food chain, and once a formula is found, it becomes resistant to change and predatory of all other formulae.

Ironically, even as the length of the urban food chain decreases, the discon-nection between the city and its ecological context seems to increase. This dis-connection probably lies at the root of why cities lack purpose or vision. If city governors do not consider that the city or the governance system is responsible for the health of both the city's internal and external condition, then we will con-tinue to produce sprawl (like Calgary), cities with chronic water shortages (like Phoenix), mega-cities with severe over-population and poverty (like Mexico City) and toxic cities where it is dangerous to breathe the air (Shanghai, Beijing).

The beginnings to a strong engineered solution for this dilemma appear to lie in the promise of the eco-footprint (Rees & Wackernagel, 1994). The eco-foot-print creates a strong measure of the use of energy, specifically carbon-based fuels, to demonstrate the relative efficiency of the lifestyle of any given city.

With the fast-growing awareness of the effects of climate change (Gore, 2007; Monbiot & Prescott, 2007), a new awareness is growing that the warning signals offered by the eco-footprint, the carbon footprint and climate warming are all critical vital signs that we need to monitor and change behaviors based on the feedback they report.

In simple terms:

1. The eco-footprint calculates the amount of space required to grow food, produce energy, erect buildings and displace waste. The more Earth space that the eco-footprint displaces over and above the actual physical foot-print of the city, the more a given city needs to import resources to sustain city life. Just as we have invented water meters to measure water consumption, it is now possible to calculate the size of each person's eco-footprint based on individual consumption. Rees and Wackernagel propose that our eco-footprint measures the land base required to support our standard of living. They estimate that if everyone on Earth lived to the standard of the developed world, we would need three Earths (Wackernagel & Rees, 1996, p. 15). Therefore they propose that we should control our lifestyles based on a sustainable land use. This is the underlying argument for the city having a direct relationship with its ecoregion and a responsibility imperative for its relationship with the rest of the world (from which it imports goods not produced in its ecoregion). Designing a proactive relationship with our eco-footprint would build in vital signs indicators that enable resilience and sustainability. It can make easily visible the positive feedback loop we need to make wise choices (like water rationing) and joint action (like electricity reduction at peak times).

2. The carbon footprint calculates the amount of carbon dioxide and greenhouse gases produced by burning carbon-based energy. The more CO_2 produced in the atmosphere, the warmer our climate becomes. Monbiot estimates that even a 1.5 degree (or less) of warming will flood low-lying land that will displace (and/or kill) 400 million people, expose another 5 million people to hunger and destroy 18 percent of the world's species (Monbiot & Prescott, 2007, p. 15). He proposes that CO_2 be rationed and that we (cities? governance authorities?) control the amount of CO_2 any lifestyle produces.

3. The relationship between eco-footprint and the carbon footprint seems to provide real constraints for the healthy functioning of cities. They are the

indicators that tell the city if it is living beyond not only its means, but the Earth's means. They are the first wake-up calls of this era that we now have enough information to measure the dissonance of the city's disconnection with its energy and matter resources. This is the feedback loop we have been waiting for. We can clearly see that these ratios of people:land:energy mean that we can no longer be ignorant of the effects cities have on the health of the planet.

If we return to our beehive analogy, we should not be surprised that all this data are relevant to sustainable living in the city. The beehive has a relationship with the environment that it co-sustains — a certain land area is required to produce the flowers that support the hive; more specifically, the bees need nectar for their carbohydrate source and pollen for their protein source.

The bees, too, have to deal with the temperature of their world. If life conditions increase the environmental heat, they are forced to forage for more water than pollen to keep their hive at an ideal temperature for them of 36°C. The shape and size of the beehive (whether wild or manufactured) has evolved to contain a certain number of bees (approximately 50,000) with optimal sized "bee-space." This ratio of the honeycomb structure to mobility space determines whether bees spend the same energy producing one kilogram of beeswax or eight kilograms of honey. Thus beekeepers with manufactured hives design and manage optimum structural conditions so the hive can keep the bees productive and sustainable (Gould & Gould, 1988).

This would lead us to speculate that, for cities, the size and density of the population, the land base and the heat output are all rational factors that should be taken into consideration for optimizing the quality of life in the city. Creating a city as livable, in a livable region, means far more than a feel-good experience for city dwellers.

Ultimately cities are not sustainable if their ecoregions are not sustainable. The city and its ecoregion need to be co-sustainable. There is a real science to the factors that contribute to city and ecoregion resilience, city and ecoregion sustainability and their contribution to planet resilience and planet sustainability.

Resilience for a city means that its nest of human systems is able to adapt to the life conditions of the city and its ecoregion. Diamond (2005), Wright (2004) and Homer-Dixon (2006) chronicle the tragic instances where cities have not been resilient and disappeared as a result of their lack of awareness, attention or action to the relationship between their eco-footprint and their heat generation. The myth of Atlantis — the city that submerged from view — takes on new meaning in light of this information. Is it possible that we are creating Earth conditions that will produce many more modern-day Atlantises?

The persuasive warnings about the cruel relationship between the city and its resource shadow (that have been documented by Diamond, Homer-Dixon and Wright) remind us that the relationship between energy, matter and information is one we constantly negotiate and is ultimately one of life and death. The city now needs to mature so that it not only pays attention to the health within its boundaries and to the health of its ecoregion, but takes responsibility for it.

How Does Who Sustain Whom, with What Resources, Drawn from Where, for What Purpose?

This could become the city's clarion question to define the parameters of its own sustainability. It is the question that calls for mining the data that the city collects and owns; mapping its functions, resources, exchange systems and energy flows, analyzing its consumption demands and developing policy and governance systems to live within its means.

The sheer challenge of trying to answer this question as it simply relates to everyday eating is being addressed by those who are introducing the slow food movement, which started in Tuscany, and the eating locally/100-mile diet movements. As we have sourced our food basket from further and further away, it appears that we have disenfranchised not only local food producers, but also local food eaters. These experiments indicate that, if everyone in a given city wanted to eat from foods sourced in the city's ecoregion, they would not be able to do so, in many cases because of a lack of local staples like wheat (or ground grains), cooking oils and legumes. (Also see sidebar on Influencing the Effluence of Affluence.)

MAKING VISIBLE THE INVISIBLE

City structures are made up both from the collective of people and from the built environment, which is the extension of our human systems that enables the large population in the city to survive in close proximity to one another. The built structures

BIOLOGICAL MIMICRY

Architect William McDonough is experimenting with buildings that live — adapted to their natural environments, responsive to sunlight and nurturing green roofs. Architect Christopher Alexander is experimenting with the "Phenomenon of Life," co-designing living worlds where building centers, hulls and space are co-created with the stakeholders and future users of the buildings. He is doing this with everyone from poor Mexican workers, to Japanese university students, to groups of house owners in rural and highly urbanized community settings.

are often referred to as artefacts — as if they were immutable tools or objects created for human use. However, the built structures in the city, taken together as systems, are not merely utilitarian but are externalized functions of human existence. We tend to classify them as infrastructures (below the surface) and superstructures (above the surface). But when we stand back far enough, we can see that the classification system developed by James Grier Miller (1978) and his team recognized the seamless interconnection between the built environment and the basic functions of the human system.

The history of the city as a built environment is the history of externalizing the internal (and generally invisible) functions of the human system so that larger and larger populations of people can live together. When we look around us at the city, we are actually seeing the basic organic functions of the body writ large. Moreover, by the simple act of being situated in the city, we become dependent on these systems for air quality, water, food, waste management, bodily protection (clothing, shelter), mobility, temperature control, information exchange and rest and renewal.

DIFFERENTIATING HUMAN SOCIAL STRUCTURES FROM ARTEFACTS

The evolution of *homo sapiens sapiens* has produced social structures in every human collective on Earth. The architecture of those social structures has always resulted in organizational structure that has some hierarchy (even if it has only a single level) and some center to it. This hierarchy of complexity arises in direct response to the complexity of life conditions.

Life conditions can be defined as the environment and ecology of the human-made world in the context of the natural world (comprising the litho-geo-bio-noetic levels of development). In this context we can see that, just as the natural world has continued to complexify structures over evolutionary history, it is perfectly natural that the human system, as a natural system, would evolve in the direction of greater complexity. It should be noted that the direction is a general one and not a guaranteed one. Complex life conditions on a universal scale assure that setbacks and reversals will occur in shorter time scales, but in general the direction of evolution is towards greater complexity.

The center to the organizational structure is not always the geometric or geographic center. It is effectively a values center from which and to which the rest of the structure flows. In that respect it is also an energy center and a power center. As the life conditions for the city change, the "center of the universe" for the city changes (as discussed in the next chapter) and so does its structural center. The organizational and structural centers of villages and towns were their marketplaces and town squares. For premodern cities, the center is city hall; for modern cities, it is the financial district; for postmodern cities, it is the community center; and for the integral city, it is a hub of networked centers with easy access to each other. Integral architects and urban planners design these centers so they can strengthen their values.

As our building technology has changed, our structures have grown dimensions that distance people from many values centers and therefore distance people from the scale of the built city. Architect Christopher Alexander invokes the criteria of life (discussed in chapter 2) to design not only from living centers, but also to locate the natural "hulls" or boundaries to which people can relate. In an Integral City, the design criteria for structures would transcend and include the values of the citizens, enabling life-giving centers and natural boundaries with qualities that served the people and functions they contained. So depending on the functions contained, the boundaries might be open and porous like a market district, closed and guarded like a public works area, semi-permeable but firm like a transportation corridor or invisible but acknowledged like a park setting.

When we consider the complexity of hierarchies and centers that make up a city, it is easy to see why cities represent the pinnacle of human social emergence. With their concentration of human populations in focused time-space continuums, they require the most complex forms of social system management ever created. In addition the translation and transfer of the extensions of human systems into built form demands the most complex form of structural system management ever needed by life.

Thus the living and the non-living are both structured, and their structures are concurrent and intertwined. The building blocks of human structures arise in order to accomplish intentional goals. We define primary work in terms of fulfilling strategies that contribute first to survival and then to achieving and supporting the hierarchy of values that we consider of prime importance for our well-being. Secondary and tertiary work support those systems that contribute to primary work.

In support of primary, secondary and tertiary work, we have created the great team, organizational and civil structures that enable collective functioning. The shape, texture and ergonomics of these structures reflect the bio-psycho-cultural-social characteristics of their creators and users. These structures in turn dictate the processes, sequences and relationships in the workforces that produce output and outcomes, and who work, live, play and rest within and around them.

Human social structures create energetic fields whose effects can be measured. At the moment, those measures are rather primitive — for example, we can measure the increase in the heat of a room when large groups are gathered. We can measure how people vote when they are hooked up to a voting machine. We can even measure statistical significance in objective outcomes from seemingly intersubjective effects of staring at a distance or of healing prayer directed by many to a single person. As our instruments and understanding improve, we will come to see that biophysical proximity creates conditions for collective epistemologies (ways of knowing) that are only just now being researched methodically. As our instruments and our understanding complexify, we will be able to measure not only time span of work roles, but mind-span of intentions, and we will understand how to structure social forms to optimize such ways of knowing and how to design built structures to amplify them. (See sidebar on Biological Mimicry for examples.)

In these ways, we can see that the extensions or artefacts of human structure become reflectors and amplifiers of human behaviors and intelligence. Perhaps the separation of human bodies from human artefacts is more illusory than real? Certainly, as long as the artefacts serve human life, they are an inextricable part of it. They leverage capacities and enable even greater complexity to emerge.

It is only when we see the artefacts through the eyes of disuse, where their functionality has long ceased to contribute to human life, that we focus on the mere elements of matter that make up the stone ghosts of Easter Island, the Mayan Temples and the deserted mining towns on the Klondike Trail. In those places, the energy field of use is no longer active, and the flow of energy and matter in the structures becomes measured by the much slower rates of change that non-living structures exhibit. But if the stones and walls could speak, they would tell tales embedded in their very structures of how they contained the information and energy fields of human systems that made past society possible. Once the relationship between place and person is broken, so that the living energy is no longer actively but merely passively contained by the non-living structures, only the residue of the inert structures reminds us of how humans once solved the equation of collective life here in this particular location.

MAPPING INFRASTRUCTURE FOR RESOURCE ALLOCATION

Urban planning abounds with theory for the planning and layout of cities. When we look at the street map of most cities, we are getting a superficial glimpse of the infrastructure that lies below the surface. We can make an educated guess that, because the streets provide access to the surface real estate, beneath (or beside or above) the streets lie the

HOW INFRASTRUCTURES CHANGE WITH INVENTION

When automobiles replaced horses as energy-consuming mobility systems, the supporting infrastructure came to dominate the streetscape and hay forage sheds were replaced by gas stations in Detroit. When computers became a favored device for information transfer and storage, the construction of wireless infrastructure to support the use of laptop computers was installed in London. When information content producers in the city changed as technology offered new options for encoding and outputting information, surfing bloggers in Astoria, Oregon, took their place alongside traditional espresso-imbibing media editors and reporters in New York. When the redesign of construction materials (matter) enabled the production of prefabricated tilt-up industrial parks in North America and residential buildings in Japan, construction techniques became faster, easier and less costly.

delivery channels for water, sewer, electricity, gas and tele-media-communications (Ascher, 2005).

The very existence of infrastructure requires the designers, engineers, technicians and construction workers who build it and all the requisite organization needed for them to operate. Moreover the creation of city infrastructure enables the creation of all the other structures that depend on it. Thus infrastructure both limits (constrains) and delimits (bounds) the city. It ultimately defines how and where resources coming into and contained within the city can be allocated.

Infrastructural systems are essentially the life grid of the city. As Kate Ascher (2005) graphically describes the *Anatomy of New York*, they enable people and freight in the city to move by street, subway, bridge and tunnel and via rail, water, air and markets; power to be distributed as electricity, gas and steam; communication systems to enable telephone, mail and electronic modes; and the flow of water, sewer and garbage. We suspect that if we attempt to go off the grid we will remove ourselves from coordinated structures and potentially suboptimize performance. Select groups are experimenting with going off the grid in numbers of ways, including self-sufficient energy and food production (McKibben, 2007; Monbiot & Prescott, 2007; Smith & MacKinnon, 2007).

The same could be said for Elliott Jaques' view of work systems (Dutrisac, Fowke, Koplowitz & Shepard, nd; Shepard, 2007b). When we have inappropriate role relationships (embedded in organization structures, organization processes and the individual values and capabilities), human systems are misconstrued (misconstructed) and performance is suboptimal.

Thus the alignment of infrastructure and human organizational structure optimizes intelligence. The exploration of Graves' research through Spiral Dynamics (Beck & Cowan, 1996) has identified eight natural structures of human organizing systems that illustrate the correlation of human structures to human values. These structures are simply illustrated in Figure 7.2. The basic description of those structures is almost a leaf out of Buckminster Fuller's exploration of the natural system of crystals or Bennett's systematics as an exploration of increasing complexity in form. The structures can be described as follows:

Level 1   Hearth circle
Level 2   Tribal gathering circle

Level 3   Power-based hierarchy

Level 4   Authority-based hierarchy

Level 5   Strategic hierarchical system

Level 6   Social network

Level 7   Self-organizing system

Level 8   Global noetic field

TAKING RESPONSIBILITY FOR RENEWING RESOURCES

One of the most fascinating structural relationships that the bees have developed in their world is with the well-being of their energy source. Not only are flowers in the fields, farms and orchards their source of green energy, but their activity with the flowers ensures a never-ending supply of energy. By pollinating the flowers, they renew the source of life that assures them an annual supply of energy.

**Figure 7.2. Archetypal genealogy of human organizing structures.
Source: Adapted from Beck and Cowan, 1996.**

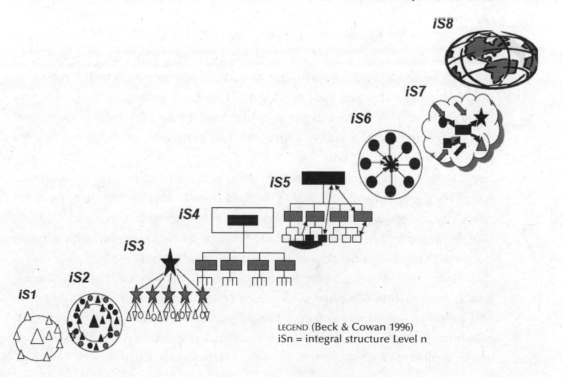

LEGEND (Beck & Cowan 1996)
iSn = integral structure Level n

An Integral City must take a similar view of its relationship with its ecoregion. Instead of taking its ecoregion for granted, or mining its resources, or simply valuing it for its landscape, or having a merely passive relationship with it, the city should be vitally concerned with the health and well-being of its watershed, its food farms and, potentially, its green energy source.

Earlier in human history, the ecoregion of any settlement was clearly its source of food, building materials and fuel. But as human populations increased in settlement size, the ecoregion was generally decimated farther and farther from the urban center.

Only experiments like Gaviotas have attempted to actually create a generative source of settlement renewables. What would happen if every city took on a stewardship role for its ecoregion? What would happen if the interdependent relationship of city and country were enshrined in responsibility and accountability agreements?

Our economies currently operate as if city and country are independent of each other. Often much of the produce from any given region is grown for export, rather than contracted to supply the city's needs. Because of this, the ecoregion's vitality is invisible to most people in the city, and they are unaware of the state of its well-being.

Likewise, ecoregions may use their land-based resources to the economic benefit of the owners, but their banking and financial transactions inevitably flow through the city. With the advent of online banking and financial transactions, this is becoming more widely dispersed, but generally the infrastructure for finance is located in the city.

Dependence on carbon-based fuel has also made cities appear independent of their ecoregions. This fuel is sourced from generally remote regions for every city and enables modern city life as we know it on such a fundamental basis that we have only recently started to visualize its replacement. Cities are as dependent on carbon-based fuel as any addict is on heroin.

Innovative developments in renewable energy sources offer a new alternative. A combination of natural sources like solar power, wind power, tidal power and green (ethanol) power create the possibility that each ecoregion has the potential to produce energy that can be continuously renewed. Such possibilities create a picture that is very similar to the relationship that the bees have with their natural energy source. What if every Integral City took responsibility for the green fields of its ecoregion as stewards of its own source for food and fuel (and became experts in the use of solar power, wind power and tidal power)?

Diversity generators and advocates of local eating, like Bill McKibben, Alisa Smith and James MacKinnon, are proponents of such a relationship. Likewise, Canadian entrepreneur Ken Field has invested in the technology that could give every city fields of renewable green fuel to power its energy needs –for both food and fuel. George Monbiot proposes harnessing a whole suite of energy sources from local resources: wind, sun, water, fossil fuel, nuclear power.

Such examples of city–country relationships invoke high appreciation for our invertebrate cousins, the bees, and remind us that biomimicry (Benyus, 1997) not only has advantages for the manufacture of goods, but can offer inspiration for the functioning of whole systems like the Integral City. Janine Benyus has spent a decade demonstrating that echoing the functions of natural systems can give us profound insights into producing fiber stronger than steel (spiders' webs), healing from natural pharmacopeia, creating closed-loop commerce, and achieving solar alchemy from photosynthesis. McKibben, Smith and MacKinnon even propose that these practices build democracy through the mesh of relationships that are developed from purchasing direct from producers rather than through supermarket distributors.

WHOLES, HEAPS AND FITNESS LANDSCAPES: INTENTIONAL DESIGN VERSUS UNINTENDED CONSEQUENCES

As we have proposed frequently throughout the book, we see the city as a whole. Our use of quadrants and the integral map are clearly not intended to convey that the map is the territory. Nevertheless, the quadrants used as mindful lenses can help us differentiate perspectives that remind us about different views. They can also help us appreciate the fractal and holonic existences of human systems and subsystems.

As in the cultural quadrant, it is tempting to see the social quadrant as simply representing a set of norms or averages, without recognizing the very real differences embedded in the biological realities of the social holon. If we make the mistake of zeroing in on the norms, we will in fact be trying to understand a "heap" of matter.

Instead, if we can keep in mind the dynamic qualities of the individual people in the social quadrant, we can appreciate that the social holon is largely characterized by the dynamics of its demographics. The research of Dychtwald (Dychtwald & Flower, 1989) and Foote (1999) on the boomer generation gave us fair warning that "demographics could become our destiny." The dynamics of the social holon are affected by specific biological typologies and their relative weightings, e.g., age, gender, race, height, weight.

Our demographics affect how we build our cities, with whom and for whom. They not only determine the type and flow of resources through the city, but they also determine to a large measure who will be making the decisions for everyone in the city. Thus the individuals who become leaders in groups will be determined by their biology and intentions, in the context of their culture and social demographics. If we think back to the relationship of conformity enforcers and diversity generators amongst our friends, the bees, it becomes apparent that the larger any set of demographics are within a social holon, the stronger will be their impact on the whole society and the more likely they will be setting the direction for enforcing conformity.

It is possible that the city has evolved to a time when this domination by the post-war baby boomers has lost one of its key feedback mechanisms that provide corrections to excesses. When we can import food, virtually from around the world, we extend the reach and influence of dominant demographic cohorts and strengthen them in the process.

The edges of the system will be defined by those who do not conform to the norm — the diversity generators. In the past the self-correcting aspect of natural systems would mean that the diversity generators in the city would offer new system solutions when the conformity enforcers had naturally exhausted their contributions and cycle. However, with the widened sphere of outsourcing, the cycle of the conformity enforcers may be so prolonged that we do not change our behaviors until it is too late. Diamond, Homer-Dixon and Wright refer to these as points of no return. Ironically they tend to occur just past the peak point of the conformity enforcers' influence. Thus societies cut down the last tree, pour out the last water and consume the last seed grain without realizing that they have passed this tipping point. Unintended consequences have resulted from under-intended design.

Complexity science construes the adaptation of living systems to their environments as "fitness landscapes." It would appear that, at this stage of evolution, virtually no city is well fitted to its landscape. This is largely because we have failed to view cities within a whole-systems perspective, including the context of its environmental fitness landscape. In order for us to attain a balance between city and environment — to make city life sustainable — we need to find a way to live that fits our city landscapes.

MANIFESTING RELATIONSHIPS: WHAT MATTERS FOR HUMANS AND ARTEFACTS?

The social quadrant embraces people and their built artefacts and ostensibly embraces structures, systems and infrastructures. It is the concretization and manifestation of relationships. So in order to bring new order to the social structures of the city, we have to appreciate how those relationships currently exist and what they are likely to change into. This will give us the direction of complexity that the city needs to structure itself towards — to create a fitness landscape for the individuals and organizations who are its citizens.

What is important to individuals in the city is vital to its success: survival, bonding, personal power, order, productivity, sharing, give-and-take, world awareness. Whether you are researching sustainability or happiness, these general values recur in people's lists of desirable characteristics of cities (Dale, Hamilton et al., 2007; Dale, Waldron et al., 2007; Hamilton, 2007b; Wills et al., 2007a, 2007b).

While it would seem that people are more in need of the appropriate fitness landscape to optimize their human priorities, in fact such a landscape is also necessary for the creation, maintenance and intentional destruction of the built landscape of artefacts.

We know now that our current built landscape is likely contributing to global warming; so it is changing the larger landscape, and we must accept responsibility for it (Monbiot & Prescott, 2007). Can we look at taking on this responsibility by redefining structure? If so, we will have to start by redefining relationships so we can approach this monumental task in a new way. In fact, we could start with redefining our relationships with the Earth itself. Effectively this means that we must transcend and include our current behaviors and the structures that emanate from them. This would start with recalibrating our underlying values of

INFLUENCING THE EFFLUENCE OF AFFLUENCE
(Owen, 2005, adapted with permission)

Mike Saley, in charge of waste diversion at the City of Calgary, recognized that the problem of waste management is not just a technical problem with a technical solution, but requires a cultural and societal solution. He responded to the City's (third person) growing waste problem, by asking what We (second person) were doing about the waste problem? He saw that, in an affluent culture and an economy based on convenience, disposability, acquisitiveness and novelty, effluence had become so insidious that an effective solution required the influence of "self-stewardship," mobilizing personal responsibility, to aid waste-managers' approaches to waste reduction.

Earth scientist, Cam Owen, proposes the quadrants framework to map out the potential factors contributing to wasteful consumption. The subjective, intersubjective, objective and interobjective realms can be considered. "Our" wasteful consumption may be because of:

- (UL) lack of awareness, lack of concern (no feeling of self-implication) or a lack of intentionality or self-empowerment (i.e., belief that I can't really make a difference)

- (UR) lack of strength or physical ability to access recycling bins

- (LL) stigmas against being "green," societal norms, e.g., "keeping up with the Joneses" or subscribing to the cultural myth that "waste is unfortunate but necessary for a healthy economy"

- (LR) lack of programs, facilities or infrastructure or inadequate laws and regulations restricting waste or encouraging reduction .

Identifying causes with the quadrant framework helps form an Integral strategy using a four-pronged approach, working in both the traditional, technical/objective (right-hand) realms and inspiring transformative subjective (left-hand) realms.

Waste Watchers, a program sponsored by the City of Calgary, revealed that conscientious families could divert from 85 to 97 percent of their waste using existing programs and facilities. Other Integral options that have been discussed include:

- "Objective/Interobjective" (Right-hand) strategies such as:
  - Improve accessibility to recycling containers (e.g., lighter lids for women and children)
  - Implementing user fees, in the form of some kind of pay-per-bag system, to penalize excessive waste (and conversely give incentives to throw out less)
  - Expanding recycling programs, especially geared towards diverting organic waste, which makes up the largest component of the waste stream (i.e., develop intensive composting system)

- "Subjective/Intersubjective" (Left-hand) strategies such as:
  - Establishing a multi-stakeholder "waste-diversion forum" to open a regular channel of com-

munication between waste services, industry, citizens, academia, government
- Establishing an education center at the landfill to accommodate awareness-building field trips
- Building on education programs in elementary and junior-high settings to promote a holistic understanding of waste (programs already exist in Grade 4 and 7)
- Linkage with post-secondary education (e.g., my own attempt at lobbying for mandatory inclusion of a course that takes an integral approach considering human ecology/sustainability in the Mount Royal College curriculum

- Open channels of communication between the municipal and other levels of government (e.g., especially since packaging regulations are under federal jurisdiction) and open communication with NGO's such as Sustainable Calgary
- Work with organizations such as the Canadian Council of Municipalities, sharing information
- Supporting additional public outreach initiatives to educate the public and engage citizenry in active dialogue about waste diversion and sustainable consumption
- Continuing to implement ideals of "Community-based Social Marketing" and promoting the ideals of "Self-stewardship" and

unrestrained expansion, our competitive but destructive relationships and our assumption of rights without responsibilities in the world. We must shift into a systemic mindset where rights, responsibilities and structures become aligned.

Even if we choose to change our structures first, we will necessarily change relationships of people interacting in those structures. We know this just by our experience in defining the size and accessibility of public space and facilities of everything from transportation to waiting rooms at bus terminals.

STRUCTURES HOLD THE MEMORY OF PATTERNS AND PROCESSES

As noted above, change in biophysical people and structures occurs more slowly than in the intentional realities of the mind, emotions and spirit. As we manifest bodily and structurally, we essentially freeze the memory of the patterns and thought processes that produced the structures. Structures become a visible history of human intentions, choices and relationships.

Structures and infrastructures reflect our social roles. They display the space we create for human performance. They allocate resources for people to daily live, relate, play, organize, work, care and create systems. And within each of the structures, they reveal how we organize ourselves to produce outcomes. By studying structures, we can determine organizational and city priorities that relate to complexity and developmental levels. (For example Level 4 priorities are purpose and principles, Level 5 is profit, Level 6 is people, Level 7 is planet). We can also determine work roles (where and how does who lead whom), work production (where and how the work is done), social relationships (pecking orders), governance systems (who rules whom), infrastructure and industrial systems, and information systems.

We can look inside each of these systems for the organizational subsystems detailed above in Figure 7.1 and discover the resource allocation that creates and maintains the flow of energy, matter and information through them. From a cross-sectional view, our structural maps could reveal the allocation of resources based on human values (what is important to maintain at capacities of complexity from Levels 1 to 8: survival, bonding, order, production, caring, sustainability, global well-being).

We could also map the roles that people perform to support those structures in terms of time span to deliver those roles. By recognizing the time factor of role contribution, we can recognize both the complexity of work and the quantity of investment required to maintain human structures. We can also see through this analysis that structure supports intentions and therefore strategy. The research of Elliott Jaques (Dutrisac et al., nd; Shepard, 2007) reveals that modern work roles fall into eight strata, each representing discretionary time spans for work decisions that are effectively doubled at every stratum. (Note that these strata are not exactly the same calibrations as those used in Spiral Dynamics, but they also convey increasing levels of complexity that transcend and include strata.) The time spans range from up to 3 months (on the shop floor) to longer than 50 years (in the international CEO office). Thus it would be possible to map not only the discretionary time spans affected by organizations but also the capacities of the workforce in the city measured in those terms. Theoretically this could be a key contributor to calculating the necessary investment in human systems throughout an entire life from birth, through the education system, work life to death. Such a calculation would come close to measuring the energy requirements to support a single life and a sustainable ecology of lives and, by aggregating the calculations, would give us the equivalent of our 40 pounds of honey. No doubt the actuarial science could be applied to this admittedly formidable but necessary calculation.

Thomas Homer-Dixon (2006) takes a similar approach to understanding the relationship between energy and structure when he calculates the amount of energy it took to build the Roman Coliseum:

> Erecting the Coliseum required more than 44 billion kilocalories of energy. Over 34 billion of these kilocalories went to feed the 1,806 oxen engaged mainly in transporting materials. More than 10 billion kilocalories powered the skilled and unskilled human laborers, which translates into 2,135 laborers working 220 days a year for five years. (p. 48)

Homer-Dixon proceeds to translate this calculation into the amount of land required to produce the grain that delivered the required calories to produce the built outcome:

> To build the Coliseum the Romans had to dedicate, every year for five years, at least 19.8 square kilometers to grow wheat and 35.3 square kilometers to grow alfalfa. That's a total equivalent of 55 square kilometers of land — or almost the area of the island of Manhattan. (p. 53)

So structures and infrastructures hold the memory of shared intentions. They are the residual patterns and processes captured in matter that first started in the minds of individuals and the shared beliefs and worldviews of the culture that built them.

EVOLVING STRUCTURES AND INFRASTRUCTURES FOR HEALTHY EDUCATION, HEALTHCARE, WORKPLACE FACILITIES

City structures and organizational structures became possible when the fourth level of human thinking had emerged the value of order (see Map 2). Without recognizing the importance of order, it is virtually impossible to create a city where the bio-psycho-cultural-social realities of the human condition can flourish. If a city is built on the predecessor Level 3 value of "power," it deteriorates to a feudal empire or military encampment without the necessary organization that enables sustainability over decades and generations.

Even as I write this, the recognition of the importance of infrastructure is being re-evaluated on world stock markets. According to CIBC Wood Gundy (Tal,

2007), close to 60 percent of the infrastructure in Canada is 50 to 150 years old, with more than half these systems having attained 80 percent of their service life. This is typical of North America's deteriorating infrastructure. The economist behind this article suggests that so great is the demand for infrastructure world-wide — but especially in China and India — that infrastructure stocks are returning 60 percent returns on investment in the last two years.

Designing appropriate structures and infrastructures for the city's vital secondary systems like education, healthcare and workplace facilities are also crucial at this time. However, in order to ensure optimum success for these systems, the city needs to do a much better job than it has done in aligning these structures with the city's vision and purpose. Without a vision the people perish — and so do the structures that should support them in the fullness of their humanity. If the infrastructures of the city only become possible with the advent of the Level 4 value of order, then the optimization of education, healthcare and workplace structures arises out of the values of productivity (level 5), caring (Level 6) and sustainability (Level 7). In reverse order, these values subsume and contain each other (sustainability subsumes caring which subsumes productivity which subsumes order).

The challenge of these higher-order structures is that they are successively more complex and more nonlinear. With the advent of new global digital technologies and global transportation options, the structures must progressively contain self-organization as well as delegated organization. Each one of these secondary systems requires design from levels of complexity that reflect over 50 years' thinking (Stratum 8 in Jaques' system). This level of complexity demands that these secondary systems be designed in conjunction with one another and not as silos separated by structures, cultures, demographics and intentions. Only by addressing the structural design needs of these systems, will we create the conditions to release the optimized intelligences of the city.

The city's greatest dilemma is that traditional forms of governance have practically guaranteed that the requisite levels of structure are not likely to be created, because the decision-makers are not sufficiently complex thinkers to create them. The decision-makers — politicians and civil servants — typically come from levels selected by the dominant conformity enforcer voters. The design of our voting systems practically guarantees that such voters are not likely to select representatives with thinking that is sufficiently complex for today's life conditions. What's more, the candidates for political office seek to please the center of gravity of the electorate, so by definition, the voters will vote for the politician who appeals to their comfort zone.

The civil servants come from ranks where performance on the job is rewarded by those who maintain the traditional order. So by definition, civil servants will serve the traditional order and tend to resist introducing more complex thinking into a system that will punish them and not reward them.

The very pressures of increased populations and thus complexity, mixed with the privileges of democracy, have evolved a panoply of new options for the structuring and operation of secondary systems in the last two decades. Into the traditional hierarchies of order, productivity and caring have been introduced the wildcards of self-organizing options. Private delivery systems are being offered side by side with public educational and healthcare institutions. Public systems are offering vouchers to parents to utilize private educational systems in competition with public systems. Private-public partnerships are producing healthcare facilities with better outcomes than either stakeholder group can produce on its own.

Interestingly, as these new options are being designed and introduced, high levels of accountability from national and international standards like International Standards Organization and Requisite Organization are creating bridges that break down silos, stovepipes and solitudes through required communications and public reporting.

The purpose of education, healthcare and workplace systems is primarily anchored in the well-being of individuals at this time. There is little or no recognition given to the importance of a collective vision. Little attention is paid to the higher value of creating a collective good for the city as a whole. Thus great city-wide effectivenesses, efficiencies, diversities and systemic benefits are not accrued for the benefit of all. Instead they accrue at the individual level without the contexting ethic of collective well-being.

For the ultimate health of the city, healthcare systems need to address collective health as well as individual health. If this were truly addressed systemically, health would embrace all four quadrants, all eight levels and health care from all the ethnic cultures that have developed multiple modes of healthcare delivery. We need integrated health care from Chinese acupuncture, Japanese shiatsu, Indian ayervedic, Swiss-German electric feedback, homeopathy, indigenous herbal and floral remedies, allopathic medicine, chiropractic, therapeutic touch and many more. It would also emphasize prevention over remedy, self- and collective responsibility instead of institutionalized treatment, research and lifelong learning.

In a similar manner, education in the city should be for optimizing collective as well as individual knowledge, skills and abilities. It would focus on lifelong learning and capacity development. It should teach people how to think and learn, not just what to think and learn. It should encourage individuals to develop competency not only for individual performance, but for team, management and leadership. It should help people discover personal purpose and enable them to utilize their natural intelligence for creativity and innovation for the five bottom lines of purpose, principles, profit, people and planet (Beck, 2004).

The education system should discover and implement the structures for educators to create the conditions for all citizens to be lifelong learners. The education system needs to integrate education across the span of the human levels of thinking complexity in all four quadrants and eight levels (and whatever evolves beyond that). The education system needs to understand the intentions of city leaders and create the conditions for new leaders to think ever-more deeply and creatively not just on their own but together in dialogue and consortia. The education system needs to be reframed to embrace not just institutional delivery but on-the-job delivery in all the other sectors of workplace, health and governance systems.

People in workplace systems should be working in conjunction with people in city governance, health systems and education systems to clearly understand how the systems contribute to the well-being of the city. Workplace opportunities, analyses and structures need to integrate the dynamics of the marketplace so that they can convey those benefits to other sectors. At the same time, workplace systems need to integrate the benefits of the public and not-for-profit sector into the private sector. They need to demonstrate the benefits of competitive approaches and structures to designing and implementing strategies, while at the same time preventing competitive approaches from overpowering and/or disempowering vulnerable and valuable elements of society.

Workplace structures, especially in profit and civil society sectors, have special roles to play with the civil service, education and healthcare sectors. They need to learn from and learn with the other sectors how to optimize performance in the city, without putting so much emphasis on profit that the well-being of individuals or the whole is compromised.

MESHWORKS, SELF-ORGANIZING SYSTEMS AND HIERARCHIES OF COMPLEXITY

"Meshworks," a term derived from brain science, integrate hierarchies and self-organizing webs of relationships. Meshworking structures in the city coordinate different capacities, functions and locations so that alignment and coherence result in an integrated operating strategy and/or emergency response. Meshworks unite data and people for effective action and outcomes. We discuss the act of creating meshworks in more detail in chapter 10.

What is important to know here is that a meshwork combines the self-organizing results of complex-adaptive human systems with the replicable backbone of hierarchical organization; it seems to capture the best of both operating systems. The practice of meshworking can originate from the bottom or the top of a system. It simultaneously recognizes boundaries that contain systems and embraces the interconnection of all systems within even larger systems. Meshworking essentially revalues and recalibrates hierarchies, so they can support and leverage self-organizing processes.

The building of bridges, connections, collaborations and links between hierarchies and across self-organizing systems means that a meshwork is highly relationship based. Governance systems make visible the relationship amongst the strata of the hierarchies and the self-organizing systems flowing amongst them.

DESIGNING APPROPRIATE GOVERNANCE SYSTEMS

Structural design in the city is ultimately about governance systems that serve the values center. For the most part, the world is in great need of new governance systems that enable the necessary hierarchies to provide accountabilities and smooth flows of energy, information and matter to serve values centers. Cities are required to deliver the largest quantity and greatest quality of resources to most citizens of any system yet created by humans. But at the same time, cities are

Figure 7.3. Summary of city structures: Mega-city (10–20 million).

STRATUM TIME SPAN	KEY VALUE	CITY HALL	HEALTH	EDUCATION	WORKPLACE
8. 50+ yr	Planet: Sustainable Gaia	Superordinate CEO/ Mayor	Superordinate CEO	Superordinate CEO/Chair	Superordinate CEO/Chair
7. 20-50 yr	Planet: Sustainable Local	Sustainability COO/Councilor	Sustainability COO	Sustainability COO/Trustee	Sustainability COO
6. 10-20 yr	People	Group VP – Infrastructure Optimization	Group VP – Wellness Optimization	Group VP – Demographic Design	Group VP - OD
5. 5-10 yr	Profit	Financial Director	Multi-Modal Delivery Director	Multi-Modal Delivery Director	CIO, CFO
4 . 2-5 yr	Purpose	Manager	Facility Manager	School Administrator	Branch Manager
3. 1-2 yr	Principles	Dept. Head	Dept. Head	Dept. Head	Dept. Head
2. 3-12 mo	Performance	Supervisor	Supervisor	Supervisor	Supervisor
1. ≤ 3mo	Persons	Lead hand	Frontline Employee	Teacher	Frontline Employee
Users	Person	Citizen	Patient	Student	Customer

Figure 7.4. Summary of city structures: Mezzo-city (5–10 million).

STRATUM TIME SPAN	KEY VALUE	CITY HALL	HEALTH	EDUCATION	WORKPLACE
7. 20-50 yr	Planet: Sustainable Glocal	Sustainability CEO/Mayor COO/Councilor	Sustainability CEO/COO	Sustainability CEO COO/Trustee	Sustainability CEO/COO
6. 10-20 yr	People	Group VP – Infrastructure Optimization	Group VP – Wellness Optimization	Group VP – Demographic Design	Group VP - OD
5. 5-10 yr	Profit	Financial Director	Multi-Modal Delivery Director	Multi-Modal Delivery Director	CIO, CFO
4 . 2-5 yr	Purpose	Manager	Facility Manager	School Administrator	Branch Manager
3. 1-2 yr	Principles	Dept. Head	Dept. Head	Dept. Head	Dept. Head
2. 3-12 mo	Performance	Supervisor	Supervisor	Supervisor	Supervisor
1. ≤ 3mo	Persons	Lead hand	Frontline Employee	Teacher	Frontline Employee
Users	Person	Citizen	Patient	Student	Customer

Figure 7.5. Summary of city structures: Mille-city (1–5 million).

STRATUM TIME SPAN	KEY VALUE	CITY HALL	HEALTH	EDUCATION	WORKPLACE
6. 10-20 yr	People, Planet: Sustainable	Sustainability CEO/Mayor COO/Councilor	Sustainability CEO/COO	Sustainability CEO COO/Trustee	Sustainability CEO/COO
5. 5-10 yr	Profit	VP – Infrastructure Optimization Financial Director	VP – Wellness Optimization Multi-Modal Delivery Director	VP – Demographic Design Multi-Modal Delivery Director	Exec. VP CIO, CFO
4 . 2-5 yr	Purpose	Manager	Facility Manager	School Administrator	Branch Manager
3. 1-2 yr	Principles	Dept. Head	Dept. Head	Dept. Head	Dept. Head
2. 3-12 mo	Performance	Supervisor	Supervisor	Supervisor	Supervisor
1. ≤ 3mo	Persons	Lead hand	Frontline Employee	Teacher	Frontline Employee
Users	Person	Citizen	Patient	Student	Customer

Figure 7.6. Summary of city structures: Mini-city (.5–1 million).

STRATUM TIME SPAN	KEY VALUE	CITY HALL	HEALTH	EDUCATION	WORKPLACE
6. 10-20 yr	Planet: Sustainable Glocal	Sustainability CEO/Mayor COO/Councilor	Sustainability CEO/COO	Sustainability CEO COO/Trustee	Sustainability CEO/COO
5. 5-10 yr	People, Profit Local	CEO/Mayor COO/Councilor Financial Director	CEO/COO Director	CEO COO/Trustee Director	CEO/COO CFO
4 . 2-5 yr	Purpose	Director Manager	Facility Director Manager	School Director Administrator	Branch Manager
3. 1-2 yr	Principles	Dept. Head	Dept. Head	Dept. Head	Dept. Head
2. 3-12 mo	Performance	Supervisor	Supervisor	Supervisor	Supervisor
1. ≤ 3mo	Persons	Lead hand	Frontline Employee	Teacher	Frontline Employee
Users	Person	Citizen	Patient	Student	Customer

Figure 7.7. Summary of city structures: Micro-city (.1–.5 million).

STRATUM TIME SPAN	KEY VALUE	CITY HALL	HEALTH	EDUCATION	WORKPLACE
4 . 2-5 yr	Profit, People, Purpose	CEO/Mayor COO/Councilor Financial Manager	CEO/COO Manager	CEO COO/Trustee Administrator	CEO Manager
3. 1-2 yr	Principles	Dept. Head	Dept. Head	Dept. Head	Dept. Head
2. 3-12 mo	Performance	Supervisor	Supervisor	Supervisor	Supervisor
1. ≤ 3mo	Persons	Lead hand	Frontline Employee	Teacher	Frontline Employee
Users	Person	Citizen	Patient	Student	Customer

subservient to higher levels of government whose operating systems for the most part are not organized around city values centers and are not sufficiently complex to respond adequately to the world, nation or city needs. These higher levels of government lack the mandate or incentive for city success. This is an impasse that must change despite the fact that higher levels of government control the financial purse strings of cities through taxation.

What we need is a progressive, systemically designed framework for the operation of the city for governments at different stages of development and different states of change. In a world where cities contain microcosms of world consciousnesses with their spectrum of cognitions, emotions and cultures, such governance systems might adapt the global governance design proposed by Steve McIntosh (2007, p. 317) with tricameral representations of legislative, executive and judicial powers. This would enable weightings of individual votes (across all levels of consciousness), neighborhood representation (using performance selection criteria), economic interests (to balance but not hijack other powers) and executive integration (using capacity criteria). Furthermore modeling this integral governance system in the city would grow the muscles to translate it to global contexts.

Such governance systems would make use of meshworking principles to evolve appropriate hierarchical structures and enable self-organizing adaptiveness. Elliott Jaques gave us a hint of what might be workable with his eight-level framework of discretionary time-span and role-span "requisite organization." Ichak Adizes also alerts us to the organizational life cycle conditions that would apply to the developmental age of the city.

What needs to be expanded on is how to apply these structures to the whole city and not just bits and pieces of it. Ideally the application would vary by the scale of the city and be adapted to fit the scale and local conditions. Figures 7.3 through 7.7 show how cities at different scales (from .1 million to 20 million) could be structured so that each of the functions of city hall, health, education and workplaces could be addressed vertically, while aligning the cross-functional capacities horizontally. Based on the concepts of Elliot Jaques' discretionary time-span structures for requisite organization (RO) (Dutrisac et al., nd; Shepard, 2007b), these tables show hypothetically that as the scale of the city increases, the values and capacities of the key stakeholders ought to develop commensurate with the impact of their decisions, measured by time. For example, the decisions of the mayor in the micro-sized city of Figure 7.7 may only have a risk horizon of two to five years, while many of the decisions of the mayor in the mega-sized city in Figure 7.3 could regularly have an impact of 50 years. The longer the time span of discretionary decision sets, the more levels are required to manage the city effectively. (Note that the tables are organized in declining scale from largest to smallest.)

From a meshworking perspective, the time-span strata in each table reveals the hierarchical meshes discussed in chapter 10. These tables demonstrate a logical evolution of governance complexity for the city as a whole. If principles like these were used, then the responsibility of states/provinces and federal governments ought to be to create accountability frameworks and capacity building opportunities and institutions for cities. Then cities could learn from each other and gain the value of mentoring and coaching from a national (and even transnational) governance development system. The roots of this possibility do not seem to exist yet in NGOs like UN-Habitat. Furthermore, even in the private sector, it is estimated that there are less than a handful of organizations that have achieved RO Level 8 capabilities, e.g., Exxon-Mobil, GE, Motorola, Walmart (Shepard, 2007a). Thus we are in the realm of extreme speculation as we observe the possibilities.

CONCLUSION

The structures, infrastructures and systems of the city derive directly from the nature of the human species. We have evolved into a stage of human history that demands we re-appreciate this relationship, for the sake of our very survival.

By remembering that cities are magnets for Earth's resources, we can take the first steps to reversing the threats to the well-being of the Earth into a direction for adding value to life on Earth. Even as our structures, infrastructures and systems have concentrated resources and blocked energy flows, we can use our intelligences to redefine what a healthy dissipative structure might look like at the scale of the city. Some of the questions we might ask ourselves follow.

QUESTIONS

1. How do we build city structures that flex and flow around centers and embrace sustainability locally and globally?

2. How do we address the dilemma of democracy where voters with a lower center of gravity have the power to elect politicians whose center of gravity is not sufficient to the level of complexity needed to create structures that contribute to sustainable life conditions?

3. How do we redefine and realign governments so that cities have the responsibility, accountability and authority to create sustainable governance systems and governments at state/province and federal levels are aligned for sustainable well-being of individuals and collectives for a network of cities?

Three simple rules for applying Integral City principles from this chapter:

1. Manage life-sustaining energy for all.

2. Design from the center, at all scales for all holons.

3. Build structures that integrate self-organizing creativity with hierarchies of order.

8

STORY INTELLIGENCE: FEEDING EACH OTHER IN THE HUMAN HIVE

*In the hive hardly a minute goes by without every bee either begging a
bit of food from others it encounters, or being solicited by them.
Indeed, if one bee is fed a bit of radioactive nectar, the majority of bees in the colony
will carry the tracer before the day is out. In some sense, a colony has a communal stomach.*

— Gould and Gould, 1988, p. 33

People need stories more than food to stay alive.

— Lopez and Pearson, 1990

THE CADENCE OF THE CITY

This chapter explores the relationships of the city in the Lower Left quadrant. We start by considering that the relationships in the city transcend boundaries that both contain and separate: for example, the individual and the group voice; multiple levels of values; and even city cultures and country cultures. When we sense the boundaries of communities and neighborhoods in the city, we are sensing the tone and cadence of the city. The boundaries are the defining edge of containers that give the city its identity and its cultural map. The relationships of the city's cultures can be heard and felt; they are the observable change states of the city.

The well-being of the city can be diagnosed by its tone and cadence. The tone is a felt sense of well-being. It relates to people's distilled assessment of their mastery of life conditions. It can be mapped easily onto the five change

179

states that characterize adaptiveness (and were discussed in more detail in chapter 4). When the city is humming, in stable alpha state, all is right with the world. The weather is sunny, hopes are high, people are optimistic. Life is stable, predictable, and our culture has figured out how to address its major problems.

When the city is tut-tut-ting and uh-ohing, people perceive that something is not quite right. The weather is cloudy, maybe even with showers, people are worried and the world is less predictable today than yesterday. We have a sense of foreboding that more change is coming, and we aren't sure if we can handle it. (This is the characteristic tone of turbulent beta state.)

When the city is complaining, fearful or stunned into inaction, when "Oh, shit, what can we do now?" is a comment on many lips, people know that we don't have the answers for the situation that has occurred. (CNN dutifully reported these conditions in New Orleans, New York and San Francisco after their disasters.) Our sense of improbability and lack of predictability is high. The weather or natural conditions can even be the cause of our angst — it is storms, tornados, earthquakes, floods, fires. We have lost our sense of control, and we don't know how to regain it. (This is the panicked, stunned, depressed, angry tone of trapped gamma state.)

When the city is elated, bursting with joy, celebrating with abandon, people feel like they can see the light or are in the light after a very long dark tunnel. The weather is inevitably clear blue sky, and the ecstatic relief in people's voices, on their faces and in their bodies inspires dancing, singing and wild outbreaks of joy. We feel that we have made a breakthrough, and we know tomorrow will bring better possibilities. This is the condition of the city when peace is declared, when the lights stay on after Year 2000 predictions of blackouts, when the electricity is restored after an ice storm. (This is the elated tone of delta state.)

When the city is humming again, and all is right with the world, we have returned to a new, more complex but stable condition of daily life. The weather is predictably fair, hope has returned, people have renewed optimism. Life is once again stable, predictable, and our culture has confidence that it knows how to address its major problems. (This is the happy tone of new stable alpha state.)

Each of these tones in the city can be related to the cadence in the container of the city itself. And like chiropractors or Feldenkreis workers or even martial artists, we can sense the state of well-being in the container by noticing the change state has not only a tonal quality, but between each change state a shift in cadence. When unpredictability creates instability of the container (when the edges are porous and without strength), the cadence is broken, uncertain and unpredictable. It is the unformed dance of the teenage sock hop. When unpredictability fails to dissipate, but instead intensifies, the instability migrates from the boundaries of the container to the actors and relationships in the container itself. The cadence is adversarial, confrontational and clashing. It is the dance of warriors in battle; jesters on stage; debaters on TV.

When the battle has ceased and before peace has been signed, the cadence in the container shifts from the frenetic, short cycle rhythms of battle to a longer cycle, to a reflective inquiry. This cadence reflects the state of deep "not knowing" but being open to a new answer. This cadence is a critical shift point. It is the dance of the long now (a term coined to describe long-term, slower, better thinking).

When the energy from battles has transformed relationships and inquiry has born fruit, the cadence shifts to one of creativity. A creative rhythm is characterized by the flex and flow of cool jazz, where the performance of individuals intertwines with the team work of the group. The container is full of potential and brimming over with innovative proactivity. This is the street dance of interpretive jazz. Thus the relationships in the city not only reflect its cultural reality, but are inextricably the touchstone of the city's health, wealth and sustainability.

RELATIONSHIPS: THE BONDS OF STRENGTH, RESILIENCE AND TRANSFORMATIVE POTENTIAL

City cultures depend totally on the quality of relationships. The city is like the beehive's giant communication dance floor on which the dancers continuously move, join, partner, group, cluster, vibrate and pattern. To the untrained eye, all is chaos and motion. We cannot see or know the shared understandings of the dancers — how they know when to smile, what it feels like to join hands, why they know where to place their feet. But using integral lenses, we can start to understand the enormous patterns of intelligence that emerge from the self-organizing relationships on the dance floor.

Relationships may be the prime currency of the Integral City. In a living system, they are the bonds that link identities (holons) and information and make exchanges possible. The formation of relationships is central to the emergence of new patterns, new intelligence and new complexity. Through the negotiation of relationships, boundaries are recognized, linked, crossed, embraced, broken, denied and redefined. Relationships arise through transaction, transformation and transmutation.

Through the simplest transactional relationship, an exchange is made, but no party to the transaction is fundamentally changed. This is the relationship of the paper boy delivering papers to your doorstep. Or you buying coffee from the barista. Or city workers picking up your garbage. Transactional relationships tend to be everyday bonds that keep us in the same patterns and cycles that enable predictability and stability. Transactions happen in the panarchic phases of investment (exploitation) and accumulation (conservation).

Through a transformative relationship, the exchange causes one or both parties to recognizably change form. The exchange amongst one or more parties redefines the dance so that another order of pattern emerges (either more or less complex than the one that existed prior to the exchange). This is the relationship of parents and their children as they develop through the stages of their lives together. Or the teacher to the students, transforming learning into knowledge. Or the employer to the factory workers, transforming metal into cars. Or the pastor to the congregation, transforming spirit into spirituality. Transformations happen in the panarchic phases of breakdown (release) or breakout and redistribution (reorganization).

Through a transmutational relationship, both (all) parties are fundamentally recombined into something completely new. The exchange between two or more parties alters the relationship so a completely new pattern emerges. In the repatterning, the relationships that existed before are transcended and included so they may not even be visible or recognizable. These are relationships that are rarely seen in cities on a city scale, because the very nature of cities relies on the predictable transactions that happen on a daily cycle along with the transformational relationships that occur more on the cycle of the seasons or stages of the actors in the relationships. Transmutational relationships can happen when organizations merge and create a new entity with entirely novel ways of operating. An example is the chaordic development of the independent banking system behind the Visa credit card system (Durrance, 1997). When collective beliefs change in the Lower Left quadrant at the transmutational level, new forms of organization and structure are also invented in the Lower Right quadrant. For example, new thinking in the 19th century produced corporations, and in the 21st century, we are seeing the creation of social enterprises.

However, at the city scale, transmutational relationships occur on the cusps of era changes. They create patterns of relationships that never before existed, relationships spawned by innovation, invention and insight. These are the relationships in the family affected by the discovery of electricity that lengthened the day and shortened the sleeping cycle in the home. These are the relationships in the workplace that collapsed time, distance and information because of the inventions by the founders of Bell Telephone, GE, Apple and Microsoft. These are the relationships in the recreational space that gave every householder visions and wings to unknown geographies and cultures revealed by television and the long-distance cheap airline flight. Every one of these transmutations affected not only life in a particular aspect of the city, but the life of the city as a whole.

Our transactional relationships tend to serve our biophysical behavioral needs. Our transformational relationships tend to serve our intentional needs. Our transmutational relationships catalyze shifts in meeting collective needs of the whole system.

Relationships can be scaled along a spectrum: simple (transactional), plural (transformational) and complex (transmutational). These are exponentially different types of relationships that occur simultaneously, each of them pulsing with a different level of energy. Transactional relationships are like two people waltzing — all they sense are each other's souls. Transformational relationships are like a group of people line dancing in synchrony — what most experience is the delight of coordinated performance. Transmutational relationships occur like a network of people coordinating their behaviors at a distance simultaneously for innovative effect — what most experience when they succeed is elated surprise; when they fail, depression and shared gloom. (al Qaeda? Stop smoking campaigns?) When transmutational relationship patterns become repeated often enough, they become institutionalized and translate into the transactions of a new cultural era.

CITY VALUES

Many cities have evolved from settlements created in the agricultural era when the majority of relationships were merely transactional. They were literally more simple relationships, requiring relatively simple governance systems. The values in these places were built on a foundation of survival, with strong family and kinship bonds and powerful individual leaders. They embodied the values of Levels 1, 2 and 3.

As those settlements evolved into towns and eventually cities, the transactional relationships continued and transformational relationships emerged. At this point the cities as relational systems became complicated and needed to transform governance systems beyond transactional capacities. Cities became dependent on the values of authority, standards and the expertise of the trades and the professions (Level 4).

Some cities were created from scratch in response to the transmutational effects of the Industrial Revolution (Washington, DC and English mill towns are examples). Their purpose was originally centralized government or manufacturing. They depended primarily on the Level 4 values for expertise in running governments and factories and training their employees, and they took for granted the values of Levels 1, 2 and 3 that maintained the basic needs of life. However, in their drive for efficiency as well as effectiveness, they evolved the Level 5 values of competitiveness, profit and performance-based results. These new cities (like Kanata, Ontario, in Canada or Boise, Idaho) encouraged relationships where competition could thrive within the city and between cities through long-distance trade.

The cultures of Level 5 cities have strategically positioned business-based relationships inside city hall to govern the relationships outside city hall. Now the over-achievement of Level 5 values requires a renegotiation of the city with the environment from which it is drawing its raw materials and to which it is returning its wastes. The relationship of city to environment has become toxic. The toxic relationship is epitomized by pollution. For a century this has been largely ignored, until the effects have become noticeably measurable in the form of climate change.

The competitive relationship between cities also produced unexpected results. In this relationship model, some cities are losers and some are winners. As capital and machinery replaced human labor, the losing cities lost economic drivers. At first they lost commodity and/or manufacturing drivers (like coal, steel, textiles) — and the jobs that go with them. Now they are losing information-based jobs, as even the professions can be sourced from lowest-cost producers. The loss of jobs shifts the relationships of organizations, employers, workers, families, partners and individuals in the city.

As the first waves of massive displacement occurred, a new set of values emerged to supply social safety nets to the unemployed, the disabled, the skill deficient and the health compromised. Out of this change emerged the values of Level 6 and the institutional relationships of caring and sharing. Progressive city halls added departments to address social needs. Charitable societies transformed into not-for-profit organizations so they could support relationships that were being shattered and torn.

Within some cities, some individuals have values that reflect the reality that relationships have a natural flex and flow. But few city relationships are easily colored by this Level 7 set of values. Long-entrenched relationships in the bureaucracies defend the rule-based values of Level 4. The competitive relationships that tend to show up in elected officials promote the strategic values of Level 5 and more recently the social justice values of Level 6. As a result, most city cultures have been largely resistant to redefining relationships in support of Level 7 systemic, ecology-based values. The superordinate dilemma of climate change may alter all that. It may be the trigger that causes a transmutational recalibration of relationships in the city and even between cities.

ADAPTIVE RELATIONSHIPS: INNER JUDGES, RESOURCE ALLOCATORS, CONFORMITY ENFORCERS, DIVERSITY GENERATORS, INTRA-GROUP TOURNAMENTS

Remembering our friends the bees, I am reminded about their survival goal to produce 40 pounds of honey for their hive through the relationships they have with one another (and even through the intra-group tournaments, with other hives). What can beehive relationships tell us about human relationships within and between cities? Perhaps the four beehive roles can give us a meta-view of relationships inside the city? Who are our inner judges, resource allocators, conformity enforcers and diversity generators? How might they contribute to adapting our relationships for survival, greater effectiveness and well-being?

As noted in chapter 4, Ichak Adizes (1999) names similar roles: integrator, administrator, producer and entrepreneur. He has studied how the relationship between these functions changes during the natural life cycle of the organization.

Adizes observes that the patterns of the stages of the organizational life cycle are the same fractal patterns of an individual human life cycle. And like individuals, organizations can die at any age or stage of the life cycle — there is no guarantee that it will be completed.

We explored in chapters 6 and 7 how James Grier Miller (1978) sees living system relationships embodied in three major biological system clusters:

1. subsystems that process both matter-energy and information (are these the judges/integrators?)

2. subsystems that process matter-energy (are these the conformity enforcers/ producers?)

3. subsystems that process information (are these the resource allocators/ administrators?)

The fourth beehive role of diversity generation/entrepreneur appears to be a special version of cluster 1 created for the special purpose of triggering adaptation. (Is it possible that, at the time of Miller's research, the technology for noticing and examining adaptive capacity did not exist and so that function was missed?)

The corporate life cycle and structuring expert Ichak Adizes, behavioral scientist/biologist James Grier Miller and biologist/impresario Howard Bloom (the teller of the bee story) all give us some indications of how human relationships adapt to life conditions. If human systems are essentially fractal, we should be able to see the same pattern of relationships at each human scale. (Holling's panarchy model gives us the lenses to see the natural flows of the life condition cycle that provide the triggers for recurring change.)

Figure 8.1. City cultural relationships in each value phase.

STAGE>>	COMPLEXITY LEVEL 4	COMPLEXITY LEVEL 5	COMPLEXITY LEVEL 6	COMPLEXITY LEVEL 7	COMPLEXITY LEVEL 8	COMPLEXITY LEVEL 9?
Driving Value>> Phase\/	Ordering-	Profiting-	Caring-	Systemizing-	Globalizing-	Solarizing-
Entry	Entrepreneur	Entrepreneur	Entrepreneur	Entrepreneur	Entrepreneur	Entrepreneur
Growth	Producer	Producer	Producer	Producer	Producer	Producer
Peak	Integrator	Integrator	Integrator	Integrator	Integrator	Integrator
Exit	Administrator	Administrator	Administrator	Administrator	Administrator	Administrator

At each phase, in each stage of complexity, the relationships between these meta-roles alter and thereby express different qualities in the cultural life of the city. Figure 8.1 suggests that, at each stage of complexity, the overriding value (order, profit, care, systemization, globalization, etc.) brings a new intention to the shared space of relationships. The enterprising diversity generator is the role that kick-starts each level, discovering the new way of adapting that solves the problems at hand. (Holling calls this phase "reorganization.") When that entry phase matures, it becomes the producer's time to generate growth and abundance using the values of that level of complexity. (Holling calls this phase "exploitation.") When growth matures, relationships peak into an integrative stage. (Holling calls this phase "conservation.") Finally when the accumulation phase peaks (Holling calls this phase "release."), the cycle is ready to move and start again at another level of complexity (assuming life conditions support this).

WHO IS AT THE CENTER OF THE UNIVERSE? EKO, ETHNO, EGO, EXCEL, EQUAL, ECO, EVO

We have seen that, because the dominant behaviors of any culture arise in response to life conditions, each level of existence behaves with increasing levels of complexity in order to maximize the organizing principle (or value) of the current life condition. This behavior results in a natural tendency to protect the status quo at its current level of complexity by means of conformity enforcement (of the organizing principle/value).

Thus a tension in favor of the values and behavior that are most coherent with the current life conditions will tend to be maintained. The flip side of this behavior is that the dominant culture will protect itself against diversity generation. When life conditions finally require the solutions that diversity generation can offer, the problems created by the conformity enforcer values will usually have become so acute that the majority are willing to change. It appears that these natural evolutionary cycles are fractal and emerge at all levels of scale: individual, family, organization, society.

When we look at the pairs of values in Graves' developmental cycle, we can see that the relationship between conformity enforcers and diversity generators is continuously cycled from one pole to the next in order to optimize the contributions of each group of people to the survival equation. And as each pole is

Figure 8.2. Worldviews: Who is the center of universe?

LEVEL OF COMPLEXITY	DRIVING VALUE	WHO IS CENTER OF UNIVERSE?
Level 1: Eko	Surviving	Individual
Level 2: Ethno	Relating	Family/tribe/clan
Level 3: Ego	Power	Kingdom
Level 4: Ethno	Authority	Nation
Level 5: Excel	Performance	World Economy
Level 6: Equal	Caring & Sharing	Social Network
Level 7: Eco	Flex & Flow	Natural System
Level 8: Evo	Global	Gaia

rounded and a new cycle begins, we can recognize the driving human values also evolve related worldviews, as set out in Figure 8.2. Essentially the worldviews describe, for any culture, who is at the center of the universe. As a culture's values altitude increases, the universe grows exponentially larger, and the culture becomes more expansive and more inclusive of others. (As noted in earlier chapters, the hyper-individualism observed by McKibben seems to indicate a blockage in the US at the ego values level. Viewed in the context of the city, this is of serious concern to the functioning of democracy, which requires at least an ethnocentric worldview — but works even better at the world, social network and systems level of relating.)

THE BLENDED FAMILY: THE DYNAMICS OF SOCIAL HOLONS

Beneath the grand sweep of cultural groupings exists the self-organizing flex and flow of social holons. As discussed in chapter 3, any group of two people is not a simple holon (a whole made up of many wholes). A cohesive group of two or more people must be considered a special kind of holon — a social holon. The characteristics of a social holon are not merely summative, but are dynamically relational. Each person in the social holon is a complex adaptive system, whose intentional and behavioral capacities demonstrate a "center of gravity" that situates them on the levels of complexity. We know that life conditions will cause any given person to respond somewhere within their capacity range. Depending on their level of mastery, they will be more or less resilient in respect to their center of gravity.

Sports and performing arts provide particularly good examples of this reality. Take the sport of golf, where generally each player plays his/her own game. When my husband plays golf, he intends to play to his handicap, a measure of his center of gravity in the sport. On a good day, he exceeds his intentions and plays better than his handicap. On a day when he is not feeling so well and the weather is rainy, he plays worse than his handicap.

When we look at a social holon, where two or more people share intentions, beliefs, values and worldviews, the performance of the social holon is determined by the individual performances of each member of the social holon. Going back to the golf example, when my husband plays in a simple tournament in a team of four, the foursome's score as a team is dependent on how each player performs. Each player has his own handicap (center of gravity) and plays the game individually. The individuals do not play as a machine made of indivisible parts. They play as a loosely connected, complex adaptive system, responding to the life conditions of the golf course and each other (not to mention all the other golfers on the course at the same time). In simple scoring terms, we can calculate the average handicap for the team by totaling and averaging their individual handicaps. However attractive this seems because of its simplicity, it is not predictive of the team's performance, or any individual's performance, because they are complex adaptive systems.

In ideal circumstances, a team can achieve supernormal performance (i.e., play beyond their handicap centers of gravity as individuals and as the team). The reasons for this result are still subject to research. Players who achieve this kind of outcome report an experience of "being in the zone," of positively influencing one another, of being embraced by a kind of bubble of telepathic communication and intuitive responsiveness. Sheldrake's research in morphic resonance or morphic fields might explain this experience of cultural cohesion. Our colloquial language refers to "being on the same wave length" or even "on the same plane." We may convey more insight than we realize with these phrases, as it appears that cultural cohesion can be measured through metrics tracking energetic noise and resonance. Most team sports report and exhibit similar phenomena.

In fact, on a larger scale, Sheldrake's research suggests that cultures emerge because, when we repeat patterns of behavior and intention often enough, we create energetic memory in the body and in the field (or space) around the body. The repetitions create a kind of energy groove from which we can access and download the collective consciousness (which is what Jung called this phenomenon). Jung called the culturally repeated behaviors stored in this energetic memory bed "archetypes." Archetypes represent the culture's typical ways of behaving and produce the characters named in every culture's traditional stories, such as, the maiden, warrior, king, hero, shaman, crone and fool.

Cultural archetypes also represent the actors and their relationships in every level of complexity. They reflect the worldviews, values and memes in play in any culture at any given level of complexity. Archetypes capture the essence of the roles and relationships at a particular "center of gravity."

However, whether or not you accept the theories of morphic resonance, fields or archetypes, the reality of cultures is that they are made up of social holons where each person's intentions can potentially make a difference. Paradoxically each person's intentions can only make a difference if the strength of the conformity enforcement is lowered sufficiently to enable the difference to be noticed and responded to. In the beehive, we know this means that the performance of the conformity enforcers is no longer reinforced by the resource allocators and the inner judges because they are not delivering survival value to the hive. This causes the conformity enforcers to become de-energized (and measurably depressed), thus allowing the system to notice the energy offered by the diversity generators.

In the Integral City, it will pay us to notice where the energy is — who are acting as conformity enforcers and who are diversity generators. We must notice this in terms of the natural subsystems or neighborhoods in the city, because it will vary by neighborhood. By paying attention to these ebbs and flows, we will know where our leverage points are and what the next natural step will be for development in any given neighborhood. Understanding this can improve actual and perceived cultural sensitivity in the city. For, as we have seen, one group's values, worldviews and wants will differ from another's, depending on the center of gravity of the social holon.

MAPPING INTEGRAL VOICES: CITIZEN, CITY MANAGER, CIVIL SOCIETY, CITY DEVELOPER

We have seen how the cultural ecology of the city ebbs and flows because the stream of individual values and collective priorities adapt to the life conditions embracing and embedded in the city. This ebb and flow can be objectively measured (see chapter 11), but it is also subjectively and intersubjectively experienced.

Subjective and intersubjective experience represents the interior realities of individuals and groups of people. Such experiences are the integral complements of peoples' objective and interobjective exterior realities. Taken together, all four realities become the basis for perspectives expressed through all languages by the use of pronouns indicating who is speaking their view: I, We/You, He/She/It, They/Its. These four perspectives are the voices of the four quadrants of the integral model of the city. The voices from each quadrant contribute to the cultural ecology of the city. Any of the voices could be at any of the levels of complexity — thus we essentially have a four-quadrant, eight-level choir of city voices. The voice of the speaker reveals their values, priorities and therefore the center of gravity of their personal capacity.

In exploring this ecology of voices, I want to hone in on four particular voices: those of the citizen, city manager, civil society and city developer. Each contributes to the intersubjective discourse of the city, while at the same time their formal functions might take them into other quadrants of the city.

When cities are smaller, these four separate voices can be heard without difficulty. But now with the population of cities spanning collectives from 100,000 to 20,000,000, the voices of individual citizens are becoming almost impossible to hear. We live in cities that are akin to Dr. Seuss's *Horton Hears a Who* — except that we rarely ask everyone to be quiet so specific voices can be heard.

Voices of the Citizen

The voice of the citizen expresses the center of gravity of the city values. It is the booming background bass that is ever-present; as independent of city managers, civil society and city developers as it is interdependent with them. The voices of citizens in democratic countries have the power to elect and criticize the other voices in the city. It is their individual power as intentional consumers used collectively and simultaneously that gives them ultimate power. When they mark their choices on a ballot card, they exercise the power of engagement and intention. The citizen voice is the very lifeblood of cultural existence in the city. It is the voice of the city spirit.

The fact that the content and intent embedded in citizen voices are counter-balanced by citizen listening capacities means that the multi-way exchange of voices requires special attention. Crafting messages that can be heard across the range of complexities is a job for the keeper of the modern-day tower of Babel. At this stage of human evolution, one message in the city is never sufficient — in most cases a minimum of four messages need to be delivered to be heard for centers of gravity that span from Level 3 to Level 6. With the maturing of the baby boomers, a growing volume of Level 7 voices can be heard, and messages need to be crafted for them too.

One of the major dilemmas of the modern city is that leadership values are frequently not at a more complex level than many citizens. When not everyone votes, the center of gravity of whoever does vote puts into office officials who may not have the capacity to even hear what leading advisors have to say, let alone to understand what issues require attention. This single dilemma may become the deciding factor in changing the governance systems of cities.

The quality of this voice varies from a rich deep bass, to a high-pitched treble. At its best it is a heavenly choir; at its worst it is a dissonant cacophony.

Voices of City Managers

The voice of the city manager (at city hall, educational institutions, healthcare agencies and other sub-holons of the city) is the needed voice of city expertise. It is the special guide that oversees and manages the demographic needs of the city. It programs the infrastructure and is the counterweight to the Tower of Babel of the voices of the citizens. It is the voice of the city brain.

The voice of the city manager includes the voices of the paid staff in city hall, school board office, healthcare facilities, justice institutions and community services. And it also includes the elected officials of mayor, council, school trustee, health board, provincial/state representatives, and federal representatives.

City managers in the developed world on the whole have gotten a bum rap. Many of their functions derive from the values of authority and order — neither of which has been highly valued in the last 40 years. The for-profit business sector in particular has been highly critical of the constraints of city managers, and they have been stereotyped as backward, resistant to change and deeply entrenched in their positions of power. Despite all that, more and more city managers have become highly skilled "meshworkers" able to coordinate the intentions, behaviors, culture and social systems of all the stakeholders of the city with skills learned both on the job and through formal study.

With more frequency, city managers are taking the lead on nationally and globally important issues, working as a cohort of influential leaders, not just in their individual cities. The US Mayors, led by the Mayor of Seattle, took the initiative on endorsing the Kyoto accords. The US President's ambassador for homelessness has invoked the power of the mayor to lead initiatives that engage the whole city in addressing the multiple roots of the issue and creating palpable change within a ten-year time span.

Without effective city managers, the city would collapse into chaos. The city managers are like the body's organs (which the Chinese refer to as "officials") — they perform vital management of energy flows through the city and enable the functions of daily life in the city to be taken for granted. If we have any doubt about the important role that city managers play, we need look no further than the recent occasions when that order has been disrupted through man-made and natural disaster: the electrical blackout in the Eastern US and Canada in the summer of 1998; the earthquakes in Osaka, Los Angeles and Mexico City in the 1990s; hurricane Katrina in New Orleans in 2005; and the World Trade Center destruction in 2001. In every case we can look to the disruption of city management to see how much we depend on the order they coordinate every day.

The public voice of the city manager is most often recognized as the elected official. But the working voice of the city manager is the everyday hum of the city water, waste management and transportation systems running. The quality of this voice is still frequently male. These are the mezzo-sopranos.

Voices of Civil Society

The civil society has become a special cultural voice of the city. Civil society has come to represent the vast army of not-for-profit organizations set up to pay special attention to the caring and sharing work in the city. They are the voice of the city's heart. In the 19th century, these voices were supported by the great industrial philanthropists and faith-based institutions, like the Salvation Army, who attended to the city's under-privileged. In the 20th century, these voices have become institutionalized into non-government organizations (NGOs) who have taken on the principal charge of attending to the social needs of the city. These needs can include everything from meals-on-wheels for shut-ins and the elderly, advocates for women and children, food banks for economically troubled families or translation services for new immigrants.

The voices of civil society have generally been those speaking on behalf of the underprivileged, the marginalized and the disabled. But increasingly, these voices are being supplemented by voices from the arts community, charitable giving (like community foundations) and special-interest service groups (like Rotary, the United Way, Institutes for the Blind, Veterans' Societies). Increasingly civil society is becoming proactive, not just reactive. Paul Hawken (2007) has noticed that this change has shifted the power of collective intention into a new force to be reckoned with, turning the life of the city on its ear. Its roots are in indigenous cultures resistance to globalization, social justice and the environmental movements. He says the new movement "is dispersed, inchoate and fiercely independent. There is no manifesto or doctrine, no authority to check with." It has the power to "bring down governments, companies and leaders through witnessing, informing and massing."

The dynamic quality of this new voice of civil society is changing how the city knows itself and why the city values its cultures. The quality of this voice has often been a massed, mixed community choir. They often sing alto but can magically produce four-part harmony.

Voices of City Developers

The plural voices of the city developers can be heard from the leading edge and bleeding edge of city emergence. Traditionally these have been the voices of the people who conceive of, invest in and build the infrastructure of the city. But more recently city developers also include those who recognize that the invisible cultural life of the city calls for development initiatives as well. Theirs are the voices of the city body/mind.

City developers are characteristically thinking of the city's future. While the voice of citizens and city managers are usually preoccupied with the affairs of the present and the voices of civil society value things of the past, the voices of city developers speak in the future tense. Thus true city developers are diversity generators, opening up new territory, new options and new facilities. Their voices are often disparaged as privileged. Just as civil society voices look to redress injustice, indifference and indecision, the voices of city developers speak of vision, engagement and promise. They convey assurance, optimism and fulfillment. These voices are often solitary and still largely male. They are the tenors.

REPORTING THE VOICES: THE ROLE OF THE MEDIA IN THE CITY

In a species of storytellers, it seems inevitable that we would invent a way of formalizing our storytelling. There is not a city in the world that does not have media to expedite the storytelling. In the free world, the media enjoys a special privilege in the governance system, in that it is allowed (and even encouraged) to criticize those in power, their policies and their privileges. Even in the unfree world, where the power of the press is commanded by the state, the state borrows the aura of respectability from the free world press to pretend that the media role is functioning in their city or state.

The role and potential of the media is ultimately limited by the capacities of its publishers (who are the resource allocators), its editors (who are its inner judges) and its reporters (who are its conformity enforcers and diversity generators). In the living body of the city, media contribute to the flow of information through the city system. Like bees pollinating a flower patch, they mediate information exchange by subjectively choosing what to focus on, gathering it, concentrating it (through mindful prioritizing, recording, interpreting and editing), sharing it through storytelling and monitoring its feedback loops.

Media that expedite, enable and interpret first-, second- and third-person voices have a powerful influence on the functioning of the city because they create and fan the flames of what they select as important to report. Thus media act as reflectors and amplifiers of information and have enormous ethical imperatives to do that responsibly. In effect, the values embedded in media practitioners become the values reflected as the city's values. Thus the media contribute to the quality of life in the city because they become the principal organs that convey the voices of the city.

Modern media have divided the market into international, national and local news. These three scales of human engagement reflect culture at different levels of engagement with distinctly different belief systems, selecting what is reported, how it is interpreted and where it is distributed. In the free world, that means that a reader/watcher/listener can choose to have their views fashioned by a media of their choice, specializing in a point of view that the information consumer accepts (and/or supports). That acceptance may be passive or active. In the passive mode, the consumer is exposed to the information without conscious choice, e.g., listening to a radio station that is publicly aired in a mall. In the active mode, the consumer is purposive in selecting the media and/or consuming the information.

Marshal McLuhan's famous koan that "the medium is the message" captures the essence of the power of the media through the lens of value attraction. With an editor who has levels of complexity equal to or exceeding the capacity of the city, the media offers the city a level of intelligence that not only honestly reflects the city's voices, but inquires into what really matters around here in a city of this scale. For instance, in Vancouver, British Columbia (with a metro population of 2 million), Patricia Graham, editor of the *Vancouver Sun* makes continuous choices that design a newspaper using the wisdom of complexity lenses and instant access to world affairs, while delivering a paper that can be appreciated by a readership with values that span the bonds of family, energy of sports and arts, standards of governance and authority, excellence of enterprise, richness of social networks and flex-flow of international ecologies.

In a smaller city, like Abbotsford, BC (population 130,000), Rick Rake, editor of the *Abbotsford News*, reflects the local concerns of mayor, council, school board, sports teams and church and temple goers. He and his newspaper do this in a way that the readers and the advertisers of Abbotsford see themselves reflected in the paper.

In the age of multimedia (particularly electronic media) where the image has been king for 50 years, and the cell-phone and iPod are transporting that capability literally to all walks of life, much media rely on selective imaging and sound bites to convey stories that titillate and stimulate without investing in the mature act of interpretation. The culture of our cities is now being served a steady stream of information that entertains and in many cases explicitly denounces values that have been shared by the majority of people.

This transnational mediated undermining of local cultural values is changing our cities. Transnational media has the capacity to exponentially expand city intelligence but, at its current state, is stuck in developing and delivering messaging that blocks or even degrades intelligence (for example, violent video games). Like all technologies, transnational electronic media is going through a life cycle that starts with immature exploration and application.

The maturity of newspapers, and now radio and television, demonstrates that values can be recalibrated, and thoughtful, productive, life-enabling programs and content can eventually emerge. This contrasts markedly with the emergence of the individuated and myopic stories exchanged on the plethora of social networking websites. The rise of blogging affirms our human fascination with storytelling but frequently belies the immature and often narcissistic preoccupation of authors with ego-based issues.

The world of wireless media is already demonstrating its capacity for accelerating intersubjective exchanges (witnessed by its influence on the 2008 US presidential campaign) even though much of it is also overwhelmed by a preoccupation with pornography and sex which seems hopelessly mired in values that register at the lowest levels of human consciousness. The city is learning how even such intelligence as that can be transmuted for greater purposes. (For example, the wide disclosure of child sex tourism has put pressure on countries to make such practices illegal; parents use V-chip technology to purposely select programming for children.) Even culturally, we must ask ourselves, how does this distraction contribute to our understanding of the human living system? What does it tell us about survival? Connecting with our environment? Reproducing? When and how will our resource allocators and inner judges reallocate our energies to more life-giving practices? What does this preoccupation tell us about a conformity that is being enforced (through participation), and how do we reward diversity generation?

RECREATING CULTURAL IMPORTANCE

The city is the container where cultural life unavoidably flourishes. But it has also been the container that has often dismissed or even repressed cultural values. In cities with histories older than the Industrial Revolution, cultural life evolved over centuries and assumed a complex and accepted influence over and in the establishment. Younger cities that emerged during and after the Industrial Revolution have less cultural depth. It brought such an importance to doing and manufacturing, that the pleasures of being, becoming and relating were sidelined. Not only that, but the worldview that arose out of it viewed human systems as machines whose visible parts could be put together like a Meccano set or Lego blocks. City managers and developers, land owners and entrepreneurs concentrated almost solely on the visible aspects of the city, with little or no understanding about the invisible relationships that weave the city together.

HOW BUILDING CONSTRUCTION IGNORES CULTURAL CONSTRUCTION

China has displaced whole cities of people in building its Three Gorges Dam project. The cultural ties to ancestors and place that are especially important in China are being sacrificed to the priorities of infrastructure and electrical energy production. Worse even than this phenomena are the new cities conceived on the drafting tables of developers from Saudi Arabia to Japan to China — where it is anticipated that people will just be "poured" into buildings — albeit beautifully designed — without any attention being paid to the realities of cultural connections. The dysfunctional purpose-built post-WWII ghettos of Glasgow, where gangs and drugs prevail, may unfortunately hold lessons that these developers are not heeding.

In pre-Industrial Revolution cities, interpersonal relationships had such an entrenched history that they anchored cities into values systems, worldviews and ways of relating that they could only be dislodged by disengaging people from one another and their territories within the city. These kinds of relationships are the true fabric of the city — the warp and woof that create the field of consciousness that becomes the felt spirit or essence of the city.

This premodern value system, with strong family and kin ties, holds the invisible culture that expresses itself in a shared aesthetic, a tangible architecture, a distinctive palate. This is the culture that arises because of the stories we tell ourselves — the oral history — that explains the lived reality of the bio-psycho-cultural-social interconnections.

Cities that have built social housing, mostly all during the 1950s and 1960s, have learned, to their discomfort and disadvantage, that simply building affordable housing does not create a great neighborhood or a viable community. When you transplant people from a place that has been dysfunctional and lacking well-being to another place built without input from these people, they bring their dysfunctional cultural experience, baggage and expectations with them from their previous lives. Where the housing developers aspired to provide great improvements to the quality of life of people who moved into new high-rises or new housing estates (e.g., Glasgow, Toronto and Chicago), the same people were aghast that all the old issues from the previous housing conditions were rapidly recreated in the new housing.

The new culture that did emerge once relationships were established was grounded in the old pathologies. Only after a generation-plus of experience can we see these experiments clearly show that cultural connections are painfully real, and they play a huge role in the viability and enjoyment of any community.

Now we know that culture is indeed a prime pillar in the sustainability of community, and countries like Canada have recently recognized the fact by officially making culture part of its sustainable communities equation. Richard Florida's Creative City (2005) model provides a framework to appreciate the effects that cultural creativity can add to the quality of city life. The Creative City network in Canada is providing the peer support on a city level to the emergence of vibrant cultural creativity that needs to be nurtured in any new community. However, in Canada, where culture was identified as the fourth pillar of sustainability by the federal government in 2005, Kat Runnalls' (2007) research indicates that the majority of municipalities have few if any strategies or resources to make this pillar meaningful.

It is as if cultural engagement is like rooting powder for the new transplants into any community. It is that kind of inducement, encouragement to connect and support, that culture adds to the wastelands of affordable housing. If its reality is neglected, it will be created anyway, because it is the nature of social holons to connect. However, when connections emerge artificially, they will respond to the life conditions and the center of gravity of those making the connections. Thus social housing so often fails its mandate to effectively shelter those most in need, because the center of gravity of those in need is frequently at a very low level. They are susceptible, therefore, to influences of predatory drug dealers or criminals, preventing residents from self-organizing in a healthy way. Overcoming values that are moderately to highly dysfunctional requires coaching support because the attaining of new values demands an environment where new capacity can be grown. (Recent experiments with homefulness that offer the right kind of peer support demonstrate it can catalyze a community in the direction of greater well-being.)

If any more evidence of the reality of the drive to culturally connect with others was needed, we should look no further than the success of the social networking software: You Tube, My Face and Face Book. Because people are so starved to make the natural connections that culture embraces, they are virtually addicted to the technological assistance that builds those bonds.

COMMUNITY AND DIALOGUE: FIELDS OF ENGAGEMENT

With an appreciation of how important interpersonal connection is, let's look at why practices and processes as old as community building and dialogue are attracting such interest. How can they deepen engagement?

When we look at the different values people bring to defining community, it seems that community can be viewed not as a place but as "a process of becoming" (Stevenson & Hamilton, 2001). In this sense, community is a process of being in a relationship that helps us to adapt, change and become who we are, through co-emergent meaning-making, discovery and inquiry.

The term "community" has its origins in the notion "of serving together"; of being "with one another in unity" (Peck, 1993). A number of authors (Gozdz, 1995) have observed that the process of "becoming community" evolves (and co-evolves) through multiple phases including chaos and breakdown. Many traditional practices and recent research show us that we can overcome this lack of coherence, mere politeness or pseudo-community through inquiry and reflection. Because inquiry and reflection require attention and intention, for which we usually do not take the time, we often live for extended periods of time in the community-building process at the edge of chaos.

This is one of the major reasons that the rediscovery of the practice of dialogue has become a powerful tool in helping people to listen to each other in new ways. Dialogue allows the process of communication to slow down, so people can tell their story, listen to others, consider new possibilities and make new meaning that potentially leads to different (more informed) behaviors.

In examining the process of dialogue, William Isaacs (1999) refers to four fields of conversation (similar to Peck's four phases of community as summarized in Figure 8.3), namely, politeness, breakdown, inquiry and flow. In the first field of "politeness," the mental models held by people that are most evident are those that suggest what is "supposed to happen." There is a "taken-for-granted" assumption about what should be

Figure 8.3. Comparative summary of phases of community. Source: Adapted from Stevenson & Hamilton, 2001.

PHASE	PECK	ISAACS – CONTAINER	ISAACS – FIELD
1	Pseudo-community	Instability of Container	Politeness
2	Chaos	Instability in Container	Breakdown
3	Emptiness	Inquiry in the Container	Inquiry
4	Community	Creativity in the Container	Flow

and about the rules that guide this level of interaction. People do not surface what they really think and feel. This is the field of normal everyday conversation.

As conversation is allowed to drift into the second field of "breakdown," conversation becomes controlled and skillful. People start to say what they think. Intensity and pressure build, and if they are in a facilitated dialogue process, they are supported by a "container" that emerges from the energy of the community. Conversation that is controlled like this is often an argument, a technical analysis or a probing challenge of one person by another. At this second stage, the elusiveness of the field may be more apparent than any sense of containment, as the community struggles with various participants. Energy seems to be projected outwards by individuals as they attempt to "heal, convert, fix or solve" (Peck, 1987) one another. This is a stage at which the meaning-making process and values of the individual members are at odds with whatever meaning-making process and values the whole community holds. Breakdown occurs. Often, many public meetings do not get past this field of dueling conversations and revert back into politeness.

If they are successful, the people with intentions to truly listen to one another can enter a third field of conversation known as "inquiry" or in formal terms, "reflective" dialogue that can be recognized by deep respect for others. This is when people begin to explore their assumptions and mental models. Different perspectives are uncovered and evaluated. Finally, there is a growing appreciation that we don't have to change others; we can agree to disagree and still be in community. The important difference between position and person comes into perspective. People begin to talk and listen differently. As Stephen Covey (1990) suggests, at this stage of community, members "first seek to understand, then to be understood."

In the fourth field of conversation, people enter the field of "flow" that transforms the conversation and people to a new state. The primacy of the whole is (re)gained, allowing people to connect in ways that can even lead to the creation of a learning community (Senge, 1995) or an action-research study group (Stringer, 1996). It is a deeper level of being "in community," one that engenders a high level of trust. New possibilities come into being as people generate new rules for interaction. A different ecology is born, one that links the collective thoughts and awareness of each person and sustains a meaning-making process that is less constrained by mental models and constructed paradigms. Synchronicity (a condition where meaningful coincidence emerges) arises here (Jaworski, 1996). This stage is often reported as a peak experience, where people feel deeply connected, seamlessly self-organizing and sustainably enabled.

Built around this notion of sustainability appear to be some simple rules that resonate with conditions for ideal interpersonal communication described by Jürgen Habermas (1984, pp. 177-178): everyone in the conversation must have equal rights to speak, all must have equal opportunities to interpret and respond to others, all are open and transparent about their own intentions and feelings, and all must be both accountable for one's conduct and demand accountability from others. The everyday dialogic practice of these four "simple rules" probably looks something like this:

- allowing each person to *speak one's voice*
- *listening deeply with discernment*
- *suspending one's assumptions/mental models and need for certainty*
- treating others with *respect*

Parker Palmer (n.d.) reminds us that community is not a wishy-washy concept — it is definitely not the same as intimacy. Rather community is about a "capacity for connectedness." He believes community must embrace "even those we perceive as 'the enemy' .... Community is that place where the person you least want to live with always lives .... and when that person moves away, someone else arises immediately to take his or her place." Palmer suggests that a capacity for connectedness is achieved through contemplation. Contemplation is any way a person has of knowing how to overcome "the illusion of separateness" and, by doing so, touch the reality of interdependence. He cites failure, loss and suffering as being deeply informative forms of contemplation. Thus the capacity for connectedness arises not from any hard work of building communal structures, but of being open to inner work and to resisting the forces of disconnection rampant in our culture and society.

While coming into community is "a process of becoming," being "in community" occurs when we are in a state of what might be termed "balance": when our minds, bodies and souls are serving each other's needs in a synchronistic manner

(Jaworski, 1996). This is reminiscent of Elisabet Sahtouris's holons being in service to one another at a level of mastery where the whole system resonates with internal coherence. Idealistically, we could perhaps say that we are living in synchrony with the Earth when we, as human complex adaptive systems, connect and serve each other's needs in a symbiotic and coherent way. In so doing we experience shared pleasure that goes beyond words.

The disarming corollary to this, however, is that to achieve this state of balanced harmony, we must be able to live at the edge of chaos, in relationships that challenge us to be self-causing and self-reflective. Maybe the indisputable purpose and outcome of our being "in community" is to ensure our survival and sustainability as complex adaptive systems? Perhaps this dualistic nature of being both in competition and in cooperation; of being explorative and exploitive at the same time; of enjoying and struggling with relationship, is how we truly achieve sufficient strength to survive as a species?

COMMUNITIES OF PRACTICE: EVOLVING CULTURES FOR HEALTHY EDUCATION, HEALTHCARE AND WORKPLACE SERVICES

A derivative of our studies of community and dialogue has led to a recognition that in our work we develop purpose-based "communities of practice." Etienne Wenger (1999) provides a helpful framing of "communities of practice" that substantively supports an integral perspective (see sidebar on Communities of Practice). Wenger acknowledges the intersubjective and objective natures of learning (the left- and right-hand sides of the integral model) and the intertwining roles of the individual and the collective in group work. Wenger talks about community in terms of three dimensions (p. 73):

- mutual engagement
- joint enterprise
- shared repertoire

The first of these dimensions emerges from shared meaning, i.e., what is of value? The second develops from the negotiation process of shared meaning and arises from the emergent relationships. The third is a set of capacities that emerge from the first two dimensions.

COMMUNITIES OF PRACTICE

Communities of professional practice at city hall, in the educational institutions, healthcare systems and workplace services make the rules. The mental models of these authority figures determine the official paradigm, study and practices applied in any given community.

Leonie Sandercock (2000) proposes four ways to respond to intransigence in these communities of practice:

1. Overhaul the planning system through legislative change (a daunting task that requires both cultural conviction and sustainable energy of the proponents of change).

2. Allow and encourage market forces to make change (usually a solution that is only partial and often inequitable).

3. Create opportunities for dialogue between the different communities.

4. Educate planners to acquire an expanded set of skills [and values].

Wenger makes a powerful case for the reality that tradeoffs in learning and communities of practice (like tradeoffs between local versus global) entail one kind of complexity replacing another, one kind of limitation being overcome at the cost of introducing another (1999, p. 132). The boundaries in which city/regional planners operate as a community of practice, he reminds us, "are important places of negotiation, learning, meaning and identity… [involving] interactions between the local and the global" (p. 133).

Wenger's proposal for a learning design (p. 232) encompasses four pairs of paradoxical dimensions that could lead to a more integral planning practice:

1. participating/distancing
2. localizing/globalizing
3. identifying/negotiating
4. designing/emerging

Thus Wenger's approach to education seems to embrace constructs of meta-paradigms, while at the same time insisting on the complex adaptive local nature of learning.

Designing Meshworks Amongst Public, Private, NFP Sectors

If communities of practice are limited by their tacit knowledge and ways of knowing, how do we move beyond these limitations? If culture is so vital to city well-being, how do we bridge the silos between the public, private and NFP sectors (Dale, 2001)? How do we bridge the stovepipes within the public, private and NFP sectors? How do we bridge the solitudes felt by individuals in the public, private and

NFP sectors? What clues does the nature of human culture offer to design appropriate community relationships that engage city cultures in ways that create healthy alignment, coherence and emergence?

While dialogue can contribute substantively to making new connections if the inclusive design capacities of Level 6 are informed by the elegant complexity capacities of Level 7, the practice of meshworking (as discussed in chapter 10) involves the Level 7 art of relating to self-organizing systems and the Level 8 science of organizing hierarchies simultaneously. The art and science of meshworking is related to making generative connections. We know the connections are generative when new capacities and/or new values emerge from the meshworking process.

Meshworking is often characterized by the presence of an intentional catalyst — a person who interacts with the system, often by witnessing, inquiring or modeling. Interestingly, in the brain sciences, it is recognized that catalytic function directs a flow of energy-matter through a system so it shifts from one steady state to another. Much cultural connecting involves using information to redirect energy-matter, for example, achieving agreement to simple rules amongst individuals and groups who are in conflict or disarray, which allows them to self-organize into new supportive relationships.

A good example is the work of Gordon Wiebe's Community Builders Benevolent Society in Vancouver's poor Downtown Eastside district. Here he has discovered that by creating habitats in rooming houses where he first gets rid of the 5% of ne'er-do-wells, the other 95% of the hard-to-house can actually self-organize a self- and peer-supportive community.

GETTIN' HIGHER CHOIR

Many of the ancient ways, like singing, by which we tell each other stories in the human hive remain genuinely enlivening and attractive and build real community. In Victoria, BC, the Gettin' Higher Choir, created by Shivon Robinsong and co-led by Dennis Donnelly, started as a non-auditioned community choir where anyone could belong. Started in 1996 by Robinsong in the belief that anyone can sing, the choir has expanded to over 300 members — so large that it must practise in three separate groups. Donnelly notes that in every other culture, outside the Western one, it is assumed that everyone can sing — there is no such thing as being excluded on the basis of "not being good enough." Members of the choir actually pay for the privilege of belonging and claim participation gives them benefits of health, energy and filling their souls. They have performed with professional soloists, global choir masters and produced a CD, aptly titled "Ubuntu" (I am because you are). More than that, they devote the entire proceeds of their annual concert (now in excess of $10,000) to the support of Kampasseni, a village in Mozambique. It appears that it takes a village to raise a choir; and a choir, to raise a village.

COMMUNITY MENTAL HEALTH SYSTEM

North of Wichita, Kansas, lie Newton and four more small cities, where after WWII, a Mennonite community group stepped into the gap abandoned by the federal government to supply a Mental Health institution. Thus was born the Prairieview Community Mental Health System, which serves individuals and groups in an integrally informed way. Prairieview provides resources to six communities to help each one provide mental health services that are culturally sensitive (the ethnicities in the communities include German, Dutch, Scottish, Swedish, Hispanic), supportive of workplaces (as varied as grain farms to Boeing Assembly plant), caring of families, spiritually engaging and individually appropriate. Employing integrally informed psychiatrists, maintaining modern healthcare facilities and utilizing a spectrum of effective modalities from around the world (including laughter yoga), for over a decade Prairieview has even sponsored "Monthly Food for Thought" keynote speakers who have informed, intrigued and invested wisdom in all of their communities.

Other developers of innovative affordable housing, from church pastors to NGOs, are finding ways for social agencies to reframe linear processes and service delivery projects into systemic, fluid and flexible processes that serve the short-term survival and long-term well-being of the homeless. Thus the bottom line for meshworking is that it builds capacity through integrating the processes of translating, transforming and transmuting.

CONCLUSION

The city's culture emerges from the quality of the relationships of its people. The richer the relationships, the more vibrant the culture. As a city grows through its natural life cycle, those relationships change from decade to decade, year to year, month to month and day to day. Our relationships in the city are how we feel the dynamics of the city. They tell us how fully alive we are because they give us an ongoing reading of ourselves as living systems. Our relationships tell us do we have the capacity to survive together? connect with our environment (including other people)? and reproduce? recreate? regenerate?

The culture of the city represents the lived values of its citizens. It is the perpetual barometer of "what is important around here." How we prioritize those values at home, work, play or in spiritual practice translates into the quality of our relationships and the character of the city's culture.

In fact, the city's culture is a multitude of sub-cultures, contained by formal and informal boundaries. How we create it, describe it and live it is a function of our living intelligence and a testament to our capacity to be conscious together.

QUESTIONS

1. How can we honor the creative process of cultural emergence?

2. How can we learn from Singapore to create the conditions for healthy expression of multiple voices, cadences and cultures?

3. How can we develop transnational media that reflect the greatest cultural capacities of homo sapiens sapiens?

Three simple rules for applying Integral City principles from this chapter:

1. Respect others.

2. Listen deeply.

3. Speak your story, and enable others to speak theirs, to co-create communities of integral practice.

9

INQUIRY INTELLIGENCE: RELEASING POTENTIAL IN THE HUMAN HIVE

This chapter was originally presented as "The Quest: Four Questions That Can
Release the Potential of Your City" at Canadian Institute of Planners Conference:
Frontiers in Planning and Design, July, 2005, Calgary, AB. Panel
Presentation: Integral Planning and Spiral Dynamics an Upcoming Model

The worry then is not that we will run out of questions, but that we will fail to
imagine the full range of possible answers — hypotheses — to test,
or be unable to dream up clever ways to perform critical experiments without
investing an inordinate amount of time or money in the effort.

— Gould and Gould, 1988, p. 225

Learn to love the questions themselves.

— Rumi

THE QUEST

Like the busy beekeeper of the human hive, it is clear that I am on a quest to unlock the potential of the city as an intelligent human system. I used to think that we needed experts to tell us what and how to change the city to optimize the quality of human life. Indeed, whole professions of urban planners, sociologists, economic advisors, social developers, healthcare and education forecasters and infrastructure and property developers have arisen to offer such expert services (Fainstein & Campbell, 2003; Gottdiener & Hutchison, 2006). They have collected vast arrays of qualitative and quantitative data, developed enormous data bases, built infrastructure management technologies and created sophisticated GIS mapping software. However, despite the fact that most of these services are technologically advanced, they are frequently disconnected from each other and the people who live the realities of everyday life in the city.

In the last ten years, I have been curious about how to build bridges between the wisdom of citizens and the knowledge of experts. My colleague Ann Dale (Dale, 2001; Dale & Onyx, 2005) has been on a similar quest to build bridges between what she calls the external silos, internal stovepipes and personal solitudes in the city. In studying the dynamics of human systems in communities and, more recently, cities, I have been taught by ordinary citizens that they are quite capable of answering four simple questions that reveal the potential of their cities. I have gathered this data through surveys, wisdom circles, archive and ethnographic analysis, focus groups and recording free conversation. Reminiscent of James Surowiecki's *Wisdom of Crowds* (2004), I am coming to believe that the questions might be the key to revealing a meta-wisdom of the city.

The four simple questions are appreciative by design, and powerful by nature.

Graceful Gardens

The first question I like to ask leads me to the city's life-giving gardens of graceful blooms.

What are the strengths of your community/city?

This question gets people to focus on what they really like about their city — what is great around here? Why did they move/stay here in the first place? Most people have wonderful, rich, illustrative stories to tell in response to this question.

"The streets are safe where I live."

"This is a great place to raise kids."

"This city has built Olympic-class sports facilities, so I've been able to train here."

"I don't need to own a car, because the public transportation system is so good."

"I have worked in the plant for 20 years, and have had fantastic career advancement as Boeing expanded its business here."

"This is a culturally diverse city, and I truly enjoy the ethnic mix. As an artist, I can be part of a really vibrant arts community."

"This place is really "wired" into the rest of the world, so I can do business around the world without leaving the comforts of my home town."

"This location is ideal for our institution to serve the world's information dis tribution needs and the expansion of cultural consciousness."

On many occasions, community focus groups gather data related to this first question. However, the community leaders and/or facilitators rarely understand how to see the unifying themes and/or cross-connections that reveal the hidden patterns in the responses to this question.

This is where values mapping can help translate the raw stories into clusters on an unfolding map like human honeycomb. Multidisciplinary science has taught us that as human systems have evolved, eight major values systems have emerged, each more complex than the one preceding it. For a truly vibrant city, each of the statements above represents a value system that must be healthy in order for the whole city to be healthy. The eight value systems are represented in these themes:

- Individual safety and survival
- Bonding, family relationships, clan and tribal customs
- Individual expressiveness, joy, personal power
- Order, authority, rules, laws, bylaws, ordinances, infrastructure
- Organization, efficiency, effectiveness, strategies, results
- Community, diversity, acceptance of differences, equal rights
- Whole-systems thinking, ecological connections
- Global worldviews, shared world emergence

Deadening Deserts

The second question I like to ask leads me to the city's "deserts" — the stony ground where no flowers bloom, where the pollen has become scarce or even toxic and where the human hive cannot sustain its activities.

What blocks potential in your community/city?

When we live as residents in cities, we are often too blind to the dynamics and com- plexities of our individual, everyday lives to be aware of the subtle ways we affect the quality of life in the city. For example, Abbotsford, BC, is one of the fastest-growing cities in Canada. Not surprisingly, most citizens grumble loudly about the gridlock that arises when parents chauffeur their children to and from school. But they fail to link that how they have voted in the last 30 years has led to short-term city/school district land use and transportation planning that prevents access to emergency services on many streets twice a day.

When we serve cities through foundations, caregiving institutions, not-for-profits and NGOs, many times we are too discouraged by the incumbent power structures of the city to adequately voice the concerns of the marginalized who cannot integrate into city life. For example, a cluster of small cities north of Wichita, Kansas, has noticed the influx of Hispanic workers into their traditionally rural areas, resulting in racism that is breaking down relationships and putting up barriers between neighbors.

When we manage cities — from the perspective of city hall, the school board or the health authority — we are often too confounded by the demands of making decisions to satisfy multiple stakeholders, to take the time to notice what is really great about our city. For example, when the city of Grapevine, Texas, faced massive development in neighboring, Dallas–Fort Worth airport 15 years ago, the loss of business from main street was a rupture to the retail core of Grapevine that drained the economic lifeblood out of city hall, city services, the school district and healthcare facilities.

When we invest in cities, as developers our interests in obtaining the highest possible return from our land development frequently makes us too preoccupied with the return on investment from sticks and bricks to notice that the social/cultural fabric of the city contributes as much or more to future returns as property values. For example, the city council of Carbondale, Colorado, approved a big-box retail store development that promised a new sales tax base, despite the fact that it was distinctly countercultural to the resident arts community and also replaced a breathtaking mountain panorama as the city's gateway.

Too blind — too discouraged — too confounded — too preoccupied. These are the causes that lead to the curse of brownfields and even desertification. The resulting deficiencies block the natural flow of resources to, within and through a healthy human hive. In our quest for city improvement, how can we overcome the causes of desertification and rediscover and recreate the vibrant gardens that sustain our human hives?

New Horizons

The third question I like to ask leads me to new horizons for the human hive, where the city's secret wishes, hopes and dreams lie in flower patches, long forgotten or not yet visited.

How would you improve your community/city?

The answer to this question usually leads us to frame the change we need to unlock the potential of our city. It tells us the answer to the question "Change from what to what?"

Very often the stories citizens tell us about their new horizons build on the strength of the city's gardens and hold the secret to creating oases from the deserts. In fact, the same values-mapping process discussed in "Gardens" can be applied to the "Deserts" and "New Horizons" stories. Returning to the four stories from the previous section, Figure 9.1 plots the corresponding "New Horizons" (and their related values system) that counteracted the "Deserts" (and their related values system).

In Abbotsford, BC, the unsafe (Level 1) and ineffective (Level 5) gridlock was addressed by the mayor and staff who created an effective (Level 5) transportation plan as part of the Official Community Plan.

In Kansas the racism behavior (Level 2) was addressed by a community mental health system creating awareness of the value of diversity (Level 6) and designing a whole community systems approach to enable resources for and from the new immigrants (Level 7).

In Grapevine, Texas, the dying city infrastructure (Level 4) was re-

Figure 9.1. New horizons overcome deserts.

LEVELS OF DESERT VALUES SYSTEM	DESERT	LEVELS OF NEW HORIZON VALUES SYSTEMS	NEW HORIZON
1. Unsafe 5. Ineffective	School time gridlock & unsafe emergency response corridors in Abbotsford	5. Effective Strategy	• City Mayor & Staff review and improve the Official Community Plan
2. Tribal/Clan customs block new citizens	• Racism in Kansas	6. Community/ Diversity 7. Whole Systems Thinking	• Community Mental Health System creates awareness of the value of healthy ethnic diversity
4. City order & infrastructure dying	• Dying town of Grapevine	2. Town Customs 5. Change Strategy	• City Manager revives respect for historical roots and implements history-based downtown revitalization strategy
5. Inappropriate competition strategy	• Big Box development mismatches city culture and environment in Carbondale	6. Citizen Protest 7. Whole Systems Thinking	• Citizens organize referendum and overturn Council decision. • City Manager sets up Roadmap Committee to gather citizen input for future vision of city.

Figure 9.2. Gardens, deserts, new horizons.
Note: The x-axis color labels correspond to the 2nd through 8th values systems.

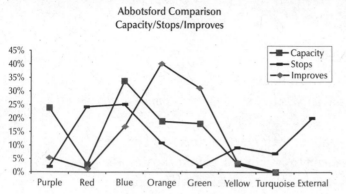

Abbotsford Comparison
Capacity/Stops/Improves

energized through the city manager creating opportunities for citizens and city staff first to rediscover and revalue the historical roots of the city (Level 2); and then to attract new commercial interests as a revitalization strategy (Level 5).

In Carbondale, Colorado, the predatory big-box strategy (Level 5) was countermanded by a citizen referendum that overturned the council decision (Level 6); followed by the city manager setting up a roadmap process to support citizens in creating a new vision for the future of the city (Level 7).

MAPPING GARDENS, DESERTS AND NEW HORIZONS

One of the most powerful outcomes of using this values-mapping process is that it creates a common language to interpret and talk about the gardens, deserts and new horizons in our human hives. Note that in each of the above examples the New Horizons inject new energy into one or more of the city's eight values systems to overcome the blocks created by the desertification process.

In fact the common language of these eight values systems gives us the capacity to actually graph the relationship between the city's gardens, deserts and new horizons — not only in spatial and temporal vectors but also values vectors. Figure 9.2 shows a comparison between one city's capacities (gardens) and stops (deserts) and improves (new horizons).

The same kind of values mapping allows us to compare the views of different populations within the same city.

Figure 9.3. Comparing gardens: Views of residents and board.

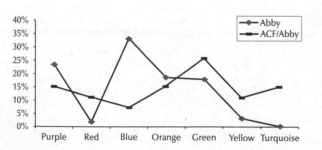

Abbotsford Residents / Abbotsford Community Foundation Board
Community Capacity

Figure 9.3 compares the views of Abbotsford's capacities/gardens from the perspective of the general population and the Community Foundation Board members.

A final advantage to using this kind of values mapping allows us to compare any or all of the Gardens, Deserts and New Horizons between cities. Figure 9.4 illustrates this with a comparison of the strengths (gardens) amongst five cities in Kansas.

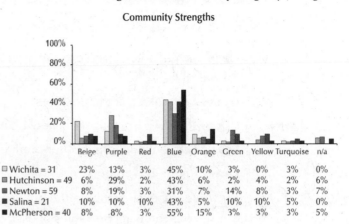

Figure 9.4. Kansas comparing city strengths.

Community Strengths

	Beige	Purple	Red	Blue	Orange	Green	Yellow	Turquoise	n/a
Wichita = 31	23%	13%	3%	45%	10%	3%	0%	3%	0%
Hutchinson = 49	6%	29%	2%	43%	6%	2%	4%	2%	6%
Newton = 59	8%	19%	3%	31%	7%	14%	8%	3%	7%
Salina = 21	10%	10%	10%	43%	5%	10%	10%	5%	0%
McPherson = 40	8%	8%	3%	55%	15%	3%	3%	3%	5%

The Wisdom of the Human Hive

Finally, the fourth question I like to ask leads me to the city's "wisdoms" — maybe even the hive wisdom of its Inner Judges and Resource Allocators?

How would you describe your community/city?

The answers to this question disclose the city's wisdoms about how various people view the city — what is the nature of the human hive's awareness about itself? The city's wisdoms are actually contained in: individual citizens; groups, organizations and collectives of all kinds; internally and externally. The wisdoms can also be mapped simply on a quadrant map like Figure 9.5.

The city wisdom map gives us the multiple perspectives of people whose lives and/or work is defined by the qualities of city life in each quadrant. Interestingly, some aspect of each person's life is located in each quadrant; for example:

Upper Left: How I intend, think, love/hate, believe (often invisible to others)

Upper Right: How I behave, physically appear (what is visible to others)

Lower Left: How my belief system influences me, e.g., family, religion, culture

Figure 9.5. City wisdom map.

	INTERNAL	EXTERNAL
Individual	• Heart, mind, spirit	• Body, traits, behaviors
Group	• Belief systems, cultures	• Infrastructure systems, workplaces, technologies

Lower Right: How my social systems influence me, e.g., workplaces, buildings, technology

In addition we have people whose work or interests give them special expertise in each quadrant. The examples we used in the second and third questions show us how.

Upper Left: City residents/parents

Upper Right: City managers; school board; healthcare specialists

Lower Left: Foundations, not-for-profit experts

Lower Right: Developers

We can even combine the quadrant maps with the values maps so that we can see the comparative values of each garden/desert/new horizon in each quadrant. (See Figure 9.7 in sidebar). Further refinements to this mapping process are described in chapter 11.

Furthermore, we are able to utilize this framework to compare the actual weighting of responses representing the qualitative values with the analysis of quantitative tax resources we invest in each quadrant, as shown in Figure 9.6.

THE POTENTIAL

Let's return to our original quest and question: How do we unlock the potential of our city? The answers to four simple questions define our quest.

1. What are the strengths of your community/city?

2. What blocks potential in your community/city?

3. How would you improve your community/city?

4. How would you describe your community/city?

When we translate the responses to these questions into a values-based framework and graph the flow, we can appreciate the beautiful synergy with which an integral system can work. Firstly, our integral language allows us to communicate with each other (like the bees do when they dance for and feed each other) and compare and contrast stories, responses and perspectives

Figure 9.6. City weighting of qualitative values compared to quantitative tax allocation.

	INTERNAL VALUES VS TAXES	EXTERNAL VALUES VS TAXES
Individual	• 16% vs <3%	• 13% vs 9%
Group	• 53% vs 12%	• 11% vs 76%

about Gardens, Deserts and New Horizons. With this common language we can much more easily compare answers between different groups of people (experts, residents, ages, gender, roles, etc.). We can recognize their varying capacities to describe what they want, don't want and what they see as their next natural horizon(s) to cross.

The integral map provides a highly useful view of the relationships between individuals and collectives and cultures and infrastructures. It lays out all the discourses, and while it can reveal the details of the landscape, it also discloses how the different elements of the map join together and/or reflect one another.

The integral map is a great resource for the resource allocators in the human hive. It breaks down the intractable but often invisible wall between quantitative and qualitative capacities in the city. It allows us to compare quantitative investments of finances and qualitative and quantitative resources, before, during and after decisions are made that affect the equation of "how to allocate resources for whom for what outcomes"?

The eight levels of complexity and the change states of the integral map disclose a picture of the natural flow-state of the city — what are the city's gardens that are its natural strengths; what are the city's deserts that block its potential; and what are the city's new horizons that will lead to improvement?

Unlocking the city's potential requires the development of a strategy to change from unbalanced and/or mismatched values systems and unbalanced wisdom quadrants to a complete set of eight balanced and flowing values systems and four balanced wisdom quadrants.

CHANGE WIZARDS

In the midst of city change scenarios, move change wizards like community sustainability activist Ann Dale (2001; Dale & Onyx, 2005; Dale, Waldron et al., 2007), human systems dynamics specialist Glenda Eoyang (1997; Eoyang & Olson, 2001) and human emergence pioneer Don Beck (Beck & Cowan, 1996; Beck & Linscott, 2006). Each is adept at adaptation, flexing and flowing, designing and disturbing systems so that exchanges occur that shift and metamorphose organizations across levels, strata and paradigms. They focus on "what is important" around here, enabling exchanges across multiple stakeholders. They ask, how are people different? They notice what sorts of change is ongoing and what kind of exchanges occur between people in the system. And they inquire about people's dreams for the future. Thus they learn about the complex adaptive behaviors of citizens and focus on designing habitats that are historically informed and future inspired, but are also the next natural developmental stage for these people in this place.

FOUR-QUADRANT COMMUNITY MAP

A research project conducted for the Abbotsford Community Foundation in 2003 produced a Spiral Integral Values Map. A four-petalled flower presented the data in a non-academic manner, using a graphical metaphor to make key learning points and later create evaluation surveys (Hamilton, 1999, 2003; Ruder & Sando, 2002.) (See Figure 9.7.) This enabled the Board to use the map to explore community values in relation to visioning, strategic planning and granting. (See chapter 11 for further refinements and application.)

The key points included on the map legend are:

1. Within the petals of the flower of community are those capacities that help make community work. If these flourish in an integrated manner, community will grow and thrive. Arrows in the background of each petal illustrate the push for the petal to bloom more fully.

2. In the gray background surrounding the petals are those barriers that prevent the flower from blooming larger. The background arrows pushing against the petals represent these negative forces.

3. There are many different ways to foster community. The four petals of the flower show how survey responses cluster into four different but essential categories. Like this flower, community is made up of all four clusters.

4. This flower is a rainbow of community values. Each of the values shown here is crucial to ensuring that the flower of community is as full and vibrant as possible. Consider these community values like multiple layers of petals — each layer is a different color that creates an award-winning flower show masterpiece. Consider the positive contributions of each color.

- **Beige** feeds people's basic survival needs for food, clothing, shelter.
- **Purple** harmonizes the values of kinship and familial traditions that bond people together most tightly.
- **Red** speaks to the pure unrestrained energy of pleasure and enjoyment in community.
- **Blue** honors commitment and order to life and work, a sense of direction for a greater good, stability, and even recognition of duty to creating and sustaining it.
- **Orange** strives towards achieving great things together with strategic and goal oriented plans.
- **Green** shares those elements that are about care and sensitivity to others, with an egalitarian perspective that celebrates diversity.
- **Yellow** meshes responses about flexibility, spontaneity, and knowledge as a spur to integrating community development.
- **Turquoise** hints at aspects of community that are about wholeness and global connections.
- **Coral** splashes represent what we might create in the future with all our good works for the common good.

Figure 9.7. Four-quadrant, multi-level city map of Abbotsford values and barriers.
Source: Hamilton, 2003.

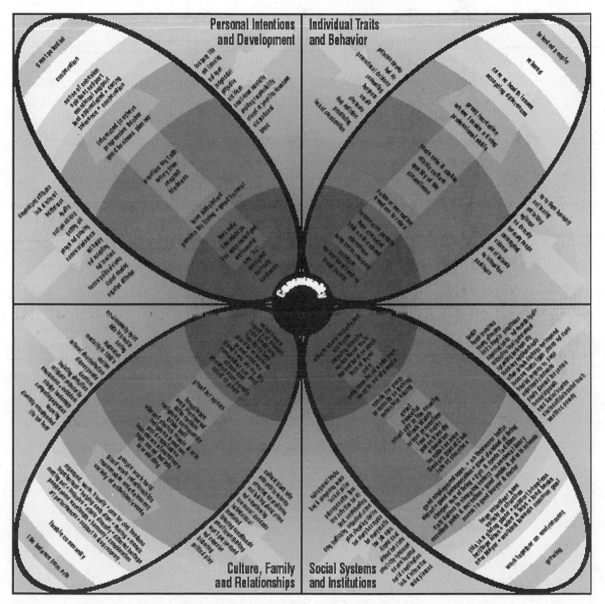

CONCLUSION

The quest for intelligence in the human hive is simplified by using the integral map to interpret the answers to four simple questions. How people answer those questions will reflect the cadence of the city (discussed in chapter 8) as well as where and why the energy of the human hive might be blocked.

The answers to the four questions tell us the natural place to start our quest and the destination we seek. The questions are the keys that let us unblock the natural flows of energy and resources, build on our strengths, attain new horizons and continuously learn from the wisdom of our quest to optimize the potential of the human hive.

QUESTIONS

1. What is working? What is not working?

2. Who is left behind? Who else needs to be in this conversation?

3. What is our vision for the future?

Three simple rules for applying Integral City principles from this chapter:

1. Ask what's working (and not) and co-generate a vision for the city's contribution to the planet.

2. Create an integral city and community plan.

3. Implement and manage the city plan appropriately at all scales in the city.

MESHING INTELLIGENCE:
ENABLING ORDER AND CREATIVITY
IN THE HUMAN HIVE

The whole fabric of honeybee society depends on communication — on an innate
ability to send and receive messages, to encode and decode
information. .... Bees use chemical, tactile, auditory and ... visual messages.

— Gould and Gould, 1988, p. 47

It may be, as philosopher Andy Clark has suggested, that our minds are a kludge
(or bricollage) of different kinds of intelligence: some intelligent abilities arise out of decentralized
and parallel processes, others from centralized and sequential ones.

— De Landa, 1995

WHAT IS MESHWORKING?

In her quest for sustainable communities, Ann Dale has long recognized that our systems of governance are fractured by solitudes, silos and stovepipes (2001). So if we are to create a view of city life that is whole and integral, how do we begin to reframe our fragmented, reductionistic, mechanistic, linear view of the city into one that is whole, integrated, natural and flowing? This chapter describes how meshworking enables whole-system capacities in the human hive.

Several years ago, I borrowed the term "meshwork" to describe the work that I do (Beck 2004, 2007b, 2008). As noted in earlier chapters, meshworking in the city integrates enabling hierarchies and self-organizing webs of relationships by aligning different capacities, functions and locations so they can be of service

MERGING THE SILOS

Research into sustainable community infrastructure by Ann Dale, Canada Research Chair on Sustainable Community Development, is a powerful example of how to merge silos by meshing hierarchies. Dale has networked together a progression of hierarchies, intentionally creating a cross-disciplinary research team from academic, NFP, private sector and public sector hierarchies. She has designed e-dialogues where participants represent hierarchies within specialized city infrastructures: energy, waste management, transportation, land use planning and governance. Within a structured online dialogue platform, Dale has catalyzed connections within sectors and across widespread geographies by inviting participants to share their views of leading-edge practices, barriers to progress and solutions to sustainability challenges. She has also made visible observed and potential connections between sectors by archiving the e-dialogues and by documenting over 20 best-practice case studies. (Check out some of Ann's work at www.sustainable infrastructure.crcresearch.org/)

to a purpose and each other. Meshworking creates the information highway that makes possible the design and implementation of highly sensitive vital signs monitors that create the feedback loops for attaining a dynamic but stable state of well-being.

Happily for the city, new integrating functionality and capacity is emerging through integral practitioners who I call meshworkers. Like honeybees that are so cosmopolitan, they can live in a myriad of environments and adapt distinctive forms of dialects and hive intelligences. Meshworkers cross the old boundaries, merge the silos and create the space for meshing perspectives.

By attracting the best from two operating systems — one that self-organizes, and the other that can replicate hierarchical structures — meshworking creates second-tier structures that flex and flow. In strict terms, the brain scientists use meshworks in relation to self-organizing neural nets and hierarchies in relation to reinforcing levels of hierarchical operations. It appears the brain builds itself by laying down large synaptic highways that become the scaffold of communication corridors from which secondary and tertiary corridors emerge, until a vast "hairnet of axons" covers the brain. Once this hairnet is in place, we have a brain that is able to self-organize an infinite number of connections, thoughts, ideas, innovations and learnings while at the same time behave and direct behaviour in dependable, learned ways.

Some researchers even relate key synaptic connections in the brain, modulated by the major neurotransmitters like serotonin, dopamine, choline, noradrenalin, to sets of values that allow for regulated brain/body function. These values appear themselves to be modifiable, based on life conditions. The appearance of this modern brain science evidence of intelligence-based values seems to vindicate Clare Graves' (2004) proposition that intelligences are triggered in the brain by dissonance (i.e., constraints) in the environment. It appears that it is the brain's very capability of reorganizing itself and releasing new potentials that allows for the emergence of new values systems. In other words, if the brain lacked its self-organizing capacity, it would be restricted from emerging new capacities. At the same time, if it lacked hierarchical capacity, it would not have the sorting and selection mechanisms that allow it to make survival choices.

What an amazing combination of qualities our brain demonstrates: an organism capable of forever reinventing itself by meshing neural nets and an organism that is able to sort and choose amongst options by producing useful hierarchies.

Moreover, it appears that meshworks link heterogeneous capacities or entities, and hierarchies link homogenous elements or functions. But as values systems emerge, a level of complexity develops where our brains meshwork hierarchies (e.g., connect organ systems like heart, lung, liver) and make hierarchies out of meshworks (e.g., the circadian sequences of the [Chinese] meridian energy system). It is this two-way combination of enabling hierarchal meshes and meshing hierarchies that lies at the heart of my use of the term "meshworking."

Is it possible that the application of meshworking is not limited to brain function? Perhaps it offers a powerful explanation of how communities and cities function? Because communities and cities are emergents and artefacts of human life, what if we considered them to be outcomes of the brains that have created them? What if communities simply reflect the capacity to meshwork hierarchies and to make hierarchies of meshworks? This might be the key to understanding how cities are working and evolving.

WHO IS MESHWORKING?

Meshworking seems to entail both an art and a science. It is tempting to associate the creativity of art with self-organizing systems and the explanatory science with organizing hierarchies. But the practice of meshworking involves both

INTEGRATING THE PERSPECTIVES

The multi-year dialogue process of Imagine BC, directed by Joanna Ashworth, Director, Dialogue Programs, Simon Fraser University at the Morris J. Wosk Centre for Dialgue has been designed to mesh hierarchies by integrating perspectives across a whole province. Ashworth has been able to network a progression of hierarchies — in this case from across British Columbia — to envision the province in 30 years. The five-year process has linked thought leaders from diverse backgrounds around three focused attractor themes: environment/economy, learning/culture and health/community. For each theme (and year), three separate face-to-face dialogues, which are also broadcast on CBC Radio, attract different stakeholders: about 15 to 20 thought leaders, policy-makers and the public.

Likewise at four regional levels, like Abbotsford in the Fraser Valley, the dialogue process is adapted to capture local voices, stakeholders and perspectives. Thus across the province, the dialogic process of Imagine BC is intentionally meshing hierarchies and using hierarchies to create new self-organizing meshes around the themes and amongst the participants and through the feedback loops. (See Imagine BC's website at sfu.ca/dialogue/imaginebc/)

simultaneously and in the process generates new connections that in turn enable new capacities and/or new values to emerge.

Meshworking is noticeable in my work when I act as an intentional catalyst. Interestingly, in the brain sciences, it is recognized that catalytic function directs a flow of energy-matter through a system so it shifts from one steady state to another. Much of my work involves using information to redirect energy-matter; for example, introducing the work of one person to another whom they have never met, so together they can combine resources and produce something that neither would be able to do on their own. Or achieving consciousness development in individuals and groups in training processes designed to discover complex integral paradigms (like Spiral Dynamics Integral, Integral Life Practice or Integral City practices, workshops and inquiries; or assisting clients to reframe linear processes and analyses into systemic, evolutionary perspectives).

Check the sidebars to meet meshworkers, some of whom are meshing existing hierarchies and others who are creating new hierarchies of existing meshes.

WHY IS MESHWORKING IMPORTANT?

Manuel De Landa (2005) says that "humanity finds it much easier to think in terms of articulated homogeneities rather than articulated heterogeneities." But he believes it is the latter that hold the secret for a better future. De Landa muses, "Perhaps we can learn from birds — and why not even rocks? — the secrets of non-homogenous thinking."

MESHING THE INTELLIGENCES

In Halifax, Nova Scotia, Mary Morrissey, co-founder of the Prior Learning Assessment Center (PLAC), is using hierarchies to create new meshes, by building on an appreciative portfolio development process for capturing individual learning. One of the unexpected outcomes of this life-changing experience is that a number of individuals in several small communities have noticed they have made connections beyond the individual level at the community development level. Their self-organizing process has led them to inquire: Why couldn't the prior learning recognition be adapted to community learning? What would happen if we adapted this to the scale of recognizing community capacities for the purpose of developing new opportunities?

Morrissey responded to this self-organizing challenge by meshing hierarchies. She organized a conference and invited stakeholders in community development from across the community and across Canada. Essentially she brought together in one room representatives of a whole community system (from education, health, private, public [federal, provincial, city], NFP, international). She created a process where participants could explore: what is working for PLAC; what to consider when changing scales; how to energize self-organizing systems; how to springboard from existing hierarchies. Morrissey also mixed the media for the discovery process, combining inquiry, graphic facilitation, PowerPoint content and face-to-face dialogue. Thus she is creating the conditions to emerge community learning from individual learning, by building on the structured hierarchical pattern that has worked for (homogenous) individuals to bridge into self-organizing clusters of heterogeneous community organizations. (You can find PLAC information at www.placentre.ns.ca)

These few (sidebar) examples of meshworking illustrate that the practice can originate from the bottom of a system or the top of a system. In both cases, as the process matures, meshworking catalyzes a shift in the system, so that new capacities emerge and the system reorganizes itself into something more internally resonant and externally coherent with life conditions.

An enormous value of meshworking is that it does not remain in the realms of the objective and interobjective space. Rather, it boldly calls forth the capacities that lie in the subjective and intersubjective zones of the city. These are the domains of intention, purpose and culture. Until we can give equal weighting to these capacities, we will never achieve the vibrant promise of an Integral City.

In a recent Integral City teleconference on meshworking, participants recognized the paradox of meshworking. It requires an understanding of boundaries that contain whole systems, along with simultaneous acceptance of the interconnection of all the systems within the larger systems.

Teleconference participants related their experiences of creating life conditions and holding space long enough for leaders to let go of old ways of doing things so they could create an entirely new approach. This process of dismantling the old so that innovation can emerge often takes a long time (years). It literally entails the rearrangement of the brain, body, relationships, expectations and paradigms. The facilitation of this act of rearranging often requires the use of non-verbal processes (like art, music, dance and other expressive arts) to access collective wisdom and tap into new ways of knowing. One meshworker suggested that this feels like a shift from entropy, where the loss of energy from a system causes it to wind down, to syntropy, where the release of energy from the disintegrating old structure, enables the creation of entirely new patterns.

We have noted above that the both/and approach of meshworking essentially revalues and recalibrates hierarchies. (This is a process of evolving complexity, into what some now call a holarchy — or a hierarchy of hierarchies.) Instead of denigrating hierarchies as outdated organizational forms, meshworking recognizes that healthy hierarchies under-gird all natural systems. In these hierarchies, the multidirectional flow of information, energy and matter is enabled for the well-being of the whole. At the same time, meshworking makes possible the newness that can be injected into a system through self-organizing processes. Through this ever-evolving meshwork emerge transformation, transcendence and transmutation of consciousness, behaviors, cultures and societies.

MESHWORKING ENABLES EMERGENCE IN THE HUMAN HIVE

Let us summarize the value of meshworking in the human hive and anticipate our needs for the Integral Vital Signs Monitor we discuss in the next chapter.

Research

- Meshworkers can help ordinary citizens to voice the change direction they value with an explicit awareness of the assets, values and capacities they experience as their reality in a changing world.

- Meshworkers can facilitate the mapping, analyses, comparisons and discussions for reconciliation and agreed direction amongst citizens, elected officials, staff and experts.

- Meshworkers can observe the expression of the different change states and ensure that these are considered in designing change processes.

- Meshworkers can catalyze the discussions amongst different sectors and different levels of authority in those sectors.

Planning

- Meshworkers can integrate intentions of social planning, land use (hard asset) planning and the integration of community education and health-care development.

- Meshworkers can use integral maps as checklists to design balanced change in all the quadrants, levels, scales, holons and structures, overcoming barriers to change because of blindnesses and/or blocks.

- Meshworkers are skilled at moving from one scale to another, integrating the fractal patterns that bring resonance, cohesion and emergence of new capacities.

Management

Meshworkers use the common language of Integral City meta-maps in order to:

- Open up options on managing conflict, allowing meshworkers to facilitate discussion amongst multiple voices when all can be heard and valued.

- Facilitate policy change across all three levels of government as well as bioregionally and globally. This allows for the potential of pooling funding and resources.

- Translate between multiple interests of many community stakeholders who would benefit from an integrated framework.

- Develop mapping strategies for: strategic planning; analyzing group differences; developing communities of professional city management practice; threats; weaknesses; opportunities.

- Ensure multiple perspectives at various scales are taken into consideration amongst diverse groups of people.

- Explore the richness of community in the context of villagizing the globe because it discloses the dynamics below the surface expressions of values.

CONCLUSION

Meshworkers depend on the relational strength of subjective and intersubjective capacities in the city. They use imagination, courage and powers of attraction. They articulate intelligent designs from the meshing of the diversities in people whose differences and uniquenesses can divide cities into heaps and messes of unarticulated heterogeneities. In so doing they release and reorganize the intelligences that are currently blocked by silos of what De Landa calls articulated homogeneities (2006).

The great contribution of meshworkers may turn out to be their talents of releasing simplicity on the other side of complexity. But, as they do so, they will quickly discover that in order for meshworking to remain effective, meshworkers need feedback and feed-forward tools like Integral Vital Signs Monitors. So that is where we will turn as our last consideration of how to create evolutionary intelligences for the human hive.

Three simple rules for applying Integral City principles from this chapter:

1. Catalyze fractal connections within the human hive.

2. Build communication bridges across silos, stovepipes and solitudes.

3. Enable meshes and hierarchies that transform, transcend and transmute capacities.

QUESTIONS

1. How do we recognize a natural and life-giving hierarchy?

2. How do we enable self-organizing creativity that transcends and includes our evolutionary cultural history?

3. How do we become the best translators in the universe so we can build bridges across the memes, silos and intelligences?

NAVIGATING INTELLIGENCE: DIRECTIONAL DASHBOARDS FOR THE HUMAN HIVE

When we look at how honeybees navigate ... we will see that they can indeed use
several sensory systems (odor, sight, light). They can detect and navigate by the sun,
or by patterns of polarized lights in the sky, or by familiar landmarks.

— Gould and Gould, 1988, p. 82

In our attempt to control the disintegrating forces that are at work in our society,
we must resume the search for unity; and to this end, we must begin with
the personality and the community in all their richness, variety, complication
and historic depth, as both the means and the end of our effort.

— Mumford, 1946, p. 216

INTEGRAL VITAL SIGNS MONITORS:
LIVING DASHBOARDS FOR THE HUMAN HIVE

Buckminster Fuller warned that humans are in a historically critical state aboard space vehicle Earth (Fuller, 1970). He proposed that we consider more intelligent ways of guiding the human hive. This chapter describes the whole-system feedback process provided by Integral Vital Signs Monitors.

If we recall the inspiration of our beehive, we will remember that bees have their own vital signs monitors. Their goal-directed behaviors are purpose driven to produce 40 pounds of honey per year. So the hive exercises a form of inner judgment that allows it to allocate resources for the most effective outcomes in achieving that goal.

VITAL SIGNS MONITORS

Many community foundations in Canada have followed the 2002 lead of the Toronto Community Foundation to create Vital Signs Monitors for their cities. With the success of Ottawa's, Vancouver's and Victoria's implementation of a Vital Signs Project, ten more cities have followed suit. Using the Toronto indicators as a universal set, all community foundations are using a Report Card (A+, B-, C, etc.) reporting on the following set of indicators: Income Gap, Safety, Learning, Housing, Getting Started, Arts and Culture, Environment, Work and Belonging and Leadership. Although these Vital Signs reports are not integral (because they are linear indicator reports), they are the first steps for inter-city comparisons on key vital signs for the human hive and will develop a time vector with annual reporting.

Defining Vital Signs Monitors

When we can talk about vital signs monitors for the human hive, we have to understand what we mean by the term. I consider a vital signs monitor to be a reporting mechanism or protocol that monitors and discloses the health of a system. When acupuncturists take your pulses, they are monitoring your vital signs. When nurses take your temperature and blood pressure, they are checking vital signs. When doctors interpret blood tests from the laboratory, they are examining data related to the baseline functioning of a healthy system. When team leaders measure team performance, they are tracking deliverables against a set of targets. When chief financial officers or internal auditors examine an organization's returns on investments, they are considering the ratios that signify optimal performance for the operation. When think-tanks review the nation's budget, they are pondering the key projections for the nation's well-being. When the World Health Organization looks at the most recent reports on zoonotic disease, they are assessing the situation of communicable viruses on behalf of the world's health. When weather forecasters project the probabilities of weather conditions from the satellite images of weather systems, they are monitoring vital signs of Earth's functioning. When NASA astronomers plot the trajectories of asteroids and space junk, they are monitoring the external life conditions of planet Earth.

A global interest in profiling indicators for health, well-being, quality of life (or even happiness) and success has become a national and global pastime since the Brundtland Report. In the last 20 years, everyone from the World Health Organization (WHO), to *Time Magazine*, to Jacksonville, Florida, to various national quality-of-life indicator groups have developed sets of indicators with a variety of characteristics.

However, despite the fact that mapping the state of community well-being has become almost a universal interest, the majority of current discussion seems to be mired in "indicators wars." These are the turf battles where a group of experts competitively promote one set of indicators for acceptance over another. Finding a common language to talk about the factors that contribute to the state of community health seems still to be an elusive goal (Hamilton, 2006b). What we really need is a meta-monitor to go with our meta-map: an Integral Vital Signs Monitor (IVSM).

My operating definition of an Integral Vital Signs Monitor (IVSM) system is this:

An IVSM is a reporting system whose design is based on an integral framework. It utilizes life-sustaining indicators and communicates its results in a universal language. An IVSM system mines existing databases, gathers new data and reports observations in a global graphic language that is accessible to all (in multiple versions and multiple translations). Its purpose is to provide life-giving data for making decisions that develop, maintain and emerge the health of local and global systems of interest, for the current generations and the generations to come. IVSMs can exist on any scale of the human system and are designed so that they can scale up and down from the individual to the planet.

E Pluribus Unum

One of the great contributions of the World Commission on Environment and Development and their Brundtland Report (Brundtland, 1987) was to identify the three imperatives of the economic, social and ecological factors in the discourse on sustainability. In the last 30 years, this has essentially become the backbone to approaches that measure and track sustainability.

So what is the state of the art in terms of models for sustainability frameworks, indicator reporting and graphical reporting?

A framework that has become increasingly endorsed around the world is The Natural Step (Cook, 2005; Naess & Rothenberg, 1989). Based on the assumptions

EVOLUTIONARY MAP FOR GOVERNANCE SYSTEMS

Steve McIntosh has created a four-quadrant map reflecting the direction of evolution, based on Swimme and Berry's cosmogenetic principles of differentiation, autopoiesis and communion. This map (Figure 11.1) identifies 12 potential domains for IVSM tracking of governance systems: Will, Thought, Feeling; Consciousness, Complexity, Unity; Morality, Science, Aesthetics; and Human Organizations, Technology, Art.

about sustainability derived from the Brundtland Report, its framework is anchored in the three imperatives: economic, social and environmental. The Natural Step has been effective in gaining global mind space for the triple bottom line. In this way environmental issues that were completely omitted from the traditional balance sheets have gained acceptance and a tracking record. The city of Whistler, BC, site of the 2010 Olympics, is a proponent of The Natural Step, using its systemic conditions of sustainability and its identification of human needs to set guidelines for municipal development and operation.

The Global Reporting Initiative has used the same economic, social and environmental categories to establish protocols for choosing indicators for sustainability reporting (Global Reporting Initiative, 2006). Its G3 Map addresses principles, strategy and profile and management approach and performance indicators for these three categories.

Finally the LOOP Iris reporting system has developed graphical presentation models that integrate a number of other sustainability reporting systems, including The Natural Step, Noisette Rose, One Planet Living Ten Principles, Harrup Spear and the Holland Barr Sustainability Matrix. LOOP Iris has a special focus on displaying eco-footprint size (Loop initiatives,

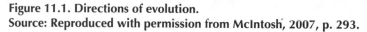

Figure 11.1. Directions of evolution.
Source: Reproduced with permission from McIntosh, 2007, p. 293.

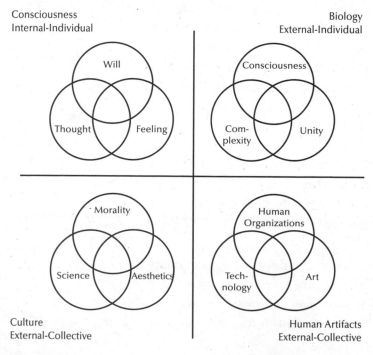

2007) that uses four quadrants to display Energy & Atmosphere, Community & Prosperity, Natural Environment, Materials & Consumables.

These three examples of indicator technology, as good as they are, are pre-integral designs. Ironically, because their focus is on sustainability, the key external context that these models only partially address is the energetic/climatic spectrum. And while all three incorporate some cultural or social elements, they are missing the vital depth metrics that correlate inner development (i.e., left-hand quadrants) with outer physical (i.e., right-hand quadrants) manifestation.

The key internal context missing in most indicator systems (or only partially represented) is human consciousness — the contribution made by the psycho-cultural quadrants of the integral model. Even in Canada where, in 2006, culture has been recognized as the fourth pillar of sustainability (Runnalls, 2007), this model remains a "flat" model because it omits the effects of change or development over time.

With the wealth of data now available in databases all over the world, the generation of innumerable indicators and the creation of multiple frameworks for reporting universal health, it has become obvious that the current stage of development for IVSMs is the Tower of Babel. As I have followed the discourse on healthy city (well-being, quality of life, happiness), sustainability and climate

Figure 11.2. GIS mapping image.
Source: Community Forum Workbook, *The State of Bowen Island*, vol. 1, 2001, p. 10.

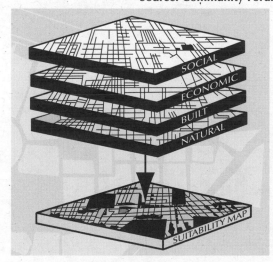

Geographic Information Systems(GIS) allow the overlay of different types of data to gain deeper understanding of the whole system. Key elements for sustainable development include:

The Natural Layer — the ecological environment including geology, soils, water, green spaces, animal, fish and other ecosystems and habitats, and the atmosphere and solar.

The Built Environment — the infrastructure and super structures, including utility and energy systems, material cycles, transportation systems and networks, communications systems and networks and buildings and artifacts.

Economic System — industry sectors (real estate, agriculture, manufacturing, services sectors, finance).

The Social Layer — this includes community governance, education, health care, culture and arts, worship, clubs and associations.

Integrating these four layers together enables communities to make land use decisions which are sensitive to each issue and therefore more sustainable.

Figure 11.3. Governance, monitoring and organisational learning framework end-to-end process. Source: Gaiasoft IP Ltd 2007, 2008. International patents pending. All rights reserved. V1.02. With permission.

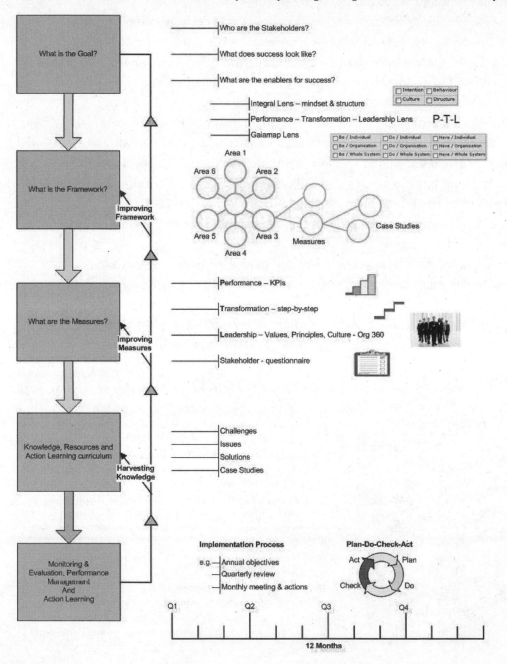

change indicators, I have come to the conclusion that the first step in creating sustainable vital signs monitors for the city (or any level of its holons) is to move to a meta-model that uses an integral design. An Integral design can translate all of the thousands of indicators that have been identified in the most advanced reporting systems around the world into meta-clusters and can report its findings in a common language (Eddy, 2006; Hamilton, 2006b).

In the last two decades, the powerful Global Information System (GIS) mapping technology has emerged. GIS has introduced the facility of layering maps in a way that discloses the interconnections of human systems and the natural environment. GIS mapping effectively reveals the boundary issues for sustainability of any given urban or regional system. Figure 11.2 identifies the natural, built, economic and social layers that this technology has the power to disclose.

While the GIS maps show us the layered relationship of people to place, another vector is required to show the timeline over which all the systems from natural to people evolve and change. This process appears in our Maps 1 and 4, in chapter 3, which disclose the change vector as a spiral unfolding over time. Figure 11.3 illustrates how this occurs with the people layers — within a governance monitoring and learning framework (Fourman, Reynolds, Firus, D'Ulizia 2008).

Each of our four maps transcends and includes the models discussed above and gives us valuable horizontal, vertical, diagonal and relational vectors for creating a more wholistic framework for an Integral Vital Signs Monitor. The Integral City model allows us to synthesize these frameworks and show how each contributes to truly mapping integral vital signs.

The Compelling Framework: Sustainable Life Conditions

However, before we do so, there is a foundational aspect and contexting piece to the vital signs monitor that relates to sustainable life conditions. Supplied by the likes of Robert Wright and Jared Diamond, it has been subsequently reinforced by the recent tornado of books on climate change (e.g., Gore, 2007; Monbiot & Prescott, 2007) . Diamond identified five factors that contribute to sustainable human society. They include paying attention to:

1. Climate change
2. Environmental health
3. Society's responses to environmental problems

4. Positive economic relationships

5. Incongruent neighbors (Diamond, 2005, p. 11)

Diamond's proposition gives us another reason to stand back from the myopic view of endless indicators and look at the sustainability equation from outer space or at least 10,000 meters. His starting point is the climate, and then the environment. Only after these elements are considered does he propose three different perspectives on the anthropic element. Diamond teaches us that, whether we are aware of these five factors or not, they are continuously interacting on each other and co-creating life conditions for city sustainability.

Diamond's argument lays the groundwork for introducing the integral framework for a vital signs monitor. The integral framework that we have been exploring in earlier chapters is essentially a meta-map that uses the four-quadrant, eight-level scaffold. But this meta-map of the city's pluralistic and dynamic qualities is totally contextualized within Diamond's critical factors of the environment and climate.

The integral meta-map is essentially dependent on Eddy's integral geographic proposition that reality has emerged from the big bang to current state through a series of progressive evolutionary complexities (2003b). This evolutionary process was introduced in chapter 1 and depicted in Figure 1.1. As Eddy notes:

> Integral Geography provides a means to explore consciousness and embodiment from a geo-spatial perspective, and conversely can be used to examine how space and place can affect both individual "minds" and "bodies" …. Consciousness remains a central focus from which human-environment interaction is explored, and from which a variety of other issues may be examined: such as geo-political tensions, ecological and environmental values, sociocultural settings, levels of techno-economic production and global trade. (2006, p. 158)

Eddy's powerful insights demonstrate the integral evolutionary principles, that any new level of development transcends and includes the capacities from which it emerges and on which it depends: "It can be seen how … certain plants require specific soil conditions, which in turn form under the influence of underlying rock types and weather patterns … which set the possibilities of patterns of emergence in the [anthropic] sphere" (2006, p. 158). As Eddy explains, each level of emergence can be examined separately through filters of differentiation and considered together through the filter of integration (p. 158).

Therefore, with Diamond's historical injunction that sustainability requires that we pay attention to his list of five factors and Eddy's integral geography, we are able to propose the framework for a vital signs monitor for an Integral City. This integral map has sufficient complexity to capture the well-being dynamics of the city (including its regional ecological context) and sufficient simplicity to make the map comprehensible to key city stakeholders.

It appears from Diamond's study that a vital signs monitor for an Integral City should develop indicators and benchmarks that recognize:

- climate systems that affect natural and human sustainability (e.g., rainfall, water tables)
- the limits of carrying capacity for the basic resources of air, land and water
- bio-psycho-cultural-social health indicators for individuals, families, workplaces, neighborhoods and city systems.
- sustainable economies
- sustainable infrastructures for transportation, health, education and commercial development
- congruent and incongruent neighbors that affect the health of the natural and human systems (e.g., air shed, water quality, transportation systems, human movement, communicable diseases)
- physical, psychological, cultural and social boundaries

How the Integral Model Reframes the Frameworks

The Integral Vital Signs Model transcends and includes all of the models presented above while incorporating Eddy's and Diamond's global frameworks. It re-contextualizes the traditional Brundtland sustainability model by placing the social and economic factors within the context of the environment as in Figure 11.4. This basically allows us to see the relationship of the I/WE social experiences in relationship to the IT/ITS economic actions. We can see that they arise simultaneously in the larger context of the environmental life conditions and the climate. This means that my internal experience is governed by environment and climate, and my external resonance with other people is also influenced by the same factors. Furthermore,

Figure 11.4. Integral sustainability framework.

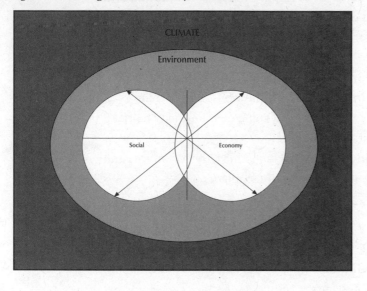

time is factored in so that the direction of growth and complexity for both human experiences and human actions can be shown traveling outward from the center of the quadrants — as shown by the arrows.

It is difficult to appreciate the simple complexity of this model when it is printed on a static two-dimensional page. To gain some appreciation of its dynamic capacity, this model must be seen or imagined in dynamic, interactive four dimensions (like an animated virtual object). As such it could disclose the plan view, the section view and the evolutionary time view to reveal its true representational qualities.

This model is both flexible and inclusive because it is a **fractal** model. That means that it can apply at multiple scales for human systems from the smallest (even within the context of an individual life) to the largest urban settlement. The model is also **holarchic**, in that it can contain multiple human systems, each being shown in context to the others that are contained within the whole. For instance it can encompass federated systems like public school boards and health systems or stand-alone systems like private enterprises. It can also embrace connecting systems, like the infrastructures of transportation, waste management, water, energy, communication.

With GIS and CAD/CAM mapping systems, it is also possible to display the **holographic** nature of this model. This means that we can turn it around and look at a subsystem of the whole from any particular perspective and see the whole reflected in the subsystem. An example of this would be seeing the whole city in a neighborhood or community (or even one of its subsystems like the infrastructures of transportation, waste management, water, energy, communication). Alternatively we could see the essence of any neighborhood in a view of the whole city.

Effectively we are designing a Vital Signs Monitor for a complex adaptive living system in the context of planet Earth. The purpose of this design is to come to know ourselves integrally and deeply. The true gauge in this IVSM is the operative information we need to know for the most intelligent way of living sustainably on this planet. By designing an IVSM, we cannot but come to know ourselves better and thereby understand more than we ever have known before about how we are embedded in the global, solar, galactic, universal system that has created us.

In the 1960s the consortium led by James Grier Miller (1978) identified 19 subsystems shared by every scale of living system from the one-celled to the most complex human social system. These subsystems were categorized into three basic clusters: those related to matter-energy-information, matter-energy and information. This work gives us some scientific analysis of the thousands of indicators from which we might choose to create IVSMs for living human systems.

However, the secret of usable IVSMs is to provide the minimum critical information for the optimum healthy performance of sustainable life. As Becker (2007) proposes, once we gain fluency in accessing indicators, it is not the volume or quantity of indicators that will provide the information we want, but the framework that reveals the messages of healthy relationships, holons, processes, patterns and structures. In integrally informed terms, this means tracking an awareness of the subjective, intersubjective, objective and interobjective feedback loops within the contexts of environmental and climatic life conditions. In other words, an IVSM not only provides the framework for reporting a taxonomy of indicators, but provides the "fuzzy logic scaffold" that discloses the relationships of the four-quadrant, eight-level patterns of complexity to one another.

The Benefits of an Integral Vital Signs Monitor

As noted above, using the technology of a book, it is difficult to truly appreciate the multi-dimen-

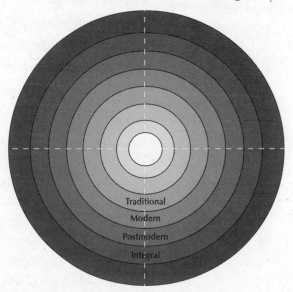

Figure 11.5. Levels of development in four quadrants and eight levels.

Traditional
Modern
Postmodern
Integral

sionality of an IVSM model, because it is conveyed in two-dimensional diagrams. An Integral Vital Signs Monitor recognizes the plurality of developmental capacities of all levels of existence, including the human individual and collective stakeholders. As Eddy has demonstrated, this plurality must be described in many layers. With an Integral Vital Signs Monitor, we can fully represent the human layers, with the four quadrants and eight levels of development, and thereby incorporate them into the principles of sustainability (see Figure 11.5).

Each of these developmental levels has its own patterns of worldviews, values, healthy expressions and unhealthy resistances to supporting sustainability or well-being as documented by Brown (2005a, 2005b, 2005c). An Integral Vital Signs Monitor recognizes the value of each level because it monitors data for the appropriate internal and external conditions for all eight levels as follows:

1. safety and supply of basic water, food, shelter, clothing
2. quality of life for family and significant other relationships
3. personal power and empowerment
4. systematic structures, protocols, rules and laws
5. proactive, rational, scientific productivity
6. social networks
7. complex, systemic, adaptive, interactive, flexible, interconnecting processes
8. planet-scale sensors of whole-system environmental and climatic well-being.

In doing so, the IVSM would reveal the healthy or unhealthy expressions of sustainability and report trigger points for action that is required to overcome any unhealthy blockages.

How Does IVSM Work?

In summary, the IVSM is an energy-matter-information-consciousness tracking system that reveals the relationship between energy, matter and information in four quadrants and eight levels of complexity, on an earthbound, human scale. It can measure the investment of energy, matter and information using multiple metrics.

However, it is also a learning system that is constantly refined by continuous usage. It provides closed-loop feedback for the city. Even though each quadrant has its own metrics, it can be related to all other quadrants through a lens of complex levels. The quadrants and levels are all hyperlinked to a database that identifies the source of the data, its properties and its desired performance target. Moreover, each indicator has an owner who is committed to supplying current data. The targets and the ownership of the indicators are selected by panels of experts (professionals, sapient circles, community members) who themselves are continuously learning by the feedback into the reporting system.

At least one prototype technology of the IVSM has been used by the private sector for the last decade. (See sidebar IVSM: Technical Implementation and Figures 11.6, 11.7.) It uses a simple but effective target-setting protocol that allows the organization to select indicators, choose targets, assign indicator owners and report on a worldwide basis into a central dashboard. This provides coverage of hugely complex data that includes both global summary and local detail that is also interculturally accessible because it uses a simple traffic-light system to display well-being. The status of the targets are displayed in the traffic-light system so that any viewer can understand at a glance if the indicator is on target (green), off target (yellow) or in crisis (red).

Selecting Integral Indicators for the Integral Vital Signs Monitor

The Integral Dashboard is a compact IVSM that tracks the achievement of target indicators corresponding to levels of emerging development, capacity or complexity. The indicators can be classified into two types: prehuman (which contribute all the elements necessary for biophysical human life) and human. Its prehuman elements are foundational and can be identified from Diamond's hypothesis and Eddy's model as:

- energy (solar and other types)
- lithosphere (rocks, minerals, land types)
- hydrosphere (water quality)
- atmosphere (air quality)
- biosphere (diverse species: biological, horticultural, zoological)

The human elements (or anthroposphere) are based on the fractals of human systems at different levels of scale, which occur in human development and human settlements and are well documented in the basic urban studies research methodologies (Eddy, 2003b, 2005, 2006), as noted in Figure 11.8.

INTEGRAL VITAL SIGNS MONITOR: TECHNICAL IMPLEMENTATION

Gaiasoft (Fourman, 2006) has created a library of information system DNA. Based on the Integral Vital Signs Monitor, its Integral Dashboard can be implemented and accessed through a Web browser.

The Integral Dashboard provides a knowledge base for storing and retrieving IVSM measures and interventions for each quadrant. They can be used on the job, at distance and when and where needed.

The Municipal home page (Figure 11.6) shows an overview of municipal indicators for:

- Foundational
- Individual
- Family
- Healthcare Systems/Education Systems/Workplace
- Community/Neighborhood
- Island/Municipality

Progress of compliance and strategy execution for indicator owners can be seen at a glance in a traffic light display (see Figure 11.7) developed by the private sector for global consolidations of financial and strategic data. As a global meta-language of its own, the colors convey information at a glance:

Blue: Target exceeded

Green: On target

Yellow: Caution – Off target

Orange: Emergency – Vital sign alert

Red: No target set – Action required to set one

A personal view shows the sapient circle, the executive team or any manager everything they are accountable for — measures, outcomes and actions. A journaling feature ensures that there is an audit trail for key compliance and strategy execution decisions. Charts show progress of key measures for assessing overall risk or traditional financial, customer or efficiency measures.

Criteria for Selecting Indicators

Indicators can be selected by a sapient circle, panel of experts and/or a modified Delphi method. The work that Global Reporting Initiative in Amsterdam has done in this area is enormously relevant and important, because they have effectively created an inventory and global body of knowledge from sectors and cities as they have wrestled with indicator selection protocols. A critical consideration for selecting relevant indicators ought to be the cultural norms of the people who will use the data. An IVSM must report data that is valued as important to the owners of the data on both local and global scales.

Thus, it is fair to say that the selection of indicators will be influenced by the filters of the choosers and users. The level of complexity represented in a given

Figure11.6. Municipal home page. Prototype by author on Gaiasoft.

Measures by Perspective in May 2005: Bowen Island

1. Foundation			2. Individual			3. Family		
Foundation			**Upper Left**			**Lower Left**		
Not Achieved	Air Quality	ON Target	Not Achieved	High school graduates	ON Target	Not Achieved	Family Services	Not Achieved
Not Achieved	Water Table	ON Target	ON Target	Education Level	ON Target	**Lower Right**		
ON Target	Boil Orders	Exceeded	**Upper Right**			Not Achieved	Housing	Not Achieved
Not Achieved	Land Forested/Developed	Not Achieved	ON Target	Population	Not Achieved	Not Achieved	Inventory Rental Rooms	Not Achieved
			Not Achieved	Visible Minorities	ON Target	Not	Personal	

4a. Healthcare				4b. Education		
Lower Left			Bowen Island Indicators	**Lower Left**		
Not Achieved	Healthcare Services	Not Achieved		Not Achieved	Education Services	Not Achieved
Lower Right				**Lower Right**		
Not Achieved	Healthcare Facilities	ON Target		ON Target	Education Facilities	ON Target

4c. Workplace			5. Community/Neighbourhood			6. Island/Municipality		
Lower Left			**Lower Left**			**Lower Left**		
Not Achieved	Chamber of Commerce	ON Target	ON Target	Parks & Recreation Programs	Exceeded	Vital Sign Alert	Social Services	Not Achieved
ON Target	Financial Services	ON Target	ON Target	Worship Belief System Cultural Services	ON Target	Not Achieved	Municipal/Provincial Services	ON Target
Lower Right			**Lower Right**			Not Achieved	Participation	Exceeded
ON Target	Local Exchange Trading System	ON Target	ON Target	Parks & Recreation Facilities	ON Target	**Lower Right**		
Not Achieved	Employers	Not Achieved				Not	Value Building	

Show Syml

Actions | Journal | **Input Data** | Chart   Executive Summary | Measur

Internet

Figure 11.7. Municipal traffic light display. Prototype by author on Gaiasoft.

Measures by Time Actual: Bowen Island

Perspective - CSF - Measure	Jan 2005	Feb 2005	Mar 2005	Apr 2005	May 2005	Jun 2005
1. Foundation						
Foundation						
Air Quality	No Target	Vital Sign Alert	Not Achieved	Not Achieved	Not Achieved	ON Target
Water Table	No Target	No Target	Not Achieved	Not Achieved	ON Target	ON Target
Boil Orders	No Target	Not Achieved	Not Achieved	ON Target	Exceeded	Exceeded
Land Forested/Developed	No Target	Not Achieved	Not Achieved	Not Achieved	Not Achieved	Not Achieved
Diverse Species	No Target	No Target	Not Achieved	Not Achieved	Not Achieved	Not Achieved
Energy	No Target	Not Achieved	Not Achieved	ON Target	ON Target	ON Target
Green Energy	No Target	Not Achieved	Vital Sign Alert	Not Achieved	ON Target	Not Achieved
2. Individual						
Upper Left						
High school graduates	No Target	Not Achieved	Not Achieved	Not Achieved	Not Achieved	ON Target
Education Level	No Target	ON Target	ON Target	ON Target	ON Target	ON Target
Upper Right						
Population	No Target	Not Achieved	Not Achieved	ON Target	ON Target	Not Achieved
Visible Minorities	No Target	No Target	Not Achieved	Not Achieved	ON Target	ON Target
Income	No Target	Not Achieved	Not Achieved	ON Target	ON Target	ON Target
Exercise	No Target	Not Achieved	ON Target	ON Target	ON Target	Exceeded
Unemployment	No Target	Not Achieved	Not Achieved	ON Target	ON Target	Exceeded
Employment	No Target	Not Achieved	Not Achieved	Not Achieved	ON Target	ON Target
Unpaid Child & Eldercare	No Target	ON Target	ON Target	ON Target	ON Target	ON Target
Crime	No Target	Not Achieved	ON Target	ON Target	Not Achieved	Vital Sign Alert

Actions | Journal | **Input Data** | Chart   Executiv

<< | < | May 2005 | > | >> | No Measure Selected. Click to the right of any Measure in the Scorecard above to select a Me

culture's human consciousness (their emotional, psychological, intellectual and spiritual development) and their shared belief systems will act as filters of what they value. If indicators are chosen from a level of complexity that exceeds that of the owners of the reports, the data will be discounted as meaningless. If the indicators are chosen from a level of complexity that is below that of the owners of the reports, the data will be disdained as simplistic. In both cases, the IVSM may serve other fractals, or even contexts, but it will not be embraced by the local data providers and/or report owners. Therefore it is vital that the creation of an IVSM be a participatory process that serves multiple needs.

The number of indicators for an IVSM is determined by the capacity of the culture to sustain reliability, recording and reporting. It is suggested that the number of indicators selected to track individuals be one to five subjective and one to five objective indicators. Within each of the collective human systems (from family to region), one to five intersubjective and interobjective indicators should be selected. These numbers can vary from location to location. The important criteria is that the people who will use these indicators consider them meaningful, and that they measure what is important to them and for (Earth-scale) sustainability.

The basic task of the designers of the Integral VSM is to organize the collection of data from existing databases and/or new data gathering methods. They then organize "owners of the data" to establish desired targets. These targets are then translated into a traffic-light system for users (from decision makers, to policy developers, to the public) to quickly assess the attainment of targets and take action where targets are in danger zones and/or suboptimal.

The entire process is one that is a form of action learning. It requires data owners to

Figure 11.8. IVSM concept diagram of nested holons.

NESTED HOLARCHY OF HUMAN SYSTEMS

- 1 = individual
- 2 = family/clan
- 3 = group/tribe
- 4 = organizations: workplaces, education, healthcare
- 5 = community(s)
- 6 = eco-system/country(s)
- 7 = world

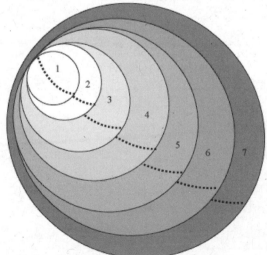

accountably self-assess and self-report against standards and best practices established in the design phase. In the process, users progressively learn and understand the standards they are meeting and wanting to attain, while at the same time learning how data sets are all interconnected. An IVSM is the technology that tracks the effectiveness of meshworks. It also maps the very hierarchies and networks that contribute to our city meshwork that have evolved from the four well-being frameworks cities could aspire to: traditional, modern, postmodern and integral.

The IVSM designers can and need to use the integral framework as a double-check to ensure that no indicator types, quadrants or levels are omitted. At the same time, they can caution users against identifying so many indicators that they will not be useable. Thus the IVSM designers should be working from a Level 7 or 8 personal and professional capacity so that they can appreciate the interconnected wholeness of the system. However, they can and should design for cities where people who will own the indicators have basic centers of gravity anywhere in the range of Level 2 through 7.

As noted previously, cities cannot really function or be managed effectively where key city managers have not achieved a complexity Level 4 capacity. However, in the developing world, many city managers will have complexity Level 3 and even Level 2 capacities that will make it very difficult for effective quadrant development or vital sign management. At the time of writing, this is only too evident in Baghdad and Kandahar where basic infrastructures of justice, health, education, water management and transportation are being continuously sabotaged by peoples whose belief systems are based on the complexity Level 2 clan and/or the complexity Level 3 kingdom. Even here (or especially here), the use of an IVSM would disclose where long-term as well as short-term resources will be needed to sustain urban well-being.

How Does the IVSM Add Value?

The IVSM adds value in four ways:

1. The essential design elements of the IVSM provide a framework, indicator organizer and common language to communicate results across cultures.

2. We can see the investment of resources that we have made in each quadrant and level, i.e., we can track energy, matter and information. We can

translate the investments into terms of any or all of: traditional financial management, strategic financial investment, density of social networks or sustainability vectors such as carbon-based resources.

3.   By the use of hyperlinking, we can see the linkage between realities (four quadrants), levels of complexity (eight-plus levels), time (development/ evolution) and scale.

4.   It allows us to compare results internally within urban systems and externally between urban systems.

In prototyping and analyzing datasets developed by others, I have noted the value of the Integral Vital Signs Monitor is that it provides common lenses, common denominators and a common language (Hamilton, 2006b).

The integral analysis deepens our understanding of change, development and evolution by opening lenses to see potential connections across studies from different domains of knowledge. Each study provides descriptors that contribute to a richer, more comprehensive, integrated indicators map than any one methodology or study could do on its own. The integral framework in turn provides the common language (and common denominators) to talk about indicators as they complexify (i.e., change) from different sources, different scales, different locations and under different life conditions. This analysis also shows us gaps in the integral data map that could help us widen our focus, strengthen our data-gathering methods and indicators and deepen our interpretation.

I have concluded that an IVSM effectively creates a quadruple bottom line for urban change. Research I have supervised or been informed of in a variety of domains has already demonstrated the utility of the four-quadrant, eight-level (4Q8L) maps for tracking change in individuals (Reams,

Figure 11.9. Measuring capacity on integral map.

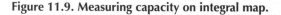
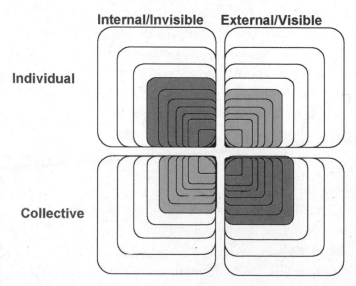

2002; V. Smith, 2002; Tupper, 2003), groups (Reynolds, 2003), organizations (Bates, 2006; Belanger, 2004; Deguire, 2005; Fisher, 2003; Hamilton, 1999), cities (Davison, 2006; Runnalls, 2007), communities (Hamilton, 1999; Nichol, 2006), bioregions (Eddy, 2003; Wight 2002, 2003), ecologies (Esbörn-Hargens, 2005) and countries (Beck et al., 2002).

This technology can provide the capability to nest, mesh and/or hyperlink multiple databases to allow a "weather mapping" approach to mining and summarizing data and mapping the dynamic complexity of land/bio/mind-scapes that Eddy (2003b) proposes "are converging in the spheres of influence of the modern community, town and city" (p. 299). I developed an early prototype by mapping the values of the city of Abbotsford. (See chapter 9 sidebar). Two more fully developed opportunities came from the prototyping of the complete eco-bio-noetic system of the Bowen Island Community (Hamilton, 2006a) and a northern self-sufficient First Nations community. In the case of Bowen Island, the source of the data came from a geo-library and a community forum process (See sidebar on Technical Implementation). In the case of the First Nations community, the data came from a community strategic plan analysis. The Integral City analysis used the data supplied in the strategic plan and mapped out the needs, gaps and visions in the four quadrants and eight levels (4Q8L). In addition, all the indicators supplied were mapped into the 4Q8L format, revealing oversights and opportunities for tracking progress.

In both cases, the IVSM design template captured existing data and translated it into the integral template. This process disclosed strong indicators where data was readily available and other indicators where data sources were either not identified or missing. In both cases, the IVSM provided an integral checklist for noticing strengths and gaps.

THE REAL "SO WHAT" OF IVSM: MAKING INFORMED CHOICES

Once an Integral Vital Signs Monitor is designed, then the Integral Dashboard (described below) can become the reporting vehicle for informing all the stakeholders of the city.

Thinking about the Integral City as the human equivalent of the beehive, the Integral Scorecard is our human equivalent of the bees' communication dance. It tells us whether we are achieving the purpose and objectives of the city in a sustainable way. It reveals to us if we are amassing the energy, matter and

Figure 11.10. Assessment of desired resources. Source: Abbotsford Community Foundation Research, Hamilton, 2003.

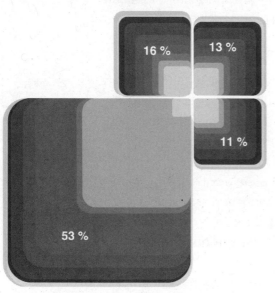

DESIRED RESOURCES

16 %

13 %

11 %

53 %

Figure 11.11. Assessment of Abbotsford Tax Allocation 2003.

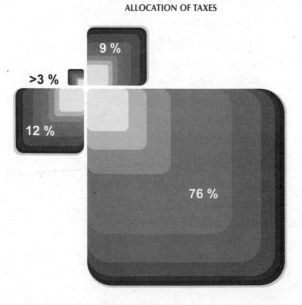

ALLOCATION OF TAXES

9 %

>3 %

12 %

76 %

information that we need to sustain ourselves. It is a way of mapping capacity and potential — as shown in Figure 11.9. The IVSM has the power to reveal the imbalances that McKibben identifies in *Deep Economy*. For example, in the situations where hyper-individualism has emerged, we would see Upper Left and Upper Right individual quadrants that were smaller than the lower collective quadrants (or vice versa). We would also see the situation where more capacity or resources were being allocated to the right-hand quadrants than the left (for example healthcare facilities at the expense of healthcare education.)

As a report on the environment and climate that produces the energy and matter, it is the information that our inner judges and Resource Allocators need to know if we should continue on course, change direction and to what degree. The IVSM can also display data from our stakeholders. For example, it can show us how resources are preferred from the perspective of multiple stakeholders in each quadrant and level (see Figure 11.10). And the IVSM can also shows us how resources are used by each quadrant and level (see Figure 11.11).

Without an IVSM, we have been blind to how our allocation of resources measures up to what we consider to be important. Moreover, as we have continued

MONITORING THE POLICY CYCLE

The diagram in Figure 11.12 illustrates the connection between monitoring and policy development (monitoring-policy cycle) on the basis of an Integral Vital Signs Monitor. Bettina Geiken used this for a project in European cities working on risk management (Geiken, Brown, & Fourman, 2005).

Policy, strategy or planning give rise to management and organizational structures, infrastructures and service provision [(1) in Figure 11.12], all of which have a positive or negative impact on the economy, environment, culture and social structure as well as on worldviews and behaviors of people. Quantitative and qualitative measurements of these by a variety of methods can be converted into indicators using appropriate frameworks.

At the same time, in order to evaluate and benchmark local development, it is necessary to measure the effectiveness and efficiency of service provision, management structures and policies, etc. against objectives and outcomes (performance indicators, outcome mapping, etc. [(2) in Figure 11.12].

Given the complexity of the measured reality and the large number of possible economic, environmental, sociocultural indicators at local and regional level [(2) in Figure 11.12], a limited number of key or meta-indicators [(3) in Figure 11.12] have to be developed and chosen as well as internal and external benchmarks [(4) in Figure 11.12]. From these meta-indicators and the results from benchmarking, policy recommendation can be drawn up [(5) in Figure 11.12].

Use of the Integral approach would ideally give rise to sociocultural indicators, benchmarks and policy recommendations that point to a more integral view of the situation in the communities in any given region.

This comprehensive information on the state of city development facilitates trend analysis and makes the interconnectedness tangible for the different economic, sociocultural and environmental phenomena arising from the implementation of sectoral policies.

11.12. Integral monitoring and policy cycle.

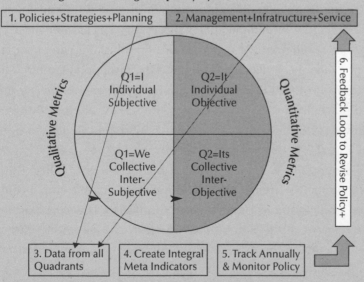

to expand the kinds and quantities of our use of resources, we need more complex maps to reflect our new knowledge, capacities, values and assets.

With an integral map of our new realities, the IVSM can show us a dynamic map of our choices and even simulations of the outcomes they might create before we put them into effect. Once we have made the choices, the IVSM can help us intelligently decide whether we are allocating resources for optimal sustainability and quality of life. With the help of GIS mapping, we can then track resources, allocations and results, as shown in Figure 11.13.

NEXT STEPS FOR IVSM

In the process of developing and prototyping the Integral Vital Signs Monitor, it has become clear that we need the flexibility to design multiple formats for a dashboard. Multiple formats are needed so that each locality can collect, analyse and display data in a locally meaningful way.

However, for city-scale collection purposes, a central hub would provide a distillation of the variety of sources, owners and states. In truth, IVSM deserves a whole book on its own; however, for the benefit of early adopters, a sidebar describes a technical implementation process for an Integral Scorecard system.

LEARNING TO CHANGE: HOW VITAL SIGNS MONITORS INFORM US

When a developer, governance authority or elected official makes a promise to citizens, he relies on others (the local municipal manager, officials and technical and administrative staff) to implement the promise. Often, with the greatest commitment and resources available, goals do not turn into the intended results.

Integral geographer Brian Eddy has shown in his research how we think about regions and places and what we say about them (i.e., whether things are good, bad or otherwise) depends in part on what boundaries we use to define them — physically in the exterior world, conceptually in our mental models and existentially in our values, worldviews and projections of reality. Eddy's research suggests that many sustainability and development issues are a continuation of boundary-conflicts among projections of various levels of consciousness and cultural development. Eddy notes that, "These cognitive and existential boundary conflicts manifest in the exterior world in a variety of complex ways — so much so that only an integral approach can begin to adequately address issues

Figure 11.13. GIS Google Earth simulation.
Source: Eddy, 2007.

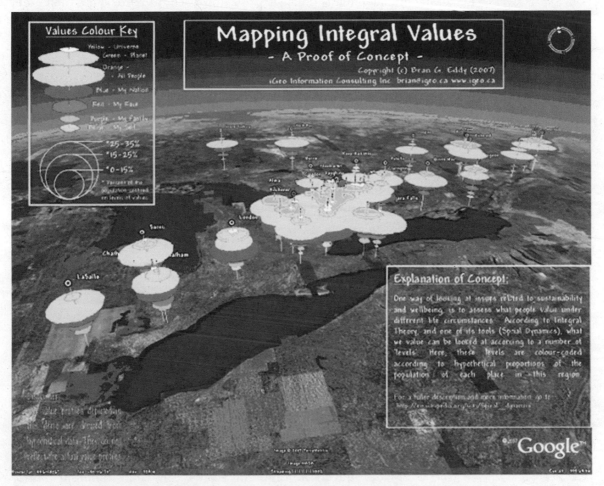

of sustainability with development in geopolitical contexts at different scales of interaction" (2003a). This important insight, combined with 20 years professional experience in working with a vast array of geo-information, allows Eddy to assess well-being, sustainability and development on regional to global scales.

VITAL SIGNS MONITORS ENABLE THE INTEGRAL CITY

In reviewing the design and use of IVSMs, we can now summarize the value of applying an integral IVSM to researching, planning and managing change in the Integral City.

Research

1. An intentional integral data gathering approach discloses more than other methodological approaches. Because the integral frameworks provide a whole-systems checklist to gather data and a common language to integrate the results from multiple data sources across nested levels of complexity, we can see both where our lenses are clear and where we are missing data. Thus we have a language to describe change that reflects different realities, indicators and values at any level of scale.

2. Other databases can be translated into a common integral/spiral "language" and thus produce an Integral Vital Signs Monitor. This means that existing databases do not have to be discounted, but can instead be integrated into the meta-map. Research results can be cross-referenced to existing:
   - census data
   - GIS surveys
   - school district data
   - university college data
   - health region data
   - agricultural surveys
   - private sector polls, etc.

3. Various prototype and pilot projects map the first steps in any change process. They identify what the community is changing from (both positive and negative) and what the community wants to change to (identified by the improvements desired). New web-based data-gathering processes indicate that dynamic data tracking will shortly become widespread.

4. The IVSMs produced at different scales can chart different world-views/values/ tensions of citizens, elected officials, staff and experts.

5. Change states and dynamic data gathering permit the tracking of dynamic complex adaptive qualities and the use of natural systems for designing change processes.

6. The meta-map qualities are GIS mappable and could be collected as change indicators by either or both government and private researchers, e.g., by census departments or creators of the Cascadia Scorecard (Northwest Environment Watch, 2004, 2005, 2006).

Planning

1. The common meta-map provides data for social planning, land use (hard asset) planning and the integration of community education and health-care development.

2. The meta-map allows meshworkers to design balanced change in all the quadrants, preventing abilities to change because of blindnesses and/ or blocks.

3. The meta-map of qualitative (left-hand quadrants) and quantitative (right-hand quadrants) data is scaleable at individual, organizational, neighborhood, city, regional and bioregional scales, thus allowing a kind of "weather mapping" of complex change usable by city planners, urban geographers, developers, etc.

Management

The common language meta-map:

1. Provides a tool for meshworkers to manage extreme complexity. The common language not only allows the use of a diversity of data to coexist, but it provides a rationale for organizing and stratifying it for decision making. It also allows for feedback loops to advise change managers of the effectiveness of their decisions.

2. Provides a synchronized set of integral vital signs indicators for meshworkers to facilitate policy change.

3. Provides the evidence and data to translate between multiple interests of many community stakeholders who would benefit from an integrated framework.

4. Provides the information for meshworkers to develop spatial, temporal and capacity mapping strategies of all kinds.

5. Discloses the meso-level of city values as a context for comprehending the interrelationship of micro-ecologies (individual/group) and macro-ecologies (bioregion, country, world).

6. Provides a mapping process that can disclose the dynamics below the surface expressions of values.

CASE STUDY T: INTEGRALLY INFORMED SUSTAINABLE CITY INDICATORS. AQAL: ALL QUADRANTS; PHYSIOSPHERE AND BIOSPHERE LEVELS

BY WILL VAREY (2008) (WITH PERMISSION)

The three main government bodies responsible for sustainable land-use planning jointly participated in a collaborative inquiry to develop the baseline indicators for a sustainable city. The inquiry was prompted by the desire to engage in long-term city planning that would endure beyond the three-year political cycle and withstand short-term changes in political power and fluctuating social policy. The initiative was prompted by the conjunction of declining indicators in a comprehensive state of the environment report and dramatically increasing projections for urban housing demand. The indicators developed looked specifically at the city's fundamental environmental needs for the sustainable carrying capacity of the urban environment. The inquiry specifically excluded from the indicator set social and economic factors that were politically influenced (e.g., crime levels, community services, unemployment, urban land-release) that may drive social changes in conflict with or independent from the underlying ecosystem integrity. This approach respected the principles of holarchical development in Integral Sustainability systems theory, being that, without underlying biosystem integrity, the social, economic and political systems integrity cannot be ultimately sustained. An expert was engaged to propose an initial set of macro-categories for the indicators (drawing from many sources, including the 1992 Bellagio Principles, international case studies from other cities, national standards, current environmental reports and state planning documents). A multipurpose stakeholder group was then formed to refine this wider category set into five essential indicator categories from a sustainable city planning perspective, being: water, waste, energy, shelter and the integrative dimension of land use. Within each category, an Integral approach was used to specify the statement of intention (UL), outcome values (LL), specific initiatives (LR) and measurable indicators of enactment (UR) to create an integral framework of macro-level citywide sustainability goals. The framework was then populated with 25 key indicators of system sustainability using location-specific information. This integral set of baseline indicators across five interlinked aspects of essential human needs for sustainable habitation provided a means to define the base system-health of the city's sustainability at any time and for any time frame. By monitoring and maintaining these lower-order dynamics, changing social policy needs could then be overlaid upon the baseline carrying capacity of the city's ecosystem health, with the view to ensuring both a sustainable and culturally evolving society as a whole. The proposed set of city planning indicators was then recommended to the main interagency planning body for widespread adoption as the main intergovernmental reporting tool for the city's overall sustainable design. (Tool: Integral Baseline Sustainable City Indicators).

CONCLUSION

With close to 60 percent of the world's population now living in cities, it is apparent that cities have a disproportionate influence on the health of the world. In making global systems healthy, they have a vast meso-scale role to play in supporting change in all scales of life in the modern world. This can only be effectively catalyzed and monitored by meshworkers who can understand an IVSM using a common language that translates all the indicators of change across different quadrants, levels and times, plus levels of scale. This integral template enables meshworkers to facilitate the insights about the vast complex interconnectedness within the quadruple bottom lines of the cosmopolis. With an IVSM intelligence system and a common language, we are ready now to create opportunities for new participatory collaboration and planning processes and a framework for choosing, monitoring and improving the quality of urban and global life.

QUESTIONS

1. How do we select the minimum number and integrate all the indicators we want to use?

2. How do we create a language that celebrates life and is shared by all?

3. How do we set a mix of sustainability targets that allow different data "owners" to report on progress towards goals and policy makers to make appropriate course corrections?

Three simple rules for applying Integral City principles from this chapter:

1. Select the future destination of the city based on its vision.

2. Design and implement integral dashboards, using integral indicators of well-being for the city.

3. Notice outcomes and make course corrections to enable progress naturally.

EVOLVING INTELLIGENCES: IMAGINING THE FUTURE FOR HUMAN HIVES

For all their efforts, though, humans have not succeeded in domesticating bees.
A swarm escaping from a commercial hive has just as good a chance of surviving in the wild
as a feral swarm, and the number of wild colonies living in trees still far exceeds the
population living in accommodations designed for them by humans. The history of beekeeping,
then, has not been a story of domestication, but rather one of
humans learning how to accommodate the needs and preferences of the bees themselves.

— Gould and Gould, 1988, p. 17

We shape ourselves to fit this world and by the world are shaped again.
The visible and the invisible working together in common cause to produce the miraculous.

— Whyte, 2001, pp. 201-202

WHERE DID WE START?

This book has been an inquiry about how to live in cities intelligently. It has drawn from discoveries in the arts, humanities, natural sciences and hard sciences to understand the city as a living system. Its principles and assumptions address key concerns of citizens, civil society, city managers at all government levels and city developers.

For curious, creative and responsible citizens, Integral City explains the dynamics of living in the city as a whole system so people can see that "everything counts." Each thought, act, belief and task is connected to everything else

257

WHO EVOLVES INTELLIGENCES IN THE HUMAN HIVE?

For executive and management civil servants, Integral City recognizes their contributions as vital functions of a living system. If these functions are not operating at a level of complexity sufficient to the scale of the city, the well-being of all parts of the city will suffer in some way. These important bureaucracies are located in: City Hall; state and provincial ministries with overlapping city mandates, e.g., Municipal Affairs, Health, Education, Children and Families, Land and Water, Energy; and federal government with overlapping city mandates, e.g., Intergovernmental Affairs/Cities, Public Health Agency, Health, Energy.

and may build momentum in any direction. Alternatively any thought, act, belief or task may be the tipping point that causes an irretrievable shift in direction and/or capacity. It is truly humbling to realize that "everything counts."

Fifteen years ago, I accepted an invitation to serve my city on an active volunteer board for a national sporting event. That experience opened my eyes to the complexity of human systems and set me on a quest to find out the answer to the question, Do leaders make the community? Or does the community make the leaders?

In the course of trying to find an answer, I have had the privilege of studying (often directly with) many of the great minds of the new sciences, new urban studies and the integral movement. I have acknowledged some of my key influencers at the beginning of this book.

This book has really been a decade in the making, for it continues where my dissertation left off. I simply moved on from considering the complexities in communities to the complexity of thinking about the whole city.

WHERE HAVE WE BEEN?

Throughout this book, I have used the beehive as a metaphor for a living system that displays patterns of intelligence analogous to a city. The analogy is not direct and often insufficient because the emergence of complexity in the vertebrate *homo sapiens sapiens* is far greater than that of the invertebrate honeybee. However, the beehive gives us surprising and even delightful provocations with which to think about the Integral City.

The four integral maps then gave us the tools to explore evolutionary intelligences in new ways — not simply the intelligence arising from the external physical evolution of climate and geography, or biology and engineering, but also the internal intelligences arising from consciousness and culture.

By starting with the climatic and geographic contexts where cities have emerged, I recognized that, even at this foundational level, the map is not the territory — but it is very useful nonetheless. The patterns with which climate and geography influence human behavior appear to have set significant conditions for the development of all distinct cultures. Moreover climate and geography have had strong influence on whether cultures are friendly or hostile to one another. Complexity science tells us that starting conditions in any system leverage the behavior of that system across time and space. And so we see that cities that were born on the seashore thousands of years ago solve problems differently than cities of the mountains or desert even today.

The maps we identified for Integral City disclosed intelligences we usually fragment or separate from one another, failing to see that all city intelligences have co-evolved. In fact the answer to my original chicken-and-egg question of whether leaders created communities or vice versa revealed that they co-emerge — one influences the other in a never-ending interaction. Likewise, the inner and outer lives of individuals and groups in the city co-evolve. In fact the self-similarity of these patterns indicate the fractal nature of human systems embedded in the city — each level of scale affecting the patterns of other levels of scale in endless feed-back loops.

So the maps that we have used to explore the intelligences of the human hive have helped us explore the city through the vectors of evolution, the individual and collective, the interior and exterior, the psychology of change and the nested holarchies of bio-psycho-cultural-social interconnections. So many of these views are just gaining ground as specialized ways of looking at vertical slices of life. But the complexity of the city merits an integration of at least these perspectives so that we can gain some better understanding of *how* leaders change themselves and others and *how* communities and cities demonstrate collective cohesive behaviors (or not).

I freely admit to speculating about the merits of the integral view as a new paradigm of the city, without a full review of the literature from earlier paradigms

HOW DOES INTEGRAL CITY EVOLVE
INTELLIGENCES IN THE HUMAN HIVE?

For elected officials, *Integral City* highlights the leadership landscape so that qualities of life are visible and achievable. These leaders are situated in all bureaucracies. But more than the functional or physical location of these leaders, *Integral City* has tried to address the inner landscapes of these leaders' minds and hearts. It is their capacities of consciousness that limits or enables the level of thriving of all whom they lead.

For executive and management in private and NFP — education, healthcare, social services institutions, agencies, and public, private, partnerships (PPP) — *Integral City* links together their work as an integrated whole, enabling the optimization of quality of city life. It is vital that these fractals of the Integral City be fully and concurrently at the table and that they contribute to decisions about city development.

For the justice sector, *Integral City* highlights the developmental and pathological nature of human systems that naturally arise from the blockage of healthy energy flows and reveals appropriate ways to restore balance.

For NFP, NGOs and social enterprises with missions in the city, *Integral City* demonstrates that their contributions often create the cultural and social capital vital to individual survival.

For teachers, professors, students and scholars, *Integral City* offers a text and a curriculum of questions for whole-systems thinking about the city that can be applied to: urban planning, social work, anthropology, psychology, social psychology, justice, geography, social geography, sociology and political science.

For First Nations, *Integral City* suggests that viewing their place-based cultures in terms of a city-state integrates whole-systems thinking with their tribal and traditional cultures.

For learning communities, *Integral City* shows the patterns of intelligent development, evolution and emergence that people in cities can choose, to optimize individual and collective learning.

— which will no doubt frustrate the whole field of urban studies. However, that task in itself is a monumental one that deserves its own book. I am confident that work will be accomplished in the not-too-distant future. My task here has been to apply the integral paradigm to the city and see how effective it might be in explaining the phenomenon of the human hive.

WHERE COULD WE GO?

Where could we go from here? In the later stages of editing this book, I embarked on a cruise that took me to three continents, fifteen cities, eight countries, uncounted cultures and subcultures and six languages. As I contemplated the feast of human systems through which I passed, I tested the maps of *Integral City* and captured these impressions:

- Seeing the city as a whole interconnected to other wholes reveals the emergent, evolving system.

- Seeing systems reveals interconnections and non-linearity.

- Non-linearity helps us to live with, prepare for and anticipate the unexpected.

- Having muscles for the unexpected creates resilience.

- Resilience means greater adaptability.

- Greater adaptability means greater survivability.

- Greater survivability means more joy, expansion, creativity, potential.

Exploring the *Integral City* has revealed to me that we have much to learn in realizing the potential of the city. In my travels, as I talked with others, I found that my most inspiring insights continued to come from parables of the beehive, stories from worldcentric leaders and the never-ending generative impulse to evolutionary intelligence. As I close this book, I share these thoughts with those who share my curiosity about the human hive.

Perhaps the bees exemplify best what natural systems have to teach us. Life is cyclical and demands that we adapt and evolve. The natural rhythms of the hive demonstrate that stability is not found in a perpetual steady state but in the adaptive responses to our life conditions. Just as the hive survives because some bees are diversity generators while other bees optimize the use of available resources, cities can borrow the lessons of adaptiveness to limit over-exploitation or under-reorganization and explore new options.

As carbon-based energy shortages start to intensify and climate changes increase pressures on those resources, we see cities naturally implementing the lessons of the bees by reducing energy consumption through green building and seeking new options through the development of energy sources like wind, solar and wave.

SUMMARY OF *INTEGRAL CITY* OBJECTIVES

This book was written for anyone who wants to see the city as a whole system so they can gain insights that will optimize their whole life. *Integral City* was framed from life-giving principles. It was based on whole-systems thinking so that the impact of the city could be appreciated in a comprehensive and integrated manner by all those who live in it and for all those who need to appreciate its impact as a whole on planet Earth.

The concept of Integral City was founded on sustainability but goes beyond it to consider the implications of emergence, i.e., it assumes that the human condition is a never-ending quest involving continuous adaptation and change. This is both good news and bad news — it means accepting that uncertainty and ambiguity are our never-ending partners and we will never know all there is to know, because the reality of the city is constantly unfolding.

Integral City considered the city in the context of the environment that is the context for economic and social capacity. This meant that we appreciated that each city had the distinctive features of its environmental Petrie dish. Every city is unique in its adaptiveness to its environment. That needs to be both respected and considered in understanding its capacity for development, its internal functioning and its potential for external contributions.

Integral City contextualized the city in terms of global and local ecology while exploring the dynamics of the city's internal human ecology. This reveals the tension that exists in the actual formation of the city. The internal human ecology has a tendency to create a centrifugal force that thrusts the city outward into its landscape, while the global and local ecologies create a natural centripetal force that define the constraints of the city.

Integral City assumed that city structures and infrastructure arise from and connect to natural systems. It has always been tempting to see the architecture and engineering of the city as apart from or imposed on natural systems. But when we examine the science of structures, we see that they are forever in the same flow states that all natural systems are subject to. These apparently non-living structures may have very slow (or seemingly arrested) flow states, but they are just as much part of the natural system as the living structures of plants, animals and humans. Likewise it appears that the infrastructures that are internal to our human systems — the marvels that are our bodies, brains and minds — are also evolutionary systems, subject to the natural flex and flow of energy, matter and information from the protein-building blocks in our DNA on up.

In fact Integral City framed human systems within the context of energetic flex and flow — not separate from global energy systems, but an integral part of them, like urban energetic acupuncture nodes. When we honor the city with this nodal capacity, we start to see what an important role it is playing in the evolution of all human capacities.

Integral City proposed that cities create dynamic energy fields that have qualities of resonance, coherence and emergence. We are just waking up to the power of the very real energy field created by collective intelligences and realizing we could harness our innate intelligences into intentional distributed networks. Even as we plumb the intricacies of human brain power to create robotics, we are learning how much more we could gain through collective communities of mental and spiritual practice. This seems the stuff of science fiction, but in fact the Integral City teaches us that it is merely the natural evolution of *homo sapiens sapiens*.

Integral City considered community to be a journey to wholeness for groups of people and that the quality of city communities contributes to the quality of city life. The fractal nature of human systems enables us to see that communities are natural, powerful levers for enabling human systems. Even as cities globalize and put much energy into looking outward, it is obvious that they must put as much energy to looking inwards and making geographic communities, special interest communities and communities of practice vibrant and well. Belonging to these kinds of communities appears to be fundamental to the human condition.

Integral City rested on the assumption that effective city leadership requires an understanding of dynamic human development, integrated with healthy workplaces, education and healthcare systems. Effective city leaders are interested and invest in leadership of themselves, other individuals, organizations and communities at the appropriate level of complexity. Effective leaders lead from about a half a level ahead of the current level of development, offering a vision that is a stretch but attainable.

Integral City considered that human systems are nested holarchies, including integral roles for parents and families. Effective city leaders transcend and include the roles of families and parents in creating meshworks that solve problems, create environments and encourage people. Leaders in every fractal aspect of the city know that they cannot achieve community growth without supporting parents and families to invest simultaneously in integral bio-psycho-cultural-social growth.

The lessons that come from worldcentric leaders are surprising and paradoxical. Who knew the ship's captain had training that could contribute to managing and leading cities? The sea captain who said "You cannot expect unless you inspect" meant that you cannot expect results unless you inspect performance. So (bio-mimicking an IVSM?) he argued for responsible control that was widely shared by all crew members. At the same time, he expected the unexpected. So the performance he expected most from his crew was to be able to respond to the unexpected. He underscored the reality of non-linearity. He also used the cycles of change so that, in periods of calm and stability, resources were prepared for the inevitable occurrence of storms, rogue waves and the unpredictable — all times when preparations for the unexpected paid dividends of responsiveness, adaptiveness and creativity.

The potential for expanding and exploring Integral City land-based lessons as they apply to human systems in sea and outer-atmosphere-based geographies remains largely untapped. What would happen if we brought together the nautical (and even aerospace) academies with the academy of city management? What would happen if city CAOs, COOs and CFOs sat down with captains, chief engineers and cruise ship hotel managers (and even their equivalents in military or space commands)? What could we learn about solving the dilemmas of cities by appreciating solutions that have been developed under much less forgiving conditions for the sea and cosmosphere?

HOW WILL WE GET THERE?

The chance to stretch my imagination for the value of Integral City beyond the confines of planet Earth came from dialogue with another worldcentric leader — a member of the NASA medical team. His lessons from aerospace reminded me that the greatest opportunity for creating new realities comes not from the past but from the future. Our history tells us where we have been in the past and how we survived, adapted and regenerated to live another day. But it is through our imaginations we can literally gain altitude from toxic cities on a beleaguered Earth. First off, from 10,000 meters we can literally see the wholeness that is in any given city. Even Google Earth gives us the tool of zooming in and zooming out at different levels of scale to appreciate the patterns and structures of the city. But it is truly from the galactic distances of the moon and solar system that we are able to see the Earth as a whole system (even in its minuteness to galactic time/space). From that perspective, we can truly marvel at the intelligence we know exists in the pinpoint of the blue planet. We can better see that not just the tiniest of individuals but the cities we have evolved are critical nodes of intelligence — literally dots of light that indicate where intelligence has coalesced in the universe.

But it is by turning our gaze to the cosmosphere and using our intelligence to identify and analyse the resources that are there that we realize the potential of our future. Every energy and material resource we need appears to be available in abundance in our solar system and the galaxy. Our job is to figure out how to access and harness those resources in the service of universal intelligence and evolution. Perhaps the answers will only emerge when we combine the intelligences of land, sea and air to optimize the potential of the city and develop the first prototype space colonies. Maybe those prototypes will even be on Earth?

The city is the best example of what a future space colony might operate like. But a city floating in space or located on other planets will need the wisdom of all the city voices (managers, developers, civil society and citizens) and the technical know-how of ship captains and crew and the investment and imagination of aerospace developers. We can only imagine the spirit and qualities of these investment and development pioneers by thinking back to the time when the Medicis funded the Renaissance (and its hundreds of artists), the Rothschilds funded the early Industrial Revolution and the Rockefellers funded the opening of the American West. Somewhere in our midst today are the pioneers who will create space colonies that will take the journey of the human species from Earth to what we now call outer space. Some day that space may be as accessible, populated and developed as the part of this world that emerged beyond the "end of the world" that was once bounded by the Straits of Gibraltar. We will look back from that future time and recount the tales of private investors who offered space vacations on the first private spaceships and developers who created the technologies that would allow us to mine meteorites and produce hydrogen, oxygen and water on demand.

But wherever we go in the future, there we will be, with whatever bio-psycho-cultural-social realities we will have evolved, quite probably in some kind of pod whose functions are likely to resemble the human hive. So exploring the intelligence of the city is not merely an investment in our own effectiveness and efficiency and its resulting comfort for today. It is not just an investment to address the social ills of cities in developing nations. It is not just an investment for the benefit of our children and grandchildren. Exploring the intelligence of the city is a necessary research project to ensure the survival of the human species on this Earth long enough for us to create the conditions where human life can be supported in space cities or colonies. Such space colonies are the natural legacy we have in our power to vest if we can attract, assemble and crystallize the intelligences inherent in the Integral City.

The prospects for this work are not guaranteed. In fact we face many threats. We need merely look to the past, present and future prospects of *apis mellifera* and Leaders to the Power of 8 to gain an understanding of how quickly we must move.

The natural history of the bee and the beehive shows us that it is possible to develop highly refined systems that serve the collective survival of a species. The evolution of the bee in every country of the world indicates its resilience and capacity to continuously learn and adapt to local conditions. However the current peril of the bees in North America is an object lesson for human systems that the unexpected can undermine even the most apparently stable system. At time of writing, up to 90 percent of many domesticated bee colonies of the United States have been wiped out in one year (Bjerga, 2007; Mittelstadt, 2007; Time Magazine, 2007). The symptom of the dilemma which threatens $75 billion of human agriculture production is that bees depart the hive and forget to return and just die outside the hive. The cause is as yet unknown. Theories include some or any of the following: infections from virus and/or mites, genetic resistance to breeding stock change, climate change and environmental toxicity. Whatever the cause, the current threat is deeply troubling to the future of human agriculture but more fundamentally to the future of the bee species as a whole. Extinction of some bee families certainly seems a worrisome possibility. If this were cities instead of beehives, we might be facing a global pandemic, a resource poisoning or a significant decimation of a selectively evolved part of the gene pool.

The sea captain reminds us that past leaders of *homo sapiens sapiens* have set out on the high seas to explore most of the planet. The intimate relationship of the captains and navigators of the high seas remind us that most cultures recount the ark story as fundamental to the survival of the human species. So we have it in our own history of planet Earth that the wisdom of survival afloat on unknown seas is the root of survival anywhere and everywhere for all living things. Thus we ignore with peril the "inconvenient truths" that are most evident from the seas around the world that the Earth and climate are changing. Although we argue still about the causes of the change, we are clearly able also to argue how to survive in the face of the change that is causing sea levels to rise and ice levels to recede. Of all the geographies on Earth, the sea reflects the larger rhythms of cosmic space through its daily tides and continuous wave motion. And despite its regularity, the sea also teaches us with greatest seriousness the lessons of non-linearity. Despite its seeming predictability of nature, it is the source of killer rogue waves, ocean currents and weather flows. And it holds the greatest biomass of any geography on Earth.

The fascination of the NASA leader with colonizing outer space parallels in many ways the fascination of historical leaders with the seas. Ironically, despite the many destinations where we have built cities along its shores, we have yet to effectively harness its diurnal energies or plumb its watery depths as thoroughly as the deep space that separates us from the moon. Nevertheless the sea has been the great trainer of leaders' skills related to vital signs monitoring; interconnectedness; short-, medium- and long life cycles; non-linearity and the unexpected. For worldcentric leaders, the sea is like a gyroscope of the Earth's well-being. It is a globe-sized tool whose indicators of health and wellness can give us a macro-means to reflect the health and wellness of humans at all levels of scale.

What lessons for cities can leaders possibly take from pondering the merits of space colonies since none yet exist? We have mere glimpses of their potential from the short history of man in space, starting with the Russians' first moon shot, to the Americans' man on the moon, to the international MIR space station. Like the planned cities in the Arabian Desert, we are imagining blue prints of possibilities. But the necessary investment and political will has yet to back up any lip service. Because the truth of the matter is that to create space colonies — like the bees who apply the intelligences (learned in either wild or designed hives) to swarm, relocate and create whole new hives in the wild — we will likely have to apply the intelligences we develop on Earth to obtain the resources to build space colonies from space. (For we do not have sufficient energy or resources to move the necessary resources from Earth to a space colony.) Thus we have many years of Integral City capacity building ahead of us — from food production and shelter construction, to inner-space people development systems, to mining meteorites — before a self-sustaining space colony can emerge. This will require us to grow the capacities of collaboration, community and colonization beyond any context the human system has ever evolved.

A SUMMARY OF THE SIMPLE RULES FOR APPLYING *INTEGRAL CITY* PRINCIPLES

When I look back at the simple rules we might apply to create Integral City (at the end of each chapter), I see the moral to the parable I have been telling. I am struck with how the rule sets of the human hive may aggregate into some macro-rules that have been discovered by others. Angeles Arrien is credited with proposing these four simple rules for building tribal community:

Show up. Be present. Speak your truth. Let go of results.

If we meshworked these self-organizing rules with a simple hierarchy of order (that I have seen credited to apocryphal high-school principals from New Zealand to New York, and heard repeated, much to my delight and surprise, by a leading-edge city planner at a recent inquiry session), I think we might distil the macro-wisdom we need for well-being in the human hive on this Earth and beyond.

Take care of yourself. Take care of each other. Take care of this place.

So by way of summary, I reprint the 11 sets of three simple rules from previous chapters and add a twelfth set for this chapter:

Chapter 1. Ecosphere Intelligence

1. Honor the climate and geography of your city.
2. Steward the environment.
3. Add value to the ecosphere.

Chapter 2. Emerging Intelligence

1. Survive so holons serve each other's existence.
2. Adapt to the environment.
3. Create a self-regenerating feedback loop, by interconnecting human regeneration cycles so that they replenish the environment.

Chapter 3. Integral Intelligence

1. Map the territory integrally (horizontally through four quadrants, vertically through eight plus levels of development, diagonally through its change states and relationally through its nested holarchies and fractals of complexity).
2. Create and sustain an integral mapping system at the highest sustainable level of complexity that is appropriate to the capacities of city management.
3. Learn from and update the maps annually or more often.

Chapter 4. Living Intelligence

1. Honor the dance of life cycles in the city.
2. Integrate the natural cycles of change within the city.
3. Learn how to zoom in and out at different scales to dance with the fractal patterns of the city.

Chapter 5. Inner Intelligence

1. Show up and be self-aware, present, mindful.
2. Notice the city intelligences and map them integrally.
3. Grow leadership in heart, mind, soul.

Chapter 6. Outer Intelligence

1. Manage personal energy.

2. Seek bio-physical well-being for self and others.

3. Nurture healthy leaders.

Chapter 7. Building Intelligence

1. Manage life-sustaining energy for all.

2. Design from the center, at all scales for all holons.

3. Build structures that integrate self-organizing creativity with hierarchies of order.

Chapter 8. Story Intelligence

1. Respect others.

2. Listen deeply.

3. Speak your story, and enable others to speak theirs, to co-create communities of integral practice.

Chapter 9. Inquiry Intelligence

1. Ask what's working (and not) and co-generate a vision for the city's contribution to the planet.

2. Create an integral city and community plan.

3. Implement and manage the plan appropriately at all scales in the city.

Chapter 10. Meshing Intelligence

1. Catalyze fractal connections within the human hive.

2. Build communication bridges across silos, stovepipes and solitudes.

3. Enable meshes and hierarchies that transform, transcend and transmute capacities.

Chapter 11. Navigating Intelligence

1. Select the future destination of the city based on its vision.

2. Design and implement integral dashboards, using integral indicators of well-being for the city.

3. Notice outcomes and make course corrections to enable progress naturally.

Chapter 12. Evolving Intelligences

1. Expect the unexpected.

2. Pay attention to the rules.

3. Enable emergence and resilience by transcending and including integral capacities at Level 8 and beyond.

With an ironic buzz across the evolutionary branches, the invertebrate bees remind us vertebrate humans that the choice of wild and tamed city will likely always be with us. Just at the point where we think we might have tamed our wandering impulses, it is highly likely that some diversity generator and/or unexpected environmental condition will motivate *homo sapiens sapiens* to swarm off in a new direction to create a wild colony that will stretch the needs and preferences of the species into yet more complex evolutionary intelligences.

Where is the leading edge of such frontiers? It is in the hearts, minds, brains and bodies of the people in the very cities we call home today. Whether our habitats are wild or designed, it is by learning the fractal rules that support intelligent sustainability wherever we live that we will create the capacities for taking our intelligence and intelligent technology into the future and into outer space.

CONCLUSION

Even now we are meshworking the highways and creating the synaptic networks that connect with our morphic fields in the Integral City. We stand on the streets of Integral City like bees (with big hearts, big minds and overactive appetites) poised at the exit from the hive, realizing that the only limitation to an amazing future is our failure to harness the intelligences we have co-evolved with the universe to date. We are called now to harness the integral capacities of the human hive and release its fullest potential. The time is now to sense the unlimited future that awaits us, integrally transcend our evolved intelligences so that we can continue our never-ending quest into yet evolving ever deeper intelligences. The time is now to share the wisdoms of natural systems exemplified by the beehive, the non-linear energies of the high seas and the evolving imagination of the universe embodied in the people of our Integral Cities.

Meshworking the intelligences of today's human hives is creating the integral DNA for tomorrow's galactic space colonies. With every co-creative act, thought, relationship and task, we are nurturing, emerging and deepening those capacities in the Integral City.

QUESTIONS

1. How can academies of city management learn from naval and aerospace academies?

2. How do we develop city visions that serve all the holons: individuals, communities, cities, Earth?

3. How does imagining the realities of space colonies contribute to our intelligent evolution of the Integral City?

POSTSCRIPT — APPLIED INTELLIGENCES: RESOURCES FOR THRIVING IN YOUR HUMAN HIVE

It may be that we are still missing something — perhaps something
already hinted at in previous experiments and buried
in the data, waiting for some keen-eyed investigator to sort it out.

Gould and Gould, 1988, p. 109

It's our greatest challenge ... to see if we can manage to mobilize the
wealth of our communities to make the transition tolerable, even sweet, instead of tragic.

McKibben, 2007, p. 232

HOW CAN WE HELP YOU?

In the course of developing the research and practices behind *Integral City*, a capability network has emerged to help cities implement these ideas. We use Integral City Systems (ICS) as a value management and development framework for meshworking in the human hive. ICS offers decision-making systems for both the built environment and quality of life, utilizing human values systems and engineering techniques that optimize available resources for strategic outcomes. It provides a common language for stakeholder participation, professional expertise and dynamic urban change. ICS meshes intelligences and technologies that have been outlined in *Integral City*.

If we wanted to summarize the advantages of using an Integral City approach, we would say it:

- reflects natural patterns of change
- reframes and integrates hierarchies of complexity
- provides a meta-framework for other frameworks
- builds capacity: physical, intellectual, social, cultural
- is based on research
- enables natural design
- uses four lenses: bio/psycho/cultural/social
- embraces multiple and diverse perspectives
- responds to horizontal, vertical, diagonal and relational adaptive conditions
- offers a multidisciplinary platform for organizing resources, expanding capacity and improving effectiveness at all levels of scale

We apply Integral City systems to six scales: Region, City, Community/ Neighborhood, Organization, Team/Group and Leader. The key work we perform includes:

- **Visioning**: Imagining Tomorrow, Facilitating Dialogue, Discovering Leaders
- **Assessing**: Culture Scans, Capacities for Change, States of Change, Preferences for Change, Priorities for Change; Risk
- **Mapping**: Leadership Development, Community Values, Social Capital, Asset Mapping
- **Capacity Building**: Competencies, Performance, Resilience, Collaboration, Social Responsibility
- **Facilitating**: Appropriate Change, Information Flow, Branding, Relationships, Processes, Structures
- **Planning**: Strategic, Scenario, Complex Adaptive, Official Community Plan (OCP) Alignment
- **Tracking**: Integral Dashboards, Well-being Indicators, Vital Signs Monitors, Organization Health, Community Wellness

We can be contacted through our website (www.integralcity.com) or reach the author directly at marilyn@integralcity.com

WHERE TO NEXT?

It has become apparent to me in writing this book that it is simply the foundation of a whole series of books that can help us to look at cities through the lenses of whole systems. One of the greatest challenges has in fact been drafting each chapter so that it addresses the focus sufficiently, without losing readers down (too many) rabbit holes. But every chapter suggests further inquiries to deepen the exploration of Integral City. As we fan the flames of human intelligences into a more coherent blaze, we want to be, do and have more insights into intelligent living. We have just thrown kindling on the fire. There is a lifetime of integral fire tending ahead of us.

Where might we go from here? The series of books below already comes to mind.

INTEGRAL CITY BOOK SERIES

- My Integral City Journal: A personal journal for seeing the city through integral lenses
- Integral City Fieldbook: A How-To Process Book for Facilitators, Planners, Developers
- Environments and Ecosystems: The Natural Opportunities and Limits to Growth for Integral City
- Integral City Governance: Meshing City Hall, the School Board and the Healthcare System; Federal, Provincial/State, City
- Optimizing and Integrating the Life and Death of Integral City-zens: Exploring What We Have to Let Go of in Order to Move On
- Thriving as an Integral Family: Re-valuing the Family in the City
- Sustaining Workplaces of Integral City: Workplaces Where Integrity Is a Way of Life and Learning Is Continuously Integrated
- The Economic Flow Within and Between Integral Cities: Revealing the Energetic Exchanges Between the Neural Network of Cities
- Lifelong Learning in the Integral City: How Education Optimizes Life
- Cradle-to-Grave Healthcare in the Integral Human Hive
- Dynamic Community Services for Vibrant Community Living

- Beyond Balanced Scorecards: Integral Vital Signs Monitors for Integral Cities

- Leadership in the Integral City: Growing Leaders for Growing Complexity

If you would like to contribute to this series, kindly let us know at emerging@integralcity.com .

GLOSSARY

Attractor: A non-linear pattern that recurs in systems, in three types: periodic, recurring in time; point, recurring in space; strange, recurring in form (De Landa, 1997; Eoyang, 1997).

Dissipative structure: An open system where the structural pattern is maintained, even as energy, matter and information flow through it and are dissipated by it.

Equilibrium: The state of balance amongst energy, matter and information maintained in a closed system.

Far from equilibrium: The state of instability that exists when energy flows through an open system, pushing it far from equilibrium and causing the system to be subject to switching from one stable state to another, often very suddenly (a condition described by Stephen Gould as punctuated equilibrium) (Capra, 1996; De Landa, 1997; Prigogine, 1967, 1989, 1997). For example, climatologists are concerned that current global warming will cause weather systems to radically change their patterns, as they believe has occurred in the past when energy from the sun and meteors have entered the Earth's atmosphere.

Fractal: A fractal is a repeated non-linear pattern that recurs at infinite scales in nature, arising from the following of simple rules embedded in the nature of the fractal entity; examples include coastlines, cloud formations, trees, villages, bodies, body parts, galaxies and neurons.

Holarchy: (A term originally coined by Arthur Koestler). A holarchy is a hierarchy of hierarchies (or holons or even a hierarchy of systems). It is a higher order system that includes all the lower order systems in its functioning.

Hologram/Holograph: A hologram is a three-dimensional image that arises from the interference patterns of two wave patterns. The hologram carries information about the whole in every part of its composition. A holograph is a three-dimensional representation of an entity, produced by bouncing two beams of laser light off a photographic plate to produce a three-dimensional image (Laszlo, 2004, p. 72).

Holon: A whole system made up of other whole systems. This term was coined by Koestler (see holarchy above) and popularized by Wilber (Wilber, 1995).

In-formation: A subtle, quasi-instant, non-evanescent and non-energetic connection between things at different locations in space and events in different points in time. Such connections are termed "non-local" in the natural sciences and "transpersonal" in consciousness research. In-formation links things (particles, atoms, molecules, organisms, ecologies, solar systems, entire galaxies, as well as the mind and consciousness associated with some of these things) regardless of how far they are from each other and how much time has passed since connections were created between them (Laszlo, 2004, pp. 68-69).

Non-linear : A condition where strong mutual interactions (like feedback and feed-forward loops of matter and/or energy and/or information) occur between components of a system (De Landa, 1997, p. 14).

Sapient Circle: A term, often attributed to Margaret Mead, to describe the gathering of the learned ones of an indigenous society or community, usually for the purpose of sharing knowledge, learning, opinions, perspectives or decision making.

REFERENCES

Abravanel, E.D., & E.A. Abravanel (1983) *Dr. Abravanel's Body Type Diet and Lifetime Nutrition Plan*. New York: Bantam.

Adger, N., et al. (2007). *Climate Change 2007: Impacts, Adaptation and Vulnerability, Summary for Policy Makers*. Retrieved June 23, 2007, from www.ipcc.ch/

Adizes, I. (1999). *Managing Corporate Life Cycles*. Paramus, NJ: Prentice Hall.

Adizes, I. (2006). *The Secrets of the Corporate Life cycle*. Retrieved May 12, 2008, from adizes.com/

Alexander, C. (2004). *The Phenomenon of Life* (September 1, 2004 ed., Vol. 1). Berkeley, CA: Center for Environmental Structure.

Andranonovich, G.D., & G. Riposa (1993). *Doing Urban Research*. Newbury Park, CA: Sage.

Ascher, K. (2005). *Anatomy of a City*. New York: Penguin.

Barnett, T.P.M. (2005). *The Pentagon's New Map: War and Peace in the Twenty-First Century*. New York: Berkley Publishing Group.

Baron-Cohen, S. (2003). *The Essential Difference: The Truth About the Male and Female Brain*. New York: Basic Books.

Bates, H. (2006). "Civilian Military Spouses: Resilience and Lifestyle Challenge." Unpublished thesis, Royal Roads University, Victoria, BC.

BC Healthy Communities (BCHC). (2005). BC *Healthy Communities Strategic Plan: 2005-2007*. Victoria, BC.

BC Healthy Communities (BCHC). (2006). An *Integral Map of Community* . Victoria, BC.

Beck, D. (2002). "Spiral Dynamics in the Integral Age." Paper presented at the Spiral Dynamics Integral, Level 1.

Beck, D. (2004). "Natural Designs and MeshWORKS: Creating our Region's Tomorrow through Second Tier Leadership, Organizational Foresight and Integral Alliances." Paper presented at the Spiral Dynamics Integral, Level 2, Natural Designs.

Beck, D. (2006). *Spiral Dynamics Integral, Level 1 Course Manual.* Denton, TX: Spiral Dynamics Group.

Beck, D. (2007). Personal communication. In M. Hamilton (Ed.), *Messaging for Change.* Winnipeg, MB.

Beck, D. (2007). The Meshworks Foundation: A New Approach to Philanthropy (Electronic Version). Retrieved January 15, 2008 from www.humanemergencemiddleeast. org/meshworks-foundation-philanthropy.html.

Beck, D. (January, 2008). A Spiral Full of Foundations. *Sense in the City,* 3.1.

Beck, D. & C. Cowan (1994, 1997). "The Future of Cities." Unpublished article. The National Values Center.

Beck, D. & C. Cowan (1996). *Spiral Dynamics: Mastering Values, Leadership and Change.* Malden, MA: Blackwell.

Beck, D. & G. Linscott (2006). *The Crucible: Forging South Africa's Future.* Columbia, MD: Center for Human Emergence.

Becker, J. (2007). "How Frameworks Can Help Operationalize Sustainable Development Indicators." *World Futures,* 63(2), 14.

Belanger, S. (2004). "Enhancing Cooperation Between Critical Infrastructure Protection Organizations." Unpublished thesis, Royal Roads University, Victoria, BC.

Benyus, J.M. (1997). *Biomimicry: Innovation Inspired by Nature.* New York: William Morrow.

Berry, W. (1977). *The Unsettling of America: Culture and Agriculture.* San Francisco: Sierra Club Books.

Bjerga, A. (June 30, 2007). "Mysterious Ailment Kills Millions of Bees in US: Disorder Poses a $75 Billion Threat to Agriculture, Washington Says." *Vancouver Sun.*

Bloom, H. (2000). *The Global Brain: The Evolution of Mass Mind from the Big Bang to the 21st Century.* New York: John Wiley.

Braudel, F. (1987). A *History of Civilizations* (R. Mayne, Trans., 1993 ed.). New York: Penguin.

Braverman, E. (2006). *The Edge Effect .* New York: Sterling

Brown, B. (2005a). "Theory and Practice of Integral Sustainable Development: An Overview. Part 1: Quadrants and the Practitioner." AQAL *Journal,* 1 (2).

Brown, B. (2005b). "Theory and Practice of Integral Sustainable Development: An Overview. Part 2: Values, Developmental Levels and Natural Design." AQAL *Journal,* 1 (2).

Brown, B. (2005c). Theory and Practice of Integral Sustainable Development: An Overview. Part 3: Current Initiatives and Applications. AOAL *Journal,* 1 (2).

Brown, B. (2006). *Integrating the Major Research Methodologies Used in Sustainable Development.* Unpublished.

Brown, T.W.H. (1989). *Integrative Medicine Diagram.* Unpublished.

Brundtland, H. (1987). *Our Common Future.* Oxford, UK: Oxford University Press.

Capra, F. (1996). *The Web of Life: A New Scientific Understanding of Living Systems* . New York: Anchor Doubleday.

Combs, A. (2002). *The Radiance of Being: Understanding the Grand Integral Vision Living the Integral Life* . St. Paul, MN: Paragon House.

Cook, D. (2005). *The Natural Step: Towards A Sustainable Society* . Totnes, Devon, UK: Green Books.

Covey, S.R. (1990). *The 7 Habits of Highly Effective People.* New York: Simon and Shuster.

Cummins, R.A. (1996a). "Assessing Quality of Life." In *Quality of Life for Handicapped People*, R.I. Brown (Ed.), London: Chapman & Hall.

Cummins, R.A. (1996b). "The Domains of Life Satisfaction: An Attempt to Order Chaos."*Social Indicators Research*, 38.

Cummins, R.A., R. Eckersley, S.K. Lo, M. Davern, B. Hunter, & E. Okerstrom (2004). "The Australian Unity Well-being Index: An Update." Paper presented at the Proceedings of the 5th Australian Conference on Quality of Life, Deakin University, Melbourne.

D'Adamo, P.J., & C. Whitney (2000). *Cook Right 4 Your Type.* New York: Berkely Books.

Dale, A. (2001). *At The Edge: Sustainable Development in the 21st Century.* Vancouver, BC: UBC Press.

Dale, A., & J. Hamilton (2007). "Sustainable Infrastructure" [Electronic Version]. Retrieved February 2008 from crcresearch.org/files-crcresearch/File/CI_Final Report.pdf

Dale, A., & J. Onyx (Eds.). (2005). *A Dynamic Balance: Social Capital and Sustainable Community Development* . Vancouver, BC: UBC Press.

Dale, A., L. Waldron, & L. Newman (2007). *Sustainable Community Infrastructure Case Studies.* Retrieved March 7, 2007, from communitycasestudies.crc research. org/casestudies/infrastructure

Davison, T. (2006). *Leisure Services: A Service Delivery Model for the Future.* Unpublished thesis, Royal Roads, Victoria, BC.

Dawson-Tunik, T.L., Commons, M.L., Wilson, M., and Fischer, K.W. (2005). The Shape of Development. *The European Journal of Development Psychology*, 2(2), 163-196.

Dawson, T. (2007). *Testing Transformation: Transformation Testing* [Electronic Version]. Retrieved from devtestservice.com

Deguire, C. (2005). *Internal Communication in the Canadian Navy.* Unpublished thesis, Royal Roads University, Victoria, BC.

De Landa, M. (1995). *Homes: Meshwork or Hierarchy?* Special Home issue. Retrieved December 4, 2004, from mediamatic.net/article-200.5956.html

De Landa, M. (1997). *A Thousand Years of Nonlinear History.* New York: Zone Books.

De Landa, M. (2006). *A New Philosophy of Society: Assemblage Theory and Social Complexity.* London: Continuum.

Diamond, J. (2005). *Collapse: How Societies Choose to Fail or Succeed.* New York: Penguin.

Durning, A. (2004). *Cascadia Scorecard*. Seattle: Northwest Environment Watch.

Durrance, B. (1997). "From Chaos to Chords: The Evolutionary Vision of Dee Hock." *Training & Development Magazine*, 4.

Dutrisac, M., D. Fowke, H. Koplowitz & K. Shepard (nd). Global Organization Design: A Dependable Path to Exceptional Business Results Based on Requisite Organization Principles. Toronto: Global Organization Design Society.

Dychtwald, K. & J. Flower (1989). *Age Wave*. Los Angeles: Jeremy P. Tarcher.

Eddy, B. (2003a). Personal communication and notes.

Eddy, B. (2003b). "Sustainable Development, Spiral Dynamics and Spatial Data: A "3i" Approach to SD." Paper presented at the Spiral Dynamics Integral, Level II, Ottawa, 2003.

Eddy, B. (2005). "Place, Space and Perspective," *World Futures*, 61, 151-163.

Eddy, B. (2006). *The Use of Maps and Map Metaphors for Integration in Geography: A Case Study of Mapping Indicators of Sustainability and Wellbeing*. Unpublished thesis, Dept. of Geography and Environmental Studies, Carleton University, Ottawa.

Eddy, B. (Cartographer). (2007). *Mapping Integral Values: A Proof of Concept on Google Earth*. Unpublished document.

Ehrlich, P.R. & A.H. Ehrlich (1997). "The Population Explosion: Why We Should Care and What We Should Do About It." *Environmental Law* (00462276), 27(4), 1187.

Eoyang, G. (1997). *Coping With Chaos: Seven Simple Tools*. Cheyenne, WY: Lagumo.

Eoyang, G. (2007). *Seeing and Learning Differently: Asset Building and Complex Change*. Minneapolis: Search Institute Webinar Series.

Eoyang, G. & E. Olson (2001). *Facilitating Organization Change: Lessons from Complexity Science*. San Francisco: Jossey-Bass Pfeiffer.

Esbörn-Hargens, S. (2005). "Integral Ecology: The What, Who, and How of Environmental Phenomena." *World Futures*, 61(1, 2), 5 - 49.

Fainstein, S. & S. Campbell (Eds.). (2003). *Readings in Urban Theory*. Malden, MA: Blackwell.

Fernandez-Armesto, F. (2001). *Civilizations: Culture, Ambition and the Transformation of Nature*. New York: Touchstone.

Fisher, M. (2003). *Fearless Leadership In and Out of the "Fear" Matrix*. Unpublished doctoral dissertation, University of British Columbia, Vancouver, BC.

Florida, R. (2005). *Cities and the Creative Class*. New York: Routledge.

Foote, D.K. (1999). *Boom, Bust & Echo 2000: Profiting from the Demographic Shift in the New Millennium*. Toronto: MacFarlane Walter & Ross.

Fourman, M. (2006). Resilience: A complex fractal, global challenge demands a systemic collaborative approach. London, UK: Gaiasoft.

Fourman, M., C. Reynolds, K. Firus & A. D'Ulizia (2008). *Online tools for developing sustainability and Resilience: Methodology, experience and cost effective solutions from MIDIR EU Reserch Project*. London, UK: European Commission.

Friedman, T.L. (2005). *The World Is Flat: A Brief History of the 21st Century*. New York: Farrar, Strauss and Giroux.

Fuller, B. (1970). "Technology and the Human Environment." In *The Ecological Conscience: Values for Survival*, R. Disch (Ed.), (pp. 174-180). Englewood Cliffs, NJ: Prentice Hall.

Gardner, H. (1999). *Intelligence Reframed: Multiple Intelligences for the 21st Century*. New York: Basic Books, Perseus Books Group.

Geiken, B., B. Brown & M. Fourman (2005). "Integral Policy Implementation and Follow-Up." Personal communication.

Global Reporting Initiative. (2006). *Reporting Guidelines*. Amsterdam: Author.

Goleman, D. (1997). *Emotional Intelligence*. New York: Bantam.

Gore, A. (2007). *An Inconvenient Truth: The Crisis of Global Warming*. New York: Viking.

Gottdiener, M. & R. Hutchison (2006). *The New Urban Sociology*, (3rd ed.). Boulder, CO: Westview Press.

Gould, J.L. & C.G. Gould (1988). *The Honey Bee*. Scientific American Library.

Gozdz, K., Ed., et al,. (1995). *Community Building: Renewing Spirit and Learning in Business*. San Francisco: New Leaders Press, Sterling & Stone Inc.

Graves, C. (1971). "A Systems Conception of Personality: Levels of Existence Theory." Paper presented at the Washington School of Psychiatry.

Graves, C. (1974). "Human Nature Prepares for a Momentous Leap." *The Futurist*.

Graves, C. (1981). *Summary Statement: The Emergent, Cyclical, Double Helix Model of the Adult Human Biopsychosocial Systems*. Retrieved July 3, 2002, from www.clarewgraves. com/articles_content/1981_handout/1981_summary.pdf

Graves, C. (2003). *Levels of Human Existence*. Santa Barbara: ECLET Publishing.

Graves, C. (2005). *The Never Ending Quest: A Treatise on an Emergent Cyclical Conception of Adult Behavioral Systems and Their Development*. Santa Barbara, CA: ECLET Publishing.

Gregory, R.L., Ed., et al,. (1987). *The Oxford Companion to The Mind*. Oxford: Oxford University Press.

Grunwald, M. (August 13, 2007). "The Threatening Storm: How Years of Misguided Policies and Bureaucratic Bungling Left New Orleans Defenseless Against Katrina — and Why It May Happen Again." *Time*, 19-31.

Gunderson, L.C. & C.S. Holling (Eds.). (2002). *Panarchy: Understanding Transformations in Human and Natural Systems*. Washington, DC: Island Press.

Habermas, J. (1984). *The Theory of Communication*. (T. McCarthy, Trans. Vol. 1). Boston: Beacon.

Hagelin, J. (June-August, 2007). "The Power of the Collective." *Shift: At the Frontiers of Consciousness*, 15, 16-20.

Hamer, D. (2004). *The God Gene: How Faith Is Hardwired into Our Genes*. New York: Doubleday.

Hamilton, M. (1999). *The Berkana Community of Conversations: A Study of Leadership Skill Development and Organizational Leadership Practices in a Self-organizing Online Microworld*. Unpublished doctoral dissertation, Columbia Pacific University, Novato, California.

Hamilton, M. (2003). Abbotsford Values Systems Flower Map [Graphical Data].

Retrieved July 24, 2008: integralcity.com/Maple%20Leaf%20Memc%20Proj/ Spiral.flower.icity pdf Abbotsford, BC.

Hamilton, M. (2005). "The Quest: Four Questions That Can Release the Potential of Your City." Paper presented at the Canadian Institute of Planners: Frontiers in Planning and Design, Calgary, AB.

Hamilton, M. (2006a). "Integral Framework for Sustainable Planning: A Prototype for Emergent Well Being." Paper presented at the World Planners Congress, Vancouver, BC.

Hamilton, M. (2006b). "Integral Meta-map Creates Common Language for Urban Change." *Journal of Organizational Change Management,* 19(3), 276-306.

Hamilton, M. (2007a). "Approaching Homelessness: An Integral Reframe." *World Futures: The Journal of General Evolution,* 63(2), 107-126.

Hamilton, M. (2007b). *Personal Wellbeing Index: Toronto.* Abbotsford, BC: Integral City, a Division of TDG Holdings.

Hamilton, M. & A. Dale (2007). *Sustainable Infrastructure Development: A Learning Framework.* In publication.

Hawken, P. (May 7, 2007). "To Remake the World Something Earth-Changing Is Afoot Among Civil Society." *Orion Magazine.*

Hertzman, C., S.A. McLean, D.E. Kohen, J. Dunn & T. Evans (2002). *Early Development in Vancouver: Report of the Community Asset Mapping Project* (CAMP). Vancouver, BC: Community Asset Mapping Project UBC.

Hochachka, G. (2005). *Developing Sustainability, Developing the Self: An Integral Approach to International and Community Development.* University of Victoria, BC: Polis Project on Ecological Governance.

Holling, C.S. (2001). "Understanding the Complexity of Economic, Ecological and Social Systems." *Ecosystems,* 4, 390-405.

Holling, C S. (2003). *From Complex Regions to Complex Worlds.* University of Florida.

Homer-Dixon, T. (2006). *The Upside of Down: Catastrophe, Creativity, and the Renewal of Civilization.* Toronto: Alfred A. Knopf.

Howard, P.J. (1994). *The Owner's Manual for the Brain: Everyday Applications from Mind-brain Research.* Austin, TX: Leornian Press.

Isaacs, W. (1999). *Dialogue and the Art of Thinking Together.* New York: Currency Doubleday.

Jacobs, J. (1970). *Economy of Cities.* New York: Vintage.

Jacobs, J. (1992). *The Death and Life of Great American Cities.* New York: Vintage

Jacobs, J. (1994). *Systems of Survival.* New York: First Vintage.

Jacobs, J. (2001). *The Nature of Economies.* New York: First Vintage.

Jacobs, J. (2004). *Dark Age Ahead.* New York: Random House.

Jaworski, J. (1996). *Synchronicity: The Inner Path of Leadership.* San Francisco: Berrett-Koehler.

Johnson, S. (2004). *Emergence: The Connected Lives of Ants, Brains, Cities, and Software.* New York: Scribener.

Kauffman, S.A. (1993). *The Origins of Order: Self-organization and Selection in Evolution.* New York: Oxford Press.

Laszlo, E. (2004). *Science and the Akashic Field: An Integral Theory of Everything.* (2007 ed.). Rochester, Vermont: Inner Traditions.

Laszlo, E. (2006a). *The Chaos Point: The World at the Crossroads.* Charlottesville, VA: Hampton Roads Publishing.

Laszlo, E. (2006b). *Science and the Reenchantment of the Cosmos: The Rise of the Integral Vision of Reality.* Rochester, VT: Inner Traditions, Bear & Co.

Leonard, G. & M. Murphy (1995). *The Life We Are Given.* New York: Jeremy P. Tarcher/Putnam.

Lipton, B. (2005). *The Biology of Belief: Unleashing the Power of Consciousness, Matter and Miracles.* Santa Rosa, CA: Mountain of Love/Elite Books.

Loop Initiatives. (2007). *LOOP Integrated Rating Indicator for Sustainability.* www.loopinitiatives. com/loopiris.html

Lopez, B. & T.C. Pearson (1990). *Crow and Weasel.* Berkeley, CA: North Point Press.

Lorenz, E. (1995). *The Essence of Chaos.* Seattle: University of Washington Press.

Margulis, L. & D. Sagan (1997). *Microcosmos: Four Billion Years of Microbial Evolution.* Los Angeles: University of California Press.

Maturana, H , & Varela, F. (1987, 1992). *The Tree of Knowledge.* Boston: Shambhala.

Mau, B. & J. Leonard (Eds.). (2004). *Massive Change.* New York: Phaidon Press.

McGregor, R. (2007). "750,000 a Year Killed by Chinese Pollution." Retrieved July 4, 2007, from *Financial Times Online*: http://www.ft.com/cms/so/8f40e248-28c7-11dc-af78-000b5df10621.html

McIntosh, S. (2007). *Integral Consciousness and the Future of Evolution: How the Integral Worldview Is Transforming Politics, Culture and Spirituality.* St. Paul, MN: Paragon House.

McKibben, B. (2007). *Deep Economy: The Wealth of Communities and the Durable Future.* New York: Time Books, Henry Holt and Co.

McQuade, A. (2005). "Reviving our Interiors: Serving the Mentally Ill Living on Our Streets." AQAL, 14.

Meller, H. (1990). *Patrick Geddes: Social Evolutionist and City Planner.* London: Routledge.

Miller, J.G. (1978). *Living Systems.* New York: McGraw-Hill.

Mittelstadt, M. (September 7, 2007). "Mysterious Die-off of Honeybees Explained." *The Globe and Mail.*

Moir, A. & D. Jessel (1991). *Brain Sex.* New York: Dell.

Monbiot, G. & M. Prescott (2007). *Heat: How to Stop the Planet from Burning.* Toronto: Anchor Canada.

Morelli, M., A. Leonard, T. Patten, J. Salzman & K. Wilber (2006). *Welcome to Integral Life Practice: Your Guide to the ILP Starter Kit* (1 ed.). Denver, CO: Integral Institute.

Morgan, G. (1998). *Images of Organization.*Thousand Oaks, CA: Sage Publications.

Mumford, L. (1946). *Values for Survival: Essays, Addresses, and Letters on Politics and Education.* New York: Harcourt, Brace and Co.

Mumford, L. (1970). "Closing Statement." In The Ecological Conscience: Values for Survival. R. Disch (Ed.), (pp. 91-102). Englewood Cliffs, NJ: Prentice Hall.

Murphy, M. (1992). The Future of the Body: Explorations into the Further Evolution of Human Nature. Los Angeles: Jeremy P. Tarcher.

Naess, A. & D. Rothenberg (trans. and rev. 1989). Ecology, Community and Lifestyle: Outline of an Ecosophy. Cambridge: Cambridge University Press.

Nichol, L. (2006). Supporting Rural and Remote Employment Counsellors. Unpublished thesis, Royal Roads University, Victoria, BC.

Owen, C. (2005). "Integral Planning Toward Sustainable Consumption and Waste Reduction in Calgary OR 'INFLUENCING THE EFFLUENCE OF AFFLUENCE'." Paper presented at the Canadian Institute of Planners Conference, July 2005, Calgary, AB.

Palmer, P. (n.d.). Thirteen Ways of Looking at Community (With a Fourteenth Thrown in for Free). Unpublished.

Peck, M.S. (1987). The Different Drum: Community-Making and Peace. New York: Touchstone, Simon & Schuster.

Peck, M.S. (1993). A World Waiting to Be Born. New York: Bantam.

Pinker, S. (2003). The Blank Slate: The Modern Denial of Human Nature. New York: Penguin.

Pointe, S.B., Lieutenant Governor. (2008). Speech from the Throne, Opening of the Fourth Session, 38th Parliament, Victoria, BC. Retrieved. from www.leg.bc.ca/38th4th/Throne_Speech_2008.pdf.

Porkert, M. & D.C. Ullmann (1988). Chinese Medicine (M. Howson, Trans.). New York: William Morrow and Co.

Prigogine, I. (1967). "Dissipative Structures in Chemical Systems," in Fast Reactions and Primary Processes in Chemical Kinetics, Stig Claesson (Ed.), Interscience.

Prigogine, I. (1989). The Philosophy of Instability, Futures, 21, 4, 396-400.

Prigogine, I. (1997). The End of Certainty. New York: The Free Press, Simon & Schuster.

Prigogine, I. & I. Stengers (1984). Order out of Chaos. New York: Bantam.

Reams, J. (2002). The Consciousness of Transpersonal Leadership. Unpublished doctoral dissertation, Gonzaga University, Spokane, WA.

Rees, W.E.P.D. & M. Wackernagel (1994). Ecological Footprints and Appropriated Carrying Capacity: Measuring the Natural Capital Requirements of the Human Economy. Washington, DC: Island Press.

Reynolds, B. (2003). Optimizing the Alternative Dispute Resolution Process at Fisheries and Oceans. Unpublished thesis, Royal Roads University, Victoria, BC.

Ridley, M. (2003). The Agile Gene: How Nature Turns on Nurture. Toronto: HarperPerennial.

Robertson, R. (October - December, 2007). "A Brighter Shade of Green: Rebooting Environmentalism for the 21st Century." What Is Enlightenment?, 42-62.

Rosas, D. & C. Rosas (2005). NIA. New York: Broadway.

Ruder, K. & D. Sando (2002). Spiral Flower System Map of Community. Seattle: Center for Ethical Leadership, www.ethicalleadership.org

Runnalls, C. (2007). *Architecting Community Sustainability: Cultural Planning and Community Development*. Unpublished thesis, Royal Roads University, Victoria, BC.

Sahtouris, E. (1999). *Earthdance: Living Systems in Evolution*. Retrieved from ratical.org/ LifeWeb/

Sandercock, L. (2000). "When Strangers Become Neighbours: Managing Cities of Difference." *Planning Theory and Practice*, 1(1).

Sandercock, L. & P. Lyssiotis (2004). *Cosmopolis II: Mongrel Cities of the 21st Century*. London: Continuum International Publishing Group.

Satin, M. (2005). "The Katrina Dialogues" [electronic version]. Retrieved October 4, 2007, from radicalmiddle.com/x_katrina_dialogues.htm.

Senge, P. M. (1995). "Creating Quality Communities." In *Community Building: Renewing Spirit and Learning in Business*, K. Gozdz (Ed.), (pp. 49-56). San Francisco: Sterling & Stone.

Sheldrake, R. (1988). *The Presence of the Past: Morphic Resonance and the Habits of Nature* (1995 ed.). Rochester, VT: Park Street Press.

Sheldrake, R. (1999). *Dogs That Know When Their Owners Are Coming Home and Other Unexplained Powers of Animals*. New York: Three Rivers Press.

Sheldrake, R. (2003). *The Sense of Being Stared At and Other Aspects of the Extended Mind*. New York: Three Rivers Press.

Shepard, K., Ed. (2007). *Organization Design, Levels of Work and Human Capability: Executive Guide*. Toronto: Global Organization Design Society.

Smith, A. & J.B. MacKinnon (2007). *The 100-Mile Diet*. New York: Random House Canada.

Smith, V. (2002). *The Evolution of Leadership*. Unpublished thesis, Royal Roads University, Victoria, BC.

The State of Bowen Island, vol.1. (2001). Bowen Island, BC.

Stevenson, B. & M. Hamilton (2001). "How Does Complexity Inform Community? How Does Community Inform Complexity?" *Emergence*, 3(2), 57-77.

Stringer, E.T. (1996). *Action Research: A Handbook for Practitioners*. Thousand Oaks, CA: Sage Publications.

Surowiecki, J. (2004). *The Wisdom of Crowds: Why the Many Are Smarter Than the Few and How Collective Wisdom Shapes Business, Economics and Nations*. New York: Doubleday.

Suzuki, D. (1989). *Inventing the Future*. Toronto: Stoddart Publishing.

Sykes, B. (2002). *The Seven Daughters of Eve*. New York: W.W. Norton.

Tal, B. (2007). "Infrastructure: The New Frontier." CIBC *Wood Gundy: Quarterly Exchange*, p. 1.

Teilhard de Chardin, P. (1966). *Man's Place in Nature* (B. Wall, Trans.). New York: Harper & Row.

Teilhard de Chardin, P. (1972). *The Phenomenon of Man* (B. Wall, Trans.). New York: Fontana.

Time. (September 24, 2007). "Beepocolypse now? Something Is Killing Honeybees in Record Numbers. Three Theories on Why."

Trager, J., Ed. (1979). *The People's Chronology: A Year-by-year Record of Human Events from Prehistory to the Present*. New York: Holt, Rinehart and Winston.

Tuckman, B.W. (1965). "Developmental sequence in small groups." *Psychological Bulletin*, 63, 384-399.

Tuckman, B.W. & M.A.C. Jensen (1977). "Stages of Small Group Development Revisited." *Group and Organizational Studies*, 2, 419-427.

Tupper, C. (2003). *Expressive Arts-based Learning for Leadership Development*. Unpublished thesis, Royal Roads University, Victoria, BC.

United Nations Human Settlements. (2005). *The State of the World's Cities 2004/5*. London: Earthscan.

Varey, W. (2008). *Integral Applications: Précis of Integral Sustainability Case Studies*. Perth, Australia: emrgnc.

Wackernagel, M. & W. Rees (1996). *Our Ecological Footprint: Reducing Human Impact on the Earth*. Gabriola Island, BC: New Society.

Weisman, A. (1998). *Gaviotas: A Village to Reinvent the World*. White River Jct., VT: Chelsea Green.

Wells, S. (2002). *The Journey of Man: A Genetic Odyssey*. Princeton, NJ: Princeton University Press.

Wenger, E. (1999). *Communities of Practice*. Cambridge: Cambridge University Press.

World Health Organization (WHO). (2004). *What Is a Healthy City?* Retrieved from www.who.dk/healthy-cities/How2MakeCities/20020114_1

Whyte, D. (2001). *Crossing the Unknown Sea*. New York: Berkley Publishing.

Wight, I. (2002). "Place, Place Making and Planning." Paper presented at the ACSP, Baltimore, MD.

Wilber, K. (1995). *Sex, Ecology and Spirituality: The Spirit of Evolution*. Boston: Shambhala Publications.

Wilber, K. (1996a). *A Brief History of Everything*. Boston: Shambhala Publications.

Wilber, K. (1996b). *Eye to Eye: The Quest for the New Paradigm*, 3rd edition. Boston: Shambhala.

Wilber, K. (2000a). *Integral Psychology*. Boston: Shambhala.

Wilber, K. (2000b). *A Theory of Everything*. Boston: Shambhala.

Wilber, K. (2001). *Marriage of Sense and Soul*. New York: Random House.

Wilber, K. (2006). *Integral Spirituality*. Boston: Shambhala.

Wilber, K. (2007). *The Integral Vision*. Boston: Shambhala.

Wills, E.H., M. Hamilton & G. Islam (2007a). "Subjective Well-being in Cities: Individual or Collective? A Cross Cultural Analysis." Paper presented at the Wellbeing in International Development Conference, University of Bath, UK.

Wills, E.H., M. Hamilton & G. Islam (2007b). *Subjective Wellbeing in Bogotá (B), Belo Horizonte (BH) and Toronto (T): A Subjective Indicator of Quality of Life for Cities*. Bogotá: World Bank.

Wright, R. (2004). *A Short History of Progress* (Avalon ed.). New York: Carroll & Graf.

100 Mile Diet, 6

INDEX

A

Abbotsford, BC, 69, 212, 213
adaptiveness
  in humans, 85-86
  and relationships, 187-189
  roles in, 36-37
  and structures of change, 67-69, 79, 93
  systems of, 31-35, 43. *See also* power of
    8 leadership; regeneration;
    renewal; resilience
Adizes, Ichak, 42, 43, 87, 88, 93, 176, 187-188
air, 79, 80, 126, 127, 131, 156, 237, 241.
  See also air pollution
air pollution, 39, 133, 134, 136, 152
Akashic field, 49
Alexander, Christopher, 10, 26-27, 31, 33-
  34, 66, 156, 157
aliveness, qualities of, 26-27
archeology, 5, 18, 44, 66, 68, 92
artefacts, 155-156. *See also* built environment
Ascher, Kate, 160
Ashkenaze, 18
Ashworth, Joanna, 224

B

baby boom, 128, 164, 192
Baghdad, 15, 134, 245
balance, in community, 202-203
Barnett, Tom, xviii, 116, 117
BC Healthy Communities, 61
Beck, Don, 86, 90, 92-93, 96, 116, 217
Becker, J., 239
bees. *See* honeybee hives
behavior, 125-126, 129
Benyus, Janine, 163
biofuels, 12, 17
biological mimicry, 156, 163
biomimicry, 163
bioregion. *See* ecoregion
birth control, 76
Bloom, Howard, 38, 42, 43, 188
Boise, 184
boundaries, of the city, 29-30, 114. *See also*
  container, city as.
Bowen Island, BC, 247
brain science, 128-129, 205, 222-223. *See
  also* senses; triune brain
Brown, Barrett, 131, 240

Brundtland, Gro, 116
Brundtland Report, 56, 231, 232
built environment, 149 178
built structures, 155-159
Burning Man, 88, 89

C

cadence, 182-183
Calgary, 108, 152, 166, 167
Capra, Fritjof, 75
Carbondale, Colorado, 141, 212, 214
carbon dioxide (CO2), 17. *See also* carbon footprint
carbon footprint, 82, 152-154
carrying capacity, 8-9, 19, 57, 77, 151-155
Case Study T, 254
Chalk, David, 92
change
    and senses, 136-137
    stages of, 33-36, 45, 56, 67-69, 75-79, 84, 87-88, 90-94, 106
    states of, 40-43, 94-96, 121-123, 176
    structures of, 67-69
Chicago, 45, 113, 198
cities
    designed, xvii, 76-77
    dynamics of, 90-94
    wild, xvii
    wisdom of, 215-216. *See also* community
citizens, voices of, 191-192
city developers, 194, 197
city managers, voices of, 192-193
city planning, 73, 74, 77, 204, 253
civil servants, 171, 258
civil society, voices of, 193-194
climate change, xviii, 7, 11, 18, 152-153, 186, 266
coherence, 46
collective, the, 27, 28-29, 35-36, 60-61, 75, 105-107, 108, 116-118, 201-202. *See also* cities; health care; social holons; social structures, and artefacts, 156-159

Combs, Alan, 104
commons, the, 16, 17, 18
communication. *See* conversation, fields of; dialogue
communities of practice, 203-206
community
    definitions of, 200, 202
    and dialogue, 200-203
    four-quadrant map of, 218-219
    improvement of, 213-214
    potential of, 211-213
    strengths of, 210-211
Community Builders Benevolent Society, 205
community foundations, 230
competitive relationships, 186-187
complexity, evolution of, 34
complex wealth, 75-79
conformity enforcement
    in cities, 41, 42, 164, 189
    in hives, 36-37
consciousness
    development of, 55-56, 67, 99-102, 236, 242, 244
    ecology of, 51-52
container, city as, 29-30, 40-41. *See also* fitness landscape
contemplation, 202
control and agreement, 39
conversation, fields of, 200-201
corporate life cycles, 87-88, 93
Covey, Stephen, 201
Cowan, Chris, 86, 90, 92-93
Creative City, 199
Cummins, R.A., 95-96
cultural life cycles, 82-83, 188-189
cultural quadrant, 163, 233. *See also* culture
culture
    and archetypes, 189-190
    and construction, 198-199
    and health care, 142, 143-145, 206, 213

importance of, 197-199
and indicators, 244
and value systems, 198-199. *See also*
  cultural quadrant; diversity

D

Dale, Ann, 121, 210, 214, 221, 222
Daly, Richard, 113
de Chardin, Teilhard, 35
degeneration, 134
De Landa, Manuel, 25, 127, 152, 224
Delhi, 134
demographics, 128-129, 143, 164
Detroit, 159
developing countries, 3, 44, 78, 80, 117, 119
development, stages of, 42-43, 94
diagonal dynamic, 90, 91-92
dialogue, 200-202
Diamond, Jared, 18, 45, 115, 236, 237
differentiation, 33
disasters, 9, 14, 39, 50, 68-69, 83, 193
disease, 133
dissipative structures, 19, 30-31, 74, 128,
  130-133
dissonance, 136-137
diversity, xxi, 16, 17, 73, 82, 87-88. *See also*
  culture
diversity generators
  in cities, 38, 42, 43, 90, 138, 163, 164,
    189, 194
  in hives, 37, 42, 164, 188, 261
Donnelly, Dennis, 205
Dychtwald, 164
dysfunction, 133-134

E

eco-footprint, 8-9, 10-13, 76, 77-79, 126,
  130, 153-154
ecological footprint. *See* eco-footprint.
ecologies, of systems, 27-28
ecoregion
  and the city, 6-7, 18-21, 39, 77-78, 153-
    154, 162
  and urban migration, 76. *See also* carrying

capacity; container, city as; food; water
  resources
Eddy, Brian, 68, 236-237, 240, 241, 247, 251
education, 40-41, 47, 76, 81, 92, 105, 167.
  See also learning systems
emergence, 46-47
energetic fields, 48, 128, 158, 159. *See also*
  morphic fields.
energy, management of, 20, 130, 160. *See
  also* eco-footprint; renewable resources
energy-matter, 19, 205, 224, 132
environment
  and the city, 57-58
  and Integral City, 262. *See also* ecoregion
Eoyang, Glenda, 30, 41-42, 43, 217
evolution, of cities, xviii, 1-2, 31, 44, 107,
  111, 152, 156, 157, 185-186, 259, 262-
  263. See also space colonies
Eysenck, Hans, 129

F

feedback processes, 5, 61, 67, 100, 154.
  See also vital signs monitors
Fernandez-Armesto, Felipe, 4
Field, Ken, 163
First Nations, 12, 18, 247, 260
fitness landscape, 39, 40, 42, 165
Florida, Richard, 199
food, 5-7, 18, 77, 80, 133, 136, 163, 164. *See
  also* food chains; Gaviotas; home
  economies; slow food movement
food chains, 127, 152, 164
Foote, D.K., 164
four quadrants. *See* integral map
fractal, definition of, xix
Friedman, Thomas, 118
Fuller, Buckminster, 229

G

Gaiasoft, 242
Gaviotas, 20-21
genes, 127, 128, 139-140, 266
geographies, 4, 6
Gettin' Higher Choir, 205

Giuliani, Rudy, 113
Glasgow, 198
Global Information System (GIS), 69-70, 209-210, 235, 238, 250, 252
globalization, 6, 18-19, 72, 76, 117, 189, 194, 263
Global Reporting Initiative, 232, 242
global warming, 165. *See also* climate change
Google Earth, 29, 251 (fig.), 264
Gore, Al, 115
governance systems
    of cities, 15-16, 78-79, 82-83, 119, 152, 170-171, 173-177, 185-186
    global, 80
    and health care, 141
    and IVSM, 232
Graham, Patricia, 196
Grapevine, Texas, 212, 213-214
Graves, Clare, 34, 38, 42, 43, 45, 87-88, 107, 223
    and consciousness, 55, 56
    and organizing systems, 160-161, 189
green building, 261
greenhouse gases, 153

H

Habermas, Jürgen, 202
Halifax, 225
happiness, 12, 106, 113, 119, 123, 165
Hawken, Paul, 114, 194
health, states of, 133-134. *See also* health care; well-being
health care
    and communities of practice, 204
    systems, 59, 80, 92, 140-144, 170, 171-172. *See also* health; Prairieview Community Mental Health System
healthy cities
    definition of, 59
    and fractal patterns, 67
    and healthy body, 133-134
    indications of, 75, 88, 96-97
    and resources, 71-72. *See also* BC Healthy Communities

hierarchies, 34-35, 157-158, 173. *See also* meshworks
Hochachka, Gail, 14
holarchy, 226
Holland America Lines, 13
Holling, C.S., 38, 41, 42, 43, 85, 94, 188, 189
holographic city, the, 46-47
hologram, definition of, xix
holons, 27-28, 34, 164
home economies, 126, 131
homefulness, 67, 85, 199
homelessness, 81, 106, 111, 193, 206
Homer-Dixon, Thomas, 19, 45, 47, 169
homo sapiens sapiens, 2, 34, 55, 78, 100, 139, 263, 269-270. *See also* life conditions; human systems
honeybee hives, 5, 10-11, 36-37, 81, 105, 126, 154, 161, 266
horizontal dynamic, 90, 91
Howard, P.J., 129
humanity, journey of, 3-4
human life cycles, 79-90
human systems, 31, 37, 40, 43, 52-57
and complexity, 157
fractal patterns of, 66-67
and Integral City, 262-263
necessities of, 130-132
nested holarchy of, 65-66
and subsystems, 132-133
and wellness, 137-138. *See also* behavior

I

Imagine BC, 224
immaturity, characteristics of, 75-79
immigration, 83, 109
indicator systems. *See* vital signs monitors
individual consciousness, 101-104
in-formation
of cities, 58-59
definition of, 53
information systems, 59-60
infrastructures, 7-8, 44, 156, 159-163. *See also* structural systems
inner judges, 36-37, 41, 42, 195, 248

in the beehive, 190
innovation, 16, 39, 88, 104, 164, 172, 185, 205-206, 226
intangible life, 48, 60-61
integral, definition of, 52
Integral City, rules for, 268-269
Integral City Framework, xvii-xviii, xix-xx, xxi, 246, 252
Integral City Systems (ICS), 271-272
Integral Dashboard, 241, 242
integral healthcare systems, 141
Integral Institute, 141
integral language, 216-217
Integral Learning System, 108
Integral Life Practice, 120, 134
integral map, 60-65
integral perspectives, 18, 112, 203. See also interobjective Its; intersubjective We; objective It; subjective I; and quadrants by name
Integral Transformative Practice, 134
Integral Vital Signs Monitors (IVSM), 231, 237-255
integral voices, 190-194
integration, 33-34, 52
intelligence capacities, 102-103. See also Integral City, rules for
intention, 14, 16, 34, 78, 140, 145
    of a city, 105-109, 111, 139, 169
    of individuals, 46, 100, 101-103, 105, 108, 111, 120, 128, 145, 164. See also Burning Man; citizens, voices of; social holons; values
intentional communities, 9-10, 15
interior environment, 14-15, 16
International Baccalaureate, 108
interobjective Its, 64
intersubjective We, 61, 64
Isaacs, William, 200-201

J

Jacobs, Jane, 29, 45, 69, 73-74, 88
Jaques, Elliott, 90, 160, 168, 176

Jensen, Mary Ann C., 91
Jung, Carl, 189

K

Kanata, 186
Kandahar, 15, 245
Kansas, 212, 213
Kauffmann, Stuart, 39
Koestler, Arthur, 27

L

land use, 11, 12, 153
Laszlo, Ervin, 47, 49, 53
leadership
    and community, xx, 112-119, 263
    and learning practices, 119-123
levels of, 115, 192, 260
learning, 81, 95, 102, 104, 137
learning systems, 108, 116, 117, 119-123, 172, 204, 240-241
legislation, 13
Leonard, George, 134
Lerner, Jaime, 113
level 1, 186, 213
level 2, 186, 213, 214, 245
level 3, 169, 186, 191-192, 245
level 4, 107, 168, 170, 186, 187, 191-192, 213, 245
level 5, 104, 107, 168, 170, 186, 187, 191-192, 213, 214
level 6, 107, 168, 168, 187, 191-192, 205, 213, 214
level 7, 107, 113, 142-143, 168, 168, 187, 205, 213, 214, 245
level 8, 107, 113, 117, 177, 205, 245. See also power of 8 leadership
life conditions
    evolution of, 53-55, 156-157
    response to, 187-188. See also adaptiveness
Lipton, Bruce, 128
living systems, 58, 127
location, 7-8, 77-79. See also geographies.

London, 49, 69, 83, 159
LOOP Iris, 232-233
Lopez, Barry, 28-29
Los Angeles, 9, 13, 92, 193
Lower Left quadrant, 59, 60-61, 64, 166, 181-207, 215, 216, 254
Lower Right quadrant, 24, 59, 60, 61, 64, 149-178, 182-183, 216, 254
Lugari, Paolo, 20

M

MacKinnon, James, 163
maps, of city life, 60-70
Maslow, Abraham, 107
mathematics, 52, 66
matter, 18-19, 31, 36, 47, 159, 169, 205
    and energy and information, 7, 31, 52, 53, 57-58, 60, 67-69, 72, 74, 100, 133, 150-151, 155, 168, 173, 186, 226, 239, 245, 262. See also energy-matter; resource consumption
mayors, as leaders, 82, 113, 192-193
McDonough, William, 10, 156
McIntosh, Steve, 106, 117, 176, 232
McKibben, Bill, 6, 81, 105, 163, 248
McLuhan, 196
media, role of, 195-197
meshworks, 173, 176-177, 204-206, 221-228
    and management, 227-228
    and planning, 227
    and research, 226-227
meta-framework, xvii-xviii, xix, xxi, 112, 272
metaphors, of the city, 24-25, 28. See also honeybee hives
Mexico City, 9, 50, 134, 152, 193
Miller, James Grier, 27, 28, 57-58, 65-66, 132-133, 150-151, 156, 186, 239
Mitchell, Edgar, xiv
Monbiot, George, 12, 17, 153, 163
monitoring systems, 72. See also vital signs monitors
Monterrey, 108
Montreal, 29
Morgan, Gareth, 24

morphic fields, 48-50, 145-146, 189
Morrissey, Mary, 225
Mumbai, 29, 82
Mumford, Lewis, xviii, xx
Murphy, Michael, 134, 138, 139

N

The Natural Step, 232
natural systems, 6, 52, 66-67, 149-150, 157, 163, 164, 226, 252-253, 261, 262
nested holarchy, 60, 65-66, 244
Neuromuscular Integration Action, 134
New Orleans, 9, 35, 49, 50, 69, 78, 83, 92, 127
Newton, 206
New York, 33, 49, 50, 113, 121, 134
not-for-profits (NFP), 15, 110-111, 123, 185, 193-194, 204-206, 212

O

objective It, 64
Osaka, 9, 50, 193
Ottawa, 15, 108, 230
over-population, 76
Owen, Cam, 166

P

Palmer, Parker, 202
panarchy, 42, 85, 94, 186
Peñalosa, Enrique, 113
Pinker, Stephen, 128, 131
place making, 44, 56
policy, and monitoring, 249
political objectives, 92-93
potential, of cities, 209-220
power of 8 leadership, 113, 115-119, 121, 123
Prairieview Community Mental Health System, 206
Prior Learning Assessment Center, 225
psychological life cycles, 81-82

Q

quality of life, 28, 31, 36, 70-71, 80-81, 113, 154, 195, 211-212, 230-231. See also healthy cities; Integral City Systems; well-being

R

Rake, Rick, 196
recycling, 166. *See also* waste
Rees, W., 153. *See also* eco-footprint
reflection, 25, 30, 59, 101, 200
regeneration, 37-38
relationships, 165-167, 181-186
renewable resources, 12, 17, 161-163
renewal, cycles of, 38, 41-42
resilience, 9-10, 17-18, 35-36, 38, 43-44, 154-155
resonance, 46, 111, 189, 190, 227, 237
resource allocation, 41, 42, 168, 217, 250
resource allocators, 43, 93, 186, 195, 217, 248
in the beehive, 36-37, 41, 42, 190
resource consumption, 11-12, 13, 17-18, 79. *See also* air; food; water resources
Rio de Janeiro, 29, 82
Robinsong, Shivon, 205
Rome, 19, 49
Runnalls, Kat, 199

S

Sahtouris, Elisabet, 75, 96, 128
Saley, Mike, 166-167
Sandercock, Leonie, 204
San Francisco, 9, 180
SARS, 14, 36, 116
Satin, Mark, 83
schools, design of, 92
secondary systems, 170
self-awareness, 130, 215
self-management, 130
self-organizing, 85, 171, 189. *See also* meshworks; social holons
senses, 135-137
Shanghai, 134, 152
Sheldrake, Rupert, 48, 128, 135, 140, 145, 189
Singapore, 18, 83, 144
slow food movement, 5-6, 155
Smith, Alisa, 163

social quadrant, 163-164, 165
social holons, 83-85
center of gravity in, 104
in corporate life cycles, 87-88
dynamics of, 189-190
life endurance expectations of, 91
social housing, 198-199
social life cycles, 83-90
social roles, 167-169
social structures, and artefacts, 156-159
space colonies, 265-266, 267
Spiral Dynamics, 160-161
Spiral Integral Values Map, 218-219
spiritual perspectives, 65
stability, 94-95
State of the World's Cities, 9
status quo, 187
stewardship, 12, 14, 21, 79, 152, 166
structural systems, 150-156
subjective I, 61, 100-101
subsystems
of cities, 36-40, 17, 58-60, 122-123
of living systems, 58, 186. *See also* hierarchies; infrastructures; Miller, James Grier
Success by Six, 143
Surowiecki, James, 210
survival, 28-29
sustainability
of the city, 43-46, 56-58
framework for, 237-239
and life conditions, 235-237
Suzuki, David, 115
Sydney, 29, 82, 139
symbiosis, 137
systems theory, 40, 67, 254

T

technology, 3-4, 67, 199, 235
and energy, 12, 163
and globalization, 6, 76, 117, 118, 170, 196-197
and infrastructure, 7-8, 157, 159, 209-210.

See also Global Information System; Integral Vital Signs Monitor
tone, 179-181
Toronto, 14, 49, 81, 83, 196, 230
traffic-light systems, 241, 242
transactional relationships, 182, 183, 184
transformative relationships, 182, 183, 184
transmutational relationships, 182-183, 184, 185
transportation, 8, 113, 159, 160, 170
triune brain, 54, 103, 139
Tuckman, Bruce, 91

U

United Nations, 78
Upper Left quadrant, 59, 60-61, 100-102, 103-104, 117, 166, 215, 216, 248, 254
Upper Right quadrant, 24, 59, 60, 61, 64, 125, 166, 215, 216, 248, 254
urban migration, 76, 84
urban planning, 159-163

V

values
    of cities, 183-185
    of citizens, 106-107, 111-112, 121, 141-142, 157, 165
    and culture, 198
    mapping of, 214-215
Vancouver, 14, 15, 33, 42, 139, 141, 196, 205, 230
Varey, Will, 254
Venice, 34, 84
vertical dynamic, 90, 92
Victoria, 205, 230
vision, of the city, 111-112, 123, 141, 152, 170. See also Gaviotas
vital signs monitors, 11, 79, 106, 144, 230-231. See also Integral Vital Signs Monitor
voting systems, 170-171

W

Wackernagel, M., 153. See also eco-footprint

waste, 18-19, 166-167
Waste Watchers, 166
water resources, 12, 79 80, 150
Wiebe, Gordon, 205
well-being
    and brain activity, 222-223
    of cities, 50, 55, 69, 74-75, 137-139, 172-173, 179-181
    of citizens, 59, 95-96, 106, 110, 118, 128-129, 171
    of the globe, 13, 21, 72, 115-119
    subjective sense of, 100-101. See also BC Healthy Communities; healthy cities; household economies; quality of life
wellness. See well-being
Wells, S., 4-5
Wenger, Etienne, 203, 204
Western world, 2-3
Westlake, 108
Whistler, BC, 232
whole-systems thinking, 23-50, 51-52, 65-67, 126, 165, 262. See also Integral City; Integral City Systems; Integral Vital Signs Monitor; meshworks
Wichita, 206, 212
Wills, E.H., 100
Wight, Ian, 44
Wilber, Ken, 58, 81, 101, 104, 120. See also integral map
Wisdom of Crowds, 39
work roles, 168
work systems, 160, 172-173
World Health Organization, 59
World Urban Forum, 78
worldviews, 14, 15-16, 26, 30, 70-71, 76-77, 90, 92, 115, 142-143, 169, 187-188, 197-198, 240. See also spiritual perspectives
Wright, Ronald, 45

Z

zoonotic diseases, 6

ABOUT THE AUTHOR

Integral City
Evolutionary Intelligences for the Human Hive

Marilyn Hamilton, PhD CGA, meshworks evolutionary intelligences in the city. She creates hope and enables community and city learning by engaging with differences of all kinds, to inspire fresh connections, open new pathways and strengthen weak signals. As a meshworker, coach, facilitator, writer, researcher and teacher she catalyzes city well-being through living, evolutionary, whole systems approaches. Generating courageous community dialogue, deliberation and design, she helps people discover invisible options for complex issues that bridge all sectors, in all quadrants: actions, ideas, relationships, structures.

Founder of Integral City and TDG Global Learning Connections; a founding Member of the Integral Institute and Integral-Ecology; Canadian Leader and International Training Board Member of the Spiral Dynamics integral Constellation; Ginger Group Affiliate; Convener of Quantum Woman Inquiries; and faculty member at Royal Roads University, UFV, Banff Centre, California Institute of Integral Studies and Adizes Graduate School, Marilyn resides in Abbotsford BC Canada with her husband Peter Dobson. She has served on the executives of many global and local organizations, recently as Chair, Abbotsford Community Foundation and Imagine Abbotsford.

If you have enjoyed *Integral City*, you might also enjoy other

BOOKS TO BUILD A NEW SOCIETY

Our books provide positive solutions for people who want to make a difference. We specialize in:

Sustainable Living • Ecological Design and Planning
Natural Building & Appropriate Technology
Environment and Justice • Conscientious Commerce
Progressive Leadership • Resistance and Community • Nonviolence
Educational and Parenting Resources

New Society Publishers

ENVIRONMENTAL BENEFITS STATEMENT

New Society Publishers has chosen to produce this book on recycled paper made with 100% post consumer waste, processed chlorine free, and old growth free.

For every 5,000 books printed, New Society saves the following resources:[1]

41	Trees
3,728	Pounds of Solid Waste
3,331	Gallons of Water
4,102	Kilowatt Hours of Electricity
5,350	Pounds of Greenhouse Gases
29	Pounds of HAPs, VOCs, and AOX Combined
10	Cubic Yards of Landfill Space

[1]Environmental benefits are calculated based on research done by the Environmental Defense Fund and other members of the Paper Task Force who study the environmental impacts of the paper industry.

For a full list of NSP's titles, please call 1-800-567-6772 or check out our web site at:

www.newsociety.com

NEW SOCIETY PUBLISHERS